FINANCIAL ADVERTISING AND PUBLIC RELATIONS

Peter Biddlecombe

BUSINESS BOOKS LIMITED London

First published 1971

© PETER BIDDLECOMBE, 1971

ISBN 0 220 99256 8

This book has been set in 10 on 12 point Times
and printed in England by
C. Tinling & Co. Ltd, Prescot, Lancs.,
for the publishers, Business Books Limited
(Registered office: 180 Fleet Street, London EC4)
Publishing offices: Mercury House, Waterloo Road, London SE1

MADE AND PRINTED IN GREAT BRITAIN

By the same author

International Public Relations Encyclopedia

Grant Helm 1968

'Communications with the shareholder and the investing public generally must be a continuous and continuing process designed with a clear understanding of the needs of those for whom it is designed and supported by the company making the communication. We in industry have the business of communications between employer and employee, manufacturer and customer, control and planning and so on. I do think, however, that amid this welter of necessary activity it is easy to overlook the importance of relations with the investor; and what this means to a company is more than simply keeping existing shareholders adequately informed and happy. It means creating good and favourable relations with the wider investing public, the City and the Press.'

Sir Martin Wilkinson,
Chairman of the London Stock Exchange,
8 May 1968

Contents

Part three Financial Advertising and Public Relations in Action

Part five Benefits of Financial Advertising and Public Relations

Foreword

by the Rt. Hon. Lord Sherfield, GCB, GCMG
Chairman, Industrial and Commercial Finance Corporation

This is apparently the first book to be published which covers the whole area of financial advertising and public relations. It therefore fills an important gap.

A company's relations with its shareholders as well as with the financial community generally are of major importance. It is of little avail to devote time and energy to sales or labour relations if, at the same time, a company's investment rating declines because it is not telling people what it is doing.

In these days it is essential for companies to keep the investment community better informed than in the past about their performance and their prospects. In doing this, they serve the interest of their employees, their customers and, of course, their shareholders.

This book will help to improve the quality and quantity of communications between business, the press and the public. It will, therefore, be a valuable addition to any business library.

Sherfield

5 November 1970.

Introduction

Half a million words—two books, hundreds of articles for magazines and newspapers in the United Kingdom, Europe and the United States as well as lectures and talks—have forced me to study every single aspect of communications. Sales promotion, industrial relations, political campaigning—they are all important. But, given our present society, nothing seems more fundamental than financial communications.

And yet nothing seems more neglected. The number of companies practising good communications policies is still in the minority. The number practising good financial communications has hardly begun to exist. Despite this, I am convinced financial advertising and public relations are vitally important—and are becoming more and more important—for every single company, public and private.

This book is the first book ever written on the whole tangled and yet immensely profitable subject of financial advertising and public relations in the United Kingdom—everything, in fact, from the urgent need for financial communications, the effectiveness of financial advertising and public relations, through choosing a financial advertising agency and a financial public relations consultancy to corporate advertising and PR campaigns. For the first time, it gives top management a practical step-by-step guide to the whole subject of financial communication. In fact, it could be worth millions of pounds to a director if it helped him to ensure nothing else but a realistic share price for his company. It also gives public relations people an easy-to-follow introduction to what, I am convinced, will be the one major growth centre in the business in years to come.

Most books on communications fail to communicate. They talk in grand terms about strategies and programmes. They are rich in theory but poor in detail. The reader, therefore, is at a loss. He can see the objectives but he still cannot for the life of him see any hope of actually reaching them. This I have tried to avoid.

Instead of writing a 'what to do' book, I have tried to write a 'how to do it' book. Where other books on communication ramble from one general observation to another, I have listed in no-nonsense terms the concrete reasons for companies following particular proposals. I believe, for example, there are ten reasons why companies should adopt a financial communications programme—and I have listed them. Nothing more. No verbose Johnsonese introductions. Just the facts. And, again, with the moves involved in hiring a financial public relations consultancy. There are eleven moves. And I have given them.

Similarly, with the actual financial public relations activities themselves. Instead of walking around the subject and describing the type of national press publicity a company can expect, I have quoted straightforward examples. This, I think, means far more to the reader trying to master the subject. The purpose of writing this book is, after all, to demonstrate the benefits of greater financial exposure. It is impossible to do that properly without quoting the press.

I have also, perhaps unusually for a text book, quoted extensively from various people in the financial communications business because—again—it is a guarantee to the reader that particular views are supported throughout the business and that I am not urging them to go out on a limb.

So much for the mechanics.

In the course of writing this book and completely re-thinking every single aspect of financial and corporate public relations, one thought has struck me again and again: perhaps financial PR advisers, like auditors, ought to be appointed by the shareholders and not by the directors of a company. Of course, shareholders generally follow directors' advice. This, I know. But I am sure it would be worth trying for three reasons. First, financial public relations advisers ought to have shareholders interests at heart right from the start. If they are appointed by directors, this might not always be the case. Second, it would guarantee shareholders that absolutely independent financial PR advice was being given to their company. This is especially vital when financial public relations can affect share prices one way or another so easily. Third, because financial public relations also covers relations with shareholders, it would ensure that the shareholders were not themselves swayed by the persuasion techniques of the man who ought to be their servant.

I know this is a radical suggestion and likely to be greeted with raised eyebrows. But I am sure the more one studies the implications of financial advertising and public relations, the more one becomes convinced of the absolute necessity of preserving the independence of the financial communications advice.

Now the credits.

I have checked, re-checked and checked again every fact and figure in this book. Similarly with the advice I have given. Where I have been uncertain, I have checked again. I would like, therefore, to thank all those people—those mentioned and those not—for suffering my questioning and helping me with their comments.

And my wife, Gay. I would like to thank her as well. To be able to write two books in three years is proof enough of how much I rely on her help.

London 1970   PETER BIDDLECOMBE

Part one

The Need for Financial Advertising and Public Relations

Chapter 1

How to Exploit the
Business News Explosion

Where there are thorns you often find roses. And its roses all the way for the giant Thorn Electrical television, radio and lighting group, comments the Daily Mirror. *Chairman, Sir Jules Thorn, delighted the Stock Exchange yesterday with profits of £54,316,000 for the last year.*

Britain's oldest aircraft firm, Handley Page, owes its creditors £13 million and is asking for a receiver and manager to be brought in. But it needn't be the end of the runway, says the Daily Mail.

The full extent of the fantastic Cowdray empire, S. Pearson and Son Limited, is revealed in the prospectus for the offer for sale to the public of 10 million shares at 25s. each. It looks as if the offer will be a knock-out success, says the Evening News, *for the record of the company in private hands has been pretty dramatic.*

Company news is big news, Twenty years ago these items would have rated, perhaps, three lines on one of the inside pages of *The Times*. Today they get front-page treatment not only in the serious press but in papers like the *Daily Mirror* and the *Daily Sketch* as well. On top of that comes radio and television coverage. For the news media is interested in business news—everything from company appointments to take over bids. There has even been a Welsh-language television series on investment. Businessmen like Lord Stokes of Leyland and Arnold Weinstock have replaced film stars as the heroes of our time.

Jim Slater, head of the fastest growing investment, banking and industrial conglomerate in the country, for example, is the darling of the City editors. In the last three years he has become their favourite financier and chalked up more than £100,000 worth of free publicity in the process. Hardly a day goes by without the *Financial Times*, *The Guardian* or *The Times* commenting on his activities. In five months he can rate over 200 column-inches of national publicity. He is the subject of one glossy feature after another in both the management and consumer press. He has only to appear on television and the shares shoot up.

> '*Interest in Slater Walker was stimulated by the chairman's television interview the previous evening, the shares rising 1s 6d further to 56s 9d.*' (*Financial Times*, 14 June 1969)

Admittedly Slater is a superb businessman. Slater Walker have doubled dividends and pushed up profits five times in three years. Which helps. Yet Slater is convinced of the value of publicity.

> 'Public relations is more important than most public companies consider. Certainly it is an important part of the acquisition business,' he says. 'It makes our acquisitions that much cheaper. That's one of the reasons we consider public relations important. We don't try to get any publicity. But we are making acquisitions all the time and the Press are always on to us as a result. The activity generates the publicity, not the other way round. I naturally want to make sure that the technical and financial press understand the details and the implications of each move we make. The press also like it that way because they like to talk to the people mainly involved.'

Lord Stokes, at one time Slater's boss at Leylands, also believes in publicity. He pays his PR adviser a handsome £8,000-a-year, one of the highest PR salaries in this country. He also made him a member of the Board, the reward for eight year's work building Stokes into a national hero. Stokes first met Keith Hopkins in 1961 when Standard Triumph were taken over by the Leyland Motor Corporation. He was made Group PR manager and given over-all responsibility for co-ordinating the PR activities of all the companies within the organisation. Between them they devised their publicity strategy. Whenever there was a major sale or an export order, Stokes would be there. But he wouldn't just smile and shake hands. He would actually drive the bus or the lorry to the customer. And Hopkins would make sure he was surrounded by photographers.

Similarly, whenever Stokes visited an exhibition or another company, they would snatch the publicity for themselves. Hence the memorable export orders announced on the eve of the Motor Show. They even went a stage further. Instead of just releasing details of staff appointments they linked them to sales and stressed their success to date.

The International Publishing Corporation is another company that has wrestled with the problems of publicity. Their call for PR started with Stafford Beer, IPC's director of development and one of Europe's leading research workers in cybernetics. Gradually it gained support from the non-publishing sectors of the organisation. The publishers were luke-warm. Yet they were persuaded by United States academic, Harold Stieglitz, when he told them bluntly at a hush-hush management conference at London's Carlton Towers

Hotel: 'I, as a stranger living over in the United States, know a helluva lot about IPC. Do your employees know as much as I—a stranger—know about IPC?' They had no answer. IPC began setting up a PR operation.

That's only one side of the coin. While the Jim Slaters and Lord Stokes' are getting all the publicity, newspapers and magazines are trying like mad to get news and still more news from every company in the country.

It is all part of the business information explosion.

1.1 The whole nature of society is becoming more money- and investment-conscious

Britain's army of investors is going up in leaps and bounds. One in ten of the adult population has a piece of the action. A survey carried out by Gallup in 1969 estimated there were about 3.2 million people—7 per cent of the whole population—investing in stocks and shares (see Table 1.1). Earlier, another Gallup Poll had estimated that 18 per cent were manual workers, 45 per cent were women and 16 per cent were under 34.

'Increasingly these days the in-thing to be is an investor,' says John Davis, City Editor of *The Observer*. 'At parties, business get-togethers or functions, a good standby for breaking the ice or for getting out of tight corners is to start talking about the state of the stock market or your latest share purchase.' (*Punch*, 25 June 1969)

The Stock Exchange has gone a stage further. 'Although they may not know it, millions more are direct investors. It is highly probable that, like five adults out of seven in this country, you are one of them,' says one of their booklets. 'If you have money in a bank, building society, savings bank, co-operative society or any similar body; or if you have any other type of insurance; or contribute to a pension fund, or a trade union; then indirectly, you are an investor on the Stock Exchange because all these associations invest a very large part of their funds—which they possess as a result of your payments and contributions—through the Stock Exchange.' Another of their booklets claims 22·5 million people are indirect investors through life assurance and pension schemes as well. The £1,329 million unit trust movement alone numbers 2,391,372 accounts, an average of £556 each holding (September 1969 figures). Then there are investment clubs, which made their debut in the UK in 1958. Today with more than 2,200 clubs operating throughout the country, they are regularly investing more than £1 million a year in stocks and shares.

That's counting the investors. But tackle it from the other direction by counting the investments and the figure is even more striking. A University of Cambridge study (*The Owners of Ordinary Quoted Shares—a survey for 1963*, J. Revell and J. Moyle, University of Cambridge, 1966) reveals that 46·9 per cent of all quoted Ordinary shares in British companies are held by individuals, including executors and trustees. Include beneficial ownership and nominee holdings and the figure shoots up to 54 per cent. More than 20 years ago the figures were 12·8 and 11·8 per cent, respectively.

Next look at the turnover. In August 1969 turnover on the London Stock Exchange was £2,111·9 million—and that was low. The previous month had been £513 million higher. Yet that still covered 380,671 bargains, an average of £100·6 million per day.

Table 1.1   Gallup survey: savings held personally or jointly*

National Savings:	
Post Office Savings Bank	13·3m
Premium bonds	12·9m
National Savings certificates	4·0m
Savings banks	10·9m
Building societies	7·7m
Stocks and shares:	
Unit trusts	2·0m
Equities	0·8m
Gilt edged	0·4m
Savings or investment clubs	0·8m
Local authority loans	0·4m

* *Financial Times*, 26 November 1969

Even the number of searches at Companies House is shooting up. For 1968 the total reached 1·10 million. And every indication is that the 1969 total will be higher still.

Fifteen years ago, however, the army was a regiment. There were half the number of investors. But as society began getting more money-conscious, business and the Stock Exchange began getting more open-minded. In 1953, for example, the Stock Exchange opened a public gallery. A public relations department was launched. Films and leaflets began pouring out. 'The Stock Exchange is a free market through which money is put to work and employment is created,' said one leaflet, which raised the charge that Stock Exchanges were 'going public' to minimise any political attacks on their position. But the Chairman of the Council at the time, Lord Ritchie, disagreed. 'We're trying to dispel the Victorian idea that the Stock Exchange is something mysterious, doing fiddles on the side,' he said.

Gradually the number of investors began rising. At the moment it is running at about 100,000 a year. It will still be some time before Britain catches up with America, where 10 per cent of the population are direct investors, or Japan where it is as high as 18 per cent.

'Mr Small Investor has come within the orbit of the Stock Exchange, though there has been nothing on the American pattern (Americans talk to their barbers about the stock market, Englishmen talk about football).

But the idea of popular investment has begun to soak through to the public. City journalists are now more widely read, and more readable, than they ever were. The *Daily Mirror* even ran a strip cartoon for a year or two called "Keeping Up with the Joneses", which told the moral tale of Joe and Prue, a young married couple waking up to the big world of investment. This was wound up rather abruptly, when Joe invented a thing called the Wedgeclamp scaffold clip one week, sold the patent for £2,000 the next, and walked off with a job as a "consultant" at £1,750 a year, an umbrella and a bowler. "The status symbols of the man who's caught up with the Joneses at last," sighed Prue.'
(Paul Ferris, *The City*, Penguin Books.)

In the meantime 17·5 per cent of all bargains on the stock exchange continue to be carried out in amounts of £100 or less. An important point to bear in mind in discussing financial advertising and public relations.

1.2 While society is becoming more business-conscious, businessmen are becoming more business-minded

The nation of shopkeepers is becoming a nation of department store managers. Imperial Tobacco and Calico Printers made their debut at the turn of the century. Imperial Chemical Industries and Unilever came with the 1920's. Clore, Wolfson, Fraser and Thomson are the takeover kings of today although they are being hustled by Slater and Weinstock. Each of them has built up a massive empire in only a few years.

Said Business News Editor of the *Sunday Times*, Peter Wilsher, reviewing the first five years of its existence from 27 September 1964 until 28 September 1969: 'There is hardly a single big company—and not many middle-sized and small ones—which have not been aggressors, defenders, willing victims, rebuffed suitors, or desperate interveners in some battle or other.'

The Monopolies Commission reported in 1969 that no less than one-fifth of the total assets of manufacturing companies with net assets of more than £½ million had been acquired in mergers and takeovers in eight years. In 1968 alone, 6·5 per cent of total assets had been transferred. And the total number of companies in the £½ million-plus category had fallen from 1,312 to 908—a fall of 31 per cent. In 1961 the 28 largest companies held 39 per cent of the net assets. By 1969, however, the 28 largest companies, not necessarily the same ones, were holding about half the net total. This meant that in the four years between 1964 and 1968 the annual number of acquisitions of non-quoted companies had been halved while that of quoted companies had doubled. Which has obvious implications for relations with the investing public.

In the past 10 years more than 1,130 companies have come to market. The total nominal value of new securities granted quotation has been in the region of £32,000 million, a yearly average of over £3,200 million including a total of £15,900 million for company stocks and shares. With 9,000 stocks being quoted their market value is more than £103,000 million or the equivalent of over £1,800 for every man, woman and child in Britain. They are also responsible for over 80 per cent of British industry and commerce and, at the same time, they provide employment for the bulk of the population.

In one year alone 1,554 applications for quotation were granted by the Stock Exchange Council. Two hundred gilt-edged quotes raised £1,679 million while the remaining 1,351 company securities drew in a further £452 million.

With about 500,000 transactions worth around £2,600 million being made on the London Stock Exchange every month, turnover hovers around the £30–£35 thousand-million mark.

In spite of this tremendous activity, there are still plenty of small private firms. At the last count there were 460,000 of them compared with about 10,538 public companies (*The Registrar of Joint Stock Companies*, 31 December 1965).

1.3 With so many people and so much money involved, society has a right to business information

It was all right when the City was a Victorian club with members doing fiddles on the side. Now everything is changed. They would no longer be fiddling their own money. Hence the need for more information. Which, of course, stimulates more interest and the demand for more information still.

Ever since the Companies Act of 1862 which gave creditors the right to appoint their own accountant, one Companies Act has followed another.

In 1962 the Jenkins Committee on company law recommended companies to detail major trade investments in their annual reports. 'The public benefit to be gained from giving shareholders sufficient information to exercise intelligently the powers which the Act bestows on them should be the overriding consideration in this matter,' said their Report.

The Companies Act, 1948, covers issues and prospectuses; annual meetings and accounts; auditors reports and so on. It insists, for example, that profit and loss accounts should be made up to date not more than nine months—or twelve if the company also operates abroad—before the annual meeting unless the company gets an extension from the Board of Trade.

The Companies Act, 1967, went on to lay down rules for disclosing turnover in spite of fears that it would lead to both increased competition for equal profits as well as pressure for lower prices. It also insisted that people interested in one-tenth or more of the company's nominal share capital should disclose their identities. And, of course, it called for companies to disclose their political contributions, their sales and their export figures.

This caused something of an earthquake in the lives of tens of thousands of privately owned companies. With the abolition of the old 'private exempt' legal status, all but the smallest companies found that the curtains were being torn back leaving them exposed to public scrutiny.

Then, of course, there is the enlarged Takeover Panel with its full-time director general; its much strengthened Bid Code as well as the Government's own merger guide-lines designed to elicit still more business information. All this has effectively ended 'the cult of the shareholder' for good. Employees, customers, suppliers and the public interest are now all taken into account as well. Thanks to that man of many parts, Lord Goodman, and Mr Charles Villiers, Managing Director of the Industrial Reorganisation Corporation. Shareholders could not be relied upon to ensure that large companies carried out policies which did not conflict with the national interest, Villiers told a Radio 3 audience. The Monopolies Commission was even more emphatic. The Monopolies Commission report on the proposed acquisition of the De La Rue Company Limited:

> 'We have to reckon with the fact that shareholders faced with an offer are more likely to be concerned with its financial implications for themselves (including tax considerations) than with the efficiency with which resources are to be used. The connection between the shareholders assessment of a takeover offer and their assessment of the effects of the takeover on efficiency . . . may indeed be tenuous, remote or even non-existent according to the circumstances. We conclude that the stock market's reaction cannot, therefore, be relied on to reflect the efficiency aspects of a takeover. Mergers now play so important a part in the reorganisation of British industry that it seems to us desirable, on general grounds, that more should be made known of the assets which have changed hands. Moreover, the need to provide more detailed information might deter companies from going ahead with mergers designed merely or largely to buy the assets and/or profits of the acquired companies cheaply and what reasonable expectations, on the basis of positive plans, that they can use the acquired assets more effectively. For all these reasons we think it would be in the public interest if more information were given by companies about the reasons for acquisitions, their real cost and, subsequently, the growth and earnings of the acquiring company and each of its major divisions or acquisitions.'

Ten years ago it was different. The City were prepared to admit they were there to protect investors from sharks. They did not feel they were there to save them from fools. Paul Ferris quoted a typical argument at the time: 'We are a capital market and our job is to get risk capital. None of the South African gold mines would have been dug if people hadn't been prepared to put up the money.'

But gradually the mood began to change. In 1963 Harold Rose published his influential *Disclosure in Company Accounts* (Institute of Economic Affairs). His theme. Disclosure begets efficiency.

'If any sweeping conclusion can be ventured at all, it is that disclosure in the United States appears to enable investors, outside those industries where current fashion blinds, to make a more confident choice between firms in the same trade and, in particular, to assess more accurately the qualities of management. The British observer of the American scene can hardly fail to be impressed by the sensitivity of management to outside opinion. Even when allowance is made for the element of self-interested propaganda in the willingness of successful firms to disclose full information, there is not much doubt that disclosure plays a material part in keeping American management at full stretch. At the very least, the argument that disclosure will curb enterprise by magnifying the risks of innovation finds little support in the experience of the US.'

The following year in August 1964, Lord Ritchie, Chairman of the Stock Exchange Council, wrote to the chairmen of all public companies. He wanted them to reveal more about themselves. Interim reports as well as the standard annual report, analyses of results and more information generally about company activities were going to be the order of the day for companies wanting a Stock Exchange quotation in the future. The dance of the seven veils had begun.

Frank H. Jones, author of the *Guide to Company Balance Sheets and Profit and Loss Accounts* (W. Heffer and Sons Limited, Cambridge, 1964)—an invaluable book—saw the reasons behind the move.

'As a natural outcome of this rapidly expanding interest in the financial affairs of quoted companies the circulation of financial papers is increasing, more space is being devoted to City news in the top Press and in the last year or two there has been a spate of books published on all aspects of investment advice. . . . It is not surprising, therefore, that the demand for company information is insatiable, not so much from the individual small saver as from those who cater for his needs—the financial journalists and authors, investment analysts, stockbrokers, etc.—and the institutional investors.'

But it was the Chairman of Wolseley-Hughes Limited, Mr N. G. Lancaster, who whole-heartedly welcomed the new open-door policy at the 1965 Accountant awards ceremony for annual reports. He spelt out the reasons from the management point-of-view:

'In the first place, it is a stimulus to ourselves, the executive, the management, to do better.

Secondly, to inform shareholders about the company in which they have been good enough to invest.

Thirdly, as a help to our employees to understand better the many financial problems of business.

And fourthly and quite definitely, to help the investment analysts, city editors, stockbrokers and investors generally to do their very important work in assessing the affairs of companies.'

The backwoodsmen led by the big bankers remained stubborn. They were against the idea of disclosure altogether.

'Full disclosure in the accounts might embarrass the banks in their policy of making large provisions in good years, while the spectacle of heavy drafts on those reserves at other times might undermine that unquestioning confidence in the stability of the banks which is acknowledged to be a national asset of the first importance.'

Playboy bunnies, commented Leftish economist Roger Opie, Fellow of New College, Oxford. The bank chairmen were always trying to see how far they could go without actually giving anything away. Now the wheel has come full-circle. The banks have finally cast their veils to the wind after 'a careful re-examination of the problems involved'. The Confederation of British Industries has even floated the idea of directors, representing shareholders interests, issuing reports on company performance separate from those of management. Which is a striking measure of the progress made over the past twenty years.

1.4 The Press reflects society. The Press, therefore, reflects the business scene more and more

Daily financial journalism made its debut on 23 January 1884 with the publication of the *Financial News*. It was followed by the *Financial Times* on 13 February 1888. Both editors, Harry Hanan Marks and Douglas Gordon MacRae, were convinced there was a need for a comprehensive daily service of financial and industrial news and comment. They were right. But they had difficulty proving their case. The turning point came with the great Kaffir boom in 1895. The flood of new flotations and prospectuses boosted the paper revenues enormously. At the same time, it greatly increased public interest in financial matters. This, in turn, coincided with the trend of many companies switching from private to general public ownership. And so it continued.

The press has become even more money- and finance-conscious. Ten years ago only the serious papers concentrated on money and investment. Today they are all in the act. The *Daily Mirror* not only has a City Page, it has launched 'Mirror Bonds', single premium endowment assurance policies redeemable after ten years, together with M. and G. Securities Limited. Designed for both *Daily Mirror* and *Sunday Mirror* readers, the repayment of the bonds is guaranteed at not less than their £20 face value although 'we would be very disappointed indeed if each £20 Mirror Bond was worth

only £30 in ten years time. We would hope it would be worth at least £40'.
Said Chairman of IPC Newspapers, Edward Pickering, 'It will also encourage
our readers to take an active interest in the financial and commercial world'.

The *Daily Mail* publishes its four-page inset, *Money Mail*, every week.
Both *The Times* and the *Sunday Times* have their Business News sections.

'From the day we started we were, as we still are, the largest-circulation
business newspaper in existence', said Peter Wilsher, editor of the *Sunday
Times Business News* on 28 September 1969. 'And the reason for this is
simple—we were the first to back the view that business is not a dull, esoteric
affair, suitable only for the trade magazines and investment news-sheets,
but a subject of passionate interest to anyone who earns a living, goes into a
shop or possesses two pound notes to rub together so long as it involves
money—the making of it, the spending of it, the mis-management of it, or the
stealing of it—then it has a place in Business News. And that brings in virtually
every human activity from the price of baby-powder to the economics of
cremation (both of which we have covered).'

And all the time the circulation of the *Financial Times*—a pretty good
indication of public interest in business and finance generally—has soared
from 95,000 to over 172,000 by 1969.

'This liberalisation of journalistic comment', says Clive Smith, Director and
group public relations controller of Astral Public Relations, 'made businessmen aware that the minimum Stock Exchange requirements were not enough.
Boards began to realise they wanted more positive information about their
activities in the papers. About the same time some top journalists began
turning to PR. And the two sides welcomed each other with open arms.'

There are also more business magazines. *Management Today*, for example,
combines the attractiveness of, say, *Queen* with the hard-headedness of
Fortune. It is the glossy bible of every business executive. Then there is radio
and television. Both are producing more and more programmes for the
businessman. Lord Kearton, Chairman of Courtaulds, even turns up on
Radio 4's 'Any Questions?'

That's the business new media. But more and more business news itself
is becoming more important as well, even when it has to face competition
with Holy Wars against Israel; Mr Callaghan finding out how much people
hate each other in Northern Ireland and so on—as, in fact, happened with the
Leasco-Pergamon battle in August 1969. Managing editor of the *Financial
Times*, Christopher Johnson, gave two reasons for the massive press coverage
of the story which dominated front pages for four or five days on end during
an interview on the BBC's Newstand on 28 August 1969:

'I think it has great elements of glamour in it. It's much more than just
a financial story. It's a story about a 29-year-old American millionaire,
and that's quite something to have made 50 million dollars, not just one
million, by the time you're 29, and Mr Maxwell, who, after all, makes

news in many different capacities. I think its been of interest to anybody who has any interest whatsoever in the City, shareholders of any company might begin to wonder just how much has been swept under the carpet by the Boards of the companies they hold shares in.'

There was so much interest in the story, he added, that the *Financial Times* ran one of its latest-ever editions to carry a statement from the Takeover Panel during the battle.

Like or not the business information explosion is taking place. Companies have no alternative. They can no longer bury their heads in small print and hope the public will disappear. If there are four reasons behind the business information explosion, there are a further ten reasons for companies taking advantage of it. And adopting a financial advertising and public relations programme.

1.4.1 BECAUSE—PROBABLY THE BEST REASON OF ALL—THEY HAVE VIRTUALLY GOT TO

The Companies Acts, the Takeover Panel, various Government guide-lines and so on make it practically impossible for companies to keep their secrets locked out of sight. There is every incentive, therefore, to make a virtue out of necessity and reveal all to one's own advantage. A number of companies, for example, were releasing details on turnover, exports, etc., before they were forced by the Companies Act, 1967. They benefitted by doing so. Similarly a number of companies are now revealing information they can still legitimately keep under wraps. But, by doing so, they are gaining the increased confidence of the investing public.

Of course, there are objections. If shareholders are protected by law why bother going any further? The reason is simple. The company stands to gain by it. A financial information programme is protection. It ensures a share valuation based on fact not fiction. And a healthy market that gives the company the credit it deserves. Information never harmed anyone. If a company is going public it has to come clean and open its books. Most of them at least. If a competitor is intent on getting facts and figures he will not rely on the company presenting them on a plate. He will hunt them out his own way.

1.4.1 BECAUSE IT ENSURES THE SHARES REFLECT THE FINANCIAL AND TRADING POSITION AS WELL AS FUTURE PROSPECTS OF THE COMPANY

'The City will recognise merit quickly enough but that merit has first to be brought to its attention', says ex-City Editor of the *Daily Sketch*, Maurice D. Cocking, Managing Director of FABUS Financial and Business PR Limited, one of the leading financial PR consultancies. This does not mean 'rigging the market' or 'puffing up the price'. It means reducing the chances of unjustified fluctuations in a share price. A completely different matter.

There is nothing wrong with this. Every Board has a duty to its shareholders and to its staff to ensure that its shares are as fully priced and as fully recognised as the facts and the performance of the company allow. It cuts down the risk of a takeover on the cheap. It gives management the continued opportunities for expansion and promotion they have planned. And it gives shareholders the maximum benefit of a realistic share price. If this is done, the company will be assured of properly valued stock. For shareholders, after all, are the people who fix the price of the stock in the first place.

'The stock of a company well known to the financial community will normally sell at a higher price-earnings ratio than will that of a lesser-known company of equal value', says *Corporate Relations*, a report on the New York Society of Security Analysts Inc. 'A high price-earnings ratio facilitates financing on the most favourable basis, makes it possible to accomplish acquisitions for stock with less dilution and renders the company less vulnerable to a raid.' Adds editor of the *Investors Chronicle*, John Cobb:

> 'It would be wrong to under-estimate the impact of City public relations on a company's share price. Shrewd investors know that if there are two strictly comparable companies, it is the one releasing a steady flow of information on its activities which will have the higher stock market rating.'
>
> (*Investors Chronicle*, October 1968)

1.4.3 BECAUSE IT MINIMISES THE DANGER OF RUMOURS SUDDENLY HITTING THE COMPANY

Psst! One word over a gin-and-tonic and a company's share price can plunge five, seven or ten shillings. Lesney Products, the 'Matchbox' toy firm, saw their shares slide from 47s to 40s in August 1969. Reason: rumours that joint managing director, Jack Odell, had died on a golf course. A similar rumour hit General Electric a few weeks earlier. This time it was supposed to be the chairman, Lord Nelson, who had come to an untimely end. Valor, the heating and lighting firm, were in trouble about the same time. Their shares fell from 3s 9d to 2s 1½d on rumours that Lloyds Bank were appointing a receiver and that merchant bankers, William Brandt, were abandoning their investigations into the company. 'Extraordinary—quite extraordinary', said chairman Michael Montague. 'There has never at any time been any suggestion of a receiver being appointed for Valor.' Yet people were still prepared to believe the rumour.

Part of the trouble, of course, is that rumour can be profitable—to the rumour-monger. If the deceiver sells say, 10,000 shares he does not own for around 45s, he can sit back and watch the price fall as he gets to work. When it falls even a few shillings he can buy the shares and, perhaps, clear about £2,000 in the process.

The only way a company can combat this kind of psychological warfare

is to provide a constant stream of information. Thus ensuring that at
investors know the true state of play.

'The more certain the public feels that it will be told all the neces
facts, the less attention it will pay to rumour', said Joint Chairman of i.
Quotations Committee of the Stock Exchange Council, Mr J. A. Hunter.
(*Stock Exchange Journal,* December 1962)

1.4.4 BECAUSE INFORMATION IS VITAL TO SHAREHOLDERS' EDUCATION

The amazing point is that although people invest their money in a company,
probably less than half understand what investment is all about. From a
company point of view this is like sitting on a keg of dynamite. One rash word,
one bad press story could spark the fuse. Opinion Research Corporation in
the United States, for example, discovered in a shareholder comprehension
study in 1961 that:

> Only 6 per cent could describe a price-earnings ratio correctly. Said one
> stockholder: 'earnings for a number of years divided by the number of
> years'.

> Only 12 per cent could describe a stock option correctly. Said one stock-
> holder: 'you have stocks to sell and you put them up for sale'.

> Only 26 per cent could describe a bond correctly. Said one stock-
> holder: 'you can buy a savings bond or different bonds and in 10 or 20
> years you can make money out of them'.

> Only 30 per cent could describe earnings correctly. Said one stockholder:
> 'it's something you work for or works for you'.

> Only 46 per cent could describe a subsidiary correctly. Said one stock-
> holder: 'receiving something in payment for not raising certain crops,
> etc'.

> Only 49 per cent could describe depreciation correctly. Said one stock-
> holder: 'term describing business conditions'.

Its the same in the UK. The *Daily Express* quoted one shareholder in Pergamon Press, a Mr Woolly, an 80-year-old retired clerical worker in Liverpool
who bought 440 shares in the company in January 1965, during the Leasco-
Pergamon battle on 17 September 1969:

> 'The whole matter is so complex it is outside the orbit of ordinary
> shareholders. It would need a lawyer or accountant to sort it out. I am
> waiting for statements from the company. You can't form an opinion
> on personalities.'

Which must be pretty typical. Yet it is in a company's interests to have a
group of shareholders who understand the business and who can vote
intelligently at company meetings. For shareholders, do not forget, can still
vote not only with their feet but with their cheque books as well. They are a

source of new capital. They are potential allies in any takeover threat. And they can be both ambassadors for the company as well as customers. For this it is worth a company's while to cultivate its shareholders. First and foremost it must deliver a good return on their investment. Then it should release sufficient information for them to judge the value of their holding as well as any price changes. This would enable them to decide whether they remain with the company; whether they invest more money with the company or not; and—in the long run—whether they would support the company in any potential bids or mergers.

> 'The need to remove ignorance on matters appertaining to company finance' has become more manifest in the last decade when a large section of political opinion in this country has tended to regard company profits as a social evil', says Frank Jones (*Guide to Company Balance Sheets and Profit and Loss Accounts*).

Similarly with the institutional shareholders. A company neglects its institutional investors at its peril. Bankers, stockbrokers, analysts, members of the Society of Investment Analysts and the Investment Protection Committee of the British Insurance Association are of key importance. Their goodwill and understanding are an indispensable asset to any company.

Lloyds Bank's new investment department, launched 1 November 1969, for example, kicked off with pension fund investments totalling around £200 million plus a further £34 million in the Lloyds Bank Unit Trusts. One pension fund alone, such as that belonging to the Post Office Corporation, can total £60 million a year—more than £1 million a week waiting to be invested.

And, of course, prospective shareholders. The company will always want somebody to buy a stake in their success. This will maintain public confidence in their operation. It will also help when the time comes for additional financing. Some companies see another advantage in increasing the number of shareholders. The more shareholders there are, the less management has to fear.

Said Sir John Braithwaite, ex-Chairman of the London Stock Exchange: 'The object and effect of all this is two-fold: to make what we may call the existing generation of shareholders more aware of their membership of the company, to make them more interested in it—to bring all the shareholders together, as it were into a family circle; and secondly, and I think more important, to assist in attracting the new generation of shareholders that it is so desirable we should have—the generation of new capitalists that ought to result from the wider distribution of wealth that has been such a feature of the post-war years.'

1.4.5 BECAUSE INFORMATION IS VITAL IN ASSESSING A BUSINESS

Take brokers, Hoare and Company. They have spent more than £350,000 on providing an on-line enquiry facility which enables clients to question their computer with its store of 230 million characters of information. It is an investment service which makes the mind boggle. Users outside the company's premises are getting the services, 'data-STREAM' 1 and 2, information retrieval on single companies and groups of companies. At a glance one can examine an individual company or one can see which companies in, say, ship-building have risen and fallen in the last three months. Basic data for any of 3,000 companies plus more sophisticated information on the top 300 concerns—the ICI's, BP's and Marks and Spencers—is available on television screens at the flick of a switch. This covers trend signals, volatility ratings and forecast earnings and P/E ratios.

The analysts recommendations are then expressed in seven different ways: buy; possible purchase; hold; slightly undervalued; neutral hold; hold but slightly overvalued; possible sale; sell. Which is a big step 'from the days when one thought that if a share wasn't worth buying then it should be sold.

If a company is going to be subjected to such rigorous examination then it must ensure that the right information is available at the right time. There is no other way if it wants to maintain realistic prices for its shares in the market.

That's not all. When dividend restraint was lifted on 6 November 1969, Hoare's worked all night to get their computer to produce a list of companies likely to go ahead and raise their dividends. Out of 1,100 stocks fed into the computer only 200 passed the test. Then only half came out with a healthy cash position. But Hoare's did not keep the details to themselves. The computer's selection appeared in the *Financial Times* on 8 November. Even more reason for companies ensuring that full information is given about their activities.

1.4.6 BECAUSE INFORMATION IS VITAL IN CHOOSING BETWEEN TWO BUSINESSES
Information is ammunition. Trying to debate without information is like trying to fight without ammunition. Most investment managers and analysts feel they have to work on less and less information. When it comes to a takeover battle, they are lost. And so is the company. Many professional investors deplored the lack of information available during the GEC–AEI battle. 'AEI did not provide enough up-to-date information', said one investor. 'We were better informed about GEC than AEI', said another. Companies should, therefore, keep shareholders and the City professional up-to-date on plans for the future before any takeover battle breaks.

Security analysis is becoming more and more important. Take the United States. In 1947 there were 1,500 members of the Financial Analysts Federation spread across just five cities. Today there are nearly 8,000 members representing brokers, investment companies, banks, insurance companies, trade associations and the press in 29 cities. And it is still growing. If this is the case in America, it will be the case in this country as well.

C

Similarly with the statistical services. The more statistics become available the more vulnerable a company becomes. The more information a company can provide the statistical services and the more up-to-date the information the better. Again, because it will ensure a realistic assessment of the company and its prospects.

Investment companies, pension and insurance companies have enormous influence. It is vital for a company to give them the facts and figures on which they can judge the company. Similarly with brokers.

1.4.7 BECAUSE A FAVOURABLE REPUTATION WILL ENHANCE THE COMPANY'S OPPORTUNITIES FOR RAISING FINANCIAL SUPPORT. IT WILL BOOST ITS REPUTATION AS AN IMPORTANT INVESTMENT

This is crucial. If a company cannot raise capital or, similarly, if it cannot raise capital at favourable rates, it will have a severe effect on corporate growth.

> 'Provided the company is soundly run, has reasonable prospects and has sensibly and widely communicated about itself to the financial and investment communities it will find that it is able to raise funds without difficulty and at the keenest rates', says Maurice Cocking, Managing Director of FABUS Financial and Business PR.
>
> 'Conversely, those companies which prefer to keep a tight clamp on news about themselves must not be disappointed if they find themselves neglected when either they bring their shares to market or, if already quoted on the Stock Exchange, they seek to raise additional capital.'

Remember Lord Keynes comparison of professional investment with a newspaper competition 'in which the competitors have to pick out the six prettiest faces from a hundred photographs, the prize being awarded to the competitor whose choice most nearly corresponds to the average preferences of the competitors as a whole; so that each competitor has to pick, not those faces which he himself finds prettiest, but those which he thinks likeliest to catch the fancy of other competitors, all of whom are looking at the problem from the same point of view. Its not a case of choosing those which, to the best of one's judgement, are really the prettiest, nor even those which average opinion genuinely thinks are the prettiest. We have reached the third degree where we devote our intelligence to anticipate what average opinion expects average opinion to be. And there are some, I believe, who practise the fourth, and fifth and even higher degrees.' (*General Theory of Employment, Interest and Money*). A company's investment rating, therefore, is important.

'No company is big enough to say that it will never need to ask its present shareholders or the public at large to subscribe for more capital', says Ian van Ammel, Managing Director of Foster, Turner and Benson, one of the top five City advertising agencies (*Financial Times*, 26 June 1967). 'If when that time eventually comes the company can raise capital just that much cheaper, then the cost of the publicity effort of past years is automatically repaid.

'No company is big enough to say that it need never fear a takeover bid. One of the factors in a successful opposition to a bid can be the spread of a company's share capital over a very large number of small investors.

'No company is big enough to say that it will never need to expand by way of acquisition. If acquisition is to be made by means of the offer of shares rather than cash, the advantages of a share price reflecting the true potential of the company making the bid are obvious. A good "image" can also facilitate acceptance of any offer.

'No company is big enough to say that "none of these things will arise with us." '

Companies have virtually got to fight to get investors to invest in them— and not with someone else. Some companies, however, are the exception. Brentford Nylons, the 10-year-old firm which stands number two in Britain's warp knitting industry, just circularised its customers in November 1969 asking them whether they would be interested in lending cash at 12 per cent to help them raise £3 million for a breakthrough into nylon tights and polyester cotton sheets. The response was astonishing. Managing Director, Kaye Metrebian, claimed they had a 12 per cent return averaging about £420 from a 9,000-strong mailing. If they contacted their million customers, he estimated, they could raise about £40 million.

Up until recently, companies only faced the problem of raising money within their own countries. Now there are four foreign capital markets open to British borrowers. They are the D-Mark, Unit of Account, Swiss Franc and the largest and freest of restriction, the Eurodollar, which came into existence in 1963 when the United States introduced an interest equalisation tax virtually barring the New York capital market to foreign borrowers. Instead the borrowers turned to the owners of foreign-owned dollars—Eurodollars. Throughout 1969 several British companies and public bodies turned to these markets to raise money. Courtaulds, for example, borrowed DM 150 million at $6\frac{3}{4}$ per cent. Watney Mann raised 12 million European Units of Account (about £5 million) at 7 per cent. The Electricity Council's DM 150 million (£15·8 million) public bond offering was so successful, both inside and outside Germany, that they decided to go back for a further DM 50 million.

All this, of course, means that companies must ensure that they are known and recognised when they go to raise money in other countries. It will become even more important as more mergers take place between companies of different nationalities. For the signs are already there. The Industrial Reorganisation Corporation, for example, in its 1969 annual report spoke of 'evidence of a keen awareness of the need to form international companies across European frontiers'. Director-General of the National Economic Development Council, Mr Fred Catherwood, has called for multinational groups. And Mr Anthony Crosland, when President of the Board of Trade, also encouraged them, although he wanted proper safeguards as well.

'If people do not invest their funds in securities, American business and American government will not have the capital they need for growth—for new products, new plants, new jobs. That capital can come from just one source: people. Not from hundreds of people with millions of dollars (there aren't many of them any more), but from millions of people with hundreds of dollars', says Merrill Lynch, Pierce, Fenner and Smith.

It's true for America and it's true for the United Kingdom.

Mr D. J. Ashton-Jones, Managing Director of BBDO Public Relations, a leading City public relations consultancy, goes a stage further. Not only will investors have to be persuaded to invest their money but they will have to be persuaded to invest their money in the right companies—from their point of view.

> 'There is some strong evidence that investors will not, in future, be pre-
> pared to purchase equity shares, other than for short-term and purely
> speculative purposes, of companies that are not forthcoming with a lot
> more intelligible relevant detail of progress than that enforced by law and
> regulation. And where will the price earnings ratios be then? They will
> be at levels which draw the hungry attention of unwelcome takeover
> bidders with unattractive offers', he says.
> (*Financial Times*, 5 November 1969)

1.4.8 BECAUSE REPUTATION IS INDIVISABLE

A company may have the finest employee relations programme in the world. But if a customer finds a beetle in a can of beans, it will make no difference at all. The company has failed—and failed bitterly. Similarly a company may have the finest sales force in the country. But if the City has to wait six months for even general figures about progress and is then brushed off without any explanation, the company's reputation will suffer. So, more likely than not, will the share prices. Goodwill and reputation, therefore, are invaluable assets for any company. Although of an intangible nature, it is frequently the most valuable asset possessed and its existence goes to the very core of the business', says Frank H. Jones (*Guide to Company Balance Sheets and Profit and Loss Accounts*). He lists six different aspects of goodwill:

1 PERSONALITY. To a small business this is crucial.
2 LOCATION. An ideal site.
3 ADVERTISING. Trade names, etc., which had become household words.
4 REPUTATION. Here its worth quoting Jones direct—mark every word:
   'Reputation, for example, may arise from a well recognised standard of
   high quality, consistently maintained, like that of a well-known motor
   car manufacturing company whose name has now almost become an

adjective in general use, to denote the best quality of any product. Reputation may also have been established as the result of reliable conscientious service and efficient organisation which has become widely accepted.'

5 LENGTH OF EXISTENCE. The longer a company has been in business, the stronger its connections.

6 MONOPOLY. Patented invention, sole rights, etc.

'The wide field of membership of a large company should be regarded as a valuable potential sphere of influence—for the creation of goodwill, for the expansion of sales, for the enhancement of customer-relations and for the marshalling of public opinion in opposition to legislation of a restrictive or onerous character,' says Jones (*Guide to Company Balance Sheets and Profit and Loss Accounts*). 'By the despatch of literature at frequent intervals—newsletters, brochures, folders and the like—or by regular, e.g. quarterly or half-yearly publications, it is claimed that much progress can be achieved in these directions.'

A favourable reputation will also help the company in any legislative battles or lobbying it undertakes.

1.4.9 BECAUSE THOSE WHO COMMUNICATE WIN AND THOSE WHO DO NOT LOSE

Or, as Michael Burrows of the British Market Research Bureau put it at the European Society for Opinion and Market Research Conference in September 1969: 'Those who communicate swallow—those who do not, get swallowed'. Out of 50 City people asked about the availability of information during the GEC–AEI battle, he said, 14 believed AEI did not provide enough information and six felt they were better informed about GEC than AEI. Such a failure to communicate could be decisive.

'It used to be said in the City of London', commented Burrows, 'that those who mattered knew and those that didn't know, didn't matter. One wonders whether this is still true. If a company doesn't say it is doing well, some people—the younger, more irreverent, but increasingly the more influential—can begin to wonder if you are as good as more senior men think you are.' He gave a four-point plan:

1 Try to offset the takeover bidders advantage by publishing as much factual data as possible about: (*a*) details of the profit record of recently recruited directors to the company; (*b*) details of improving profit trends in selected product fields; (*c*) evidence of expanding shares in specified market sectors at home or abroad; (*d*) evidence of new, tighter budgetary control systems.

2 Circulate as much technical data about potential price/earnings ratios, for example, as possible to financial editors and investment analysts.

3 Issue bank managers and other advisers with objective summaries of facts and Press comment.

4 Prepare easily-understood and objective but persuasive 'direct mail' circulars to shareholders.

Do not forget companies are vulnerable to a raid when it is worth more than the stock it is selling for—and when the raider can rally the stockholders to his cause. But if the shares are selling for what they are worth a raider will not be able to get something for nothing. Neither will he be able to rally discontented shareholders behind him.

1.4.10 BECAUSE—LIKE IT OR NOT—THE PRESS IS THERE. THEY HAVE A DUTY TO
      REPORT THE NEWS—AND THEY HAVE INFLUENCE

If the press are going to report the news, it's much better if they report the good news about a company instead of just the bad news. On top of that, press comment has a tremendous effect on a company.

> 'When I mentioned some six weeks ago that buyers of Slater Walker would have few regrets in a year's time, I did not expect quite so swift a response in the share price, even allowing for a certain amount of overdue bear covering.'
> (Questor, *Daily Telegraph*, 15 September 1969)

Daily Stock Exchange reports in the press often list as many as 20 different examples of shares being affected by press comment. It can also effect prices in the long-term. Investors tend to take into account the corporate image of the companies concerned and, more often than not, come down on the side of the company with the right image. General Electric and Westinghouse prove the theory among United States companies. The price/earnings ratio of General Electric shows a slow steady growth. Westinghouse's ratio, however, switched back and forth year after year. Similarly with GEC and AEI before the takeover. Almost as soon as Arnold Weinstock joined the GEC board, the publicity machine started building him up as a whizz kid.

The price/earnings ratio started to climb along with the increased dividends and profits. AEI's ratio went down and down. So the strength of GEC's corporate image helped the takeover. United States industrial design and marketing consultants, Lippincott and Margulies, have gone a stage further and quantified their belief that the shares of a company with a good growth record and a good image are generally higher than those of an equally successful company without a good image. To get the growth record across, however, one needs the news media.

The press is also a major source of advice and information. A British Market Research Bureau enquiry into the factors which influenced institutional investors, stockholders and private shareholders involved in the GEC–AEI takeover bid discovered that press comment rated a high 69 points compared with company circulars (96) and stockbrokers (95). But then the stockbrokers admitted that they were also influenced by the press as well.

Sir Joseph Latham, Deputy Chairman and Managing Director of AEI at the time, seemed to recognise their short-comings with the press in his book on the battle (*Takeover: the facts and the myths of the GEC/AEI battle*, Iliffe Books, London). With hindsight, he wrote, AEI might have briefed reporters more effectively, though he doubted whether it would have affected the result.

A Stock Exchange survey released in May 1966 revealed that while only 10 per cent of shareholders consulted a stockbroker when deciding which shares to buy no less than 20 per cent relied on the columns of the financial press.

This was reinforced in a survey among professional investors carried out by the British Market Research Bureau for the *Investors Chronicle* and published in 1969. Three reasons, they discovered, were given for considering the purchase of a particular share:

1 Suggested by the research department—33 per cent.
2 Suggested by a stockbroker—18 per cent.
3 Read about in the press—15 per cent.

The researchers went a stage further. When prompted, those mentioning their research departments rose to 43 per cent and those who had read about it in the press jumped to 28 per cent. But which newspapers? Ninety-three per cent said they read or looked at the *Financial Times* six times a week. Next came *The Times Business News* with 61 per cent followed by the *Daily Mail* with 43 per cent, which on 30 August 1969 immediately labelled itself, 'The newspaper that shareholders trust'.

Ten reasons for a vigorous and effective financial advertising and public relations programme.

A market research survey in March 1968 for United Artists revealed that only 4 per cent of the public had heard of the making of their multi-million pound film, 'Chitty Chitty Bang Bang'. By the end of the year public awareness had shot up to 70 per cent. Reason: the efficient use of advertising and related arts.

Similar opportunities for increasing public awareness are open to every company.

Part two

Preparing for Action

Chapter 2

Financial Advertising and Its Media

The first thing about advertising is to forget the bally-hoo.

Legend has piled upon legend since a young Texan-Jewish salesman, Albert Lasker, devised the concept of 'salesmanship in print' in 1904 which transformed straightforward announcements into seductive inducements—making him 45 million dollars in the process. 'Advertising is not (as some people seem to imagine) something in its own right, some separate estate of the realm, like civil administration or the services or law. Advertising is an integral part of industry', said John Hobson, Chairman of Hobson, Bates and Partners, one of the top agencies in the country, in the *Journal of the Royal Society of Arts*, July 1964.

As soon as a company becomes a company, financial advertising becomes an integral part of their commercial life.

It is not like consumer or trade advertising which is designed to boost sales or classified advertising which seeks staff. Financial advertising is first of all essential. It is virtually laid down by the Stock Exchange. It is a mixture of straightforward informative advertising and reputation-building advertising not for the company's products or staff but for the company itself. Anthony Sampson in his mammoth *The Anatomy of Britain Today* lists five different names for it: prestige advertising; reputation advertising; company advertising; institutional advertising; goodwill advertising—'the multiplicity of names, as for lavatories, suggest embarrassment', he adds. Which is nonsense. The Institute of Practitioners in Advertising gives the key definition:

> 'Company advertisements can influence the public to regard the company in a certain way: as forward-looking people with a vigorous policy of scientific research; as friendly, helpful people with enough humanity to laugh at themselves; or as craftsmen in the English tradition to whom "automation" and "assembly line" are naughty words.'

This covers everything from the 'fairy tale' story of Holt Williams and Company Limited—'after a lot of head scratching their designer John Bramhill came up with a Retractable Twist Lock'—to the smooth, sophisticated advertisements of the Algemene Bank Nederland—'The case of the doubling diamonds'—which grace the pages of *Time* magazine. Don't confuse it with advertising by financial institutions, such as banks, building societies and insurance companies. That is also labelled financial advertising. Which is crazy. As Rupert Chetwynd, managing director of his own agency, says, 'This form of financial advertising is the same as any other kind of advertising. You can market money the same as you can market dog food.' True, financial advertising, probably better called business or company advertising, is advertising which promotes the company as a whole rather than its products or services, primarily, to the financial communities.

2.1 Reasons for advertising

Why advertise? To present information to a selected audience. Or, as PR adviser, Trevor Russell-Cobb says, 'To be quite sure what you want said is said the way you want it said'. Buying advertising space ensures that the company maintains complete control not only over the content of the advertisement but over the timing of its publication as well. This is something which is impossible through any other form of publicity. It also ensures that a company can throw its full technical and design expertise behind the operation in order to make the maximum impact.

'Properly done, financial advertising can surely achieve a great deal', says Ian van Ammel (*Financial Times*, 26 June 1967) who is Managing Director of Foster, Turner and Benson, one of the big five financial advertising agencies in the UK. 'It builds goodwill in the City, and among the investing public— and that can be most valuable in times of stress. I do not want to suggest that such goodwill can come only from financial advertising: that would be foolish. But advertising can certainly help if, I repeat, it is properly done.' And he adds, 'Investors don't see every item of company news—there is too much of it—and the same goes for City men. They may miss things which are good for a company's image—large export orders, record profits, higher dividends. Financial advertising presents an opportunity to draw these things to the public's attention and let them sink in.'

Russell Cobb makes a similar point. 'Financial advertising helps to keep the name of the company before the people. It might help, for example, to point a financial analyst in the right direction and don't forget, financial analysts are also part of the general public. Their research departments can influence them. But so can their wife's papers and magazines as well as their own non-technical reading.'

With more than £30,000 million changing hands every year on the Stock Exchange, its worth the effort—and it works as well. The *Investors Chronicle* survey into professional investors, published in 1969, revealed that few of them read the printed version of the chairmans' annual statements, unless they wanted a close analysis of the company concerned. Sixty-seven per cent, however, read extracts or comments in the press, often in the train on their way to the City. They gave two reasons: partly because it was a convenient time for them to get their reading done and partly because of the need to be aware of the main points of an important company statement by the time the market opened or the first investment meeting was held. By comparison, the printed company statements arrived by post. If they arrived at the office,

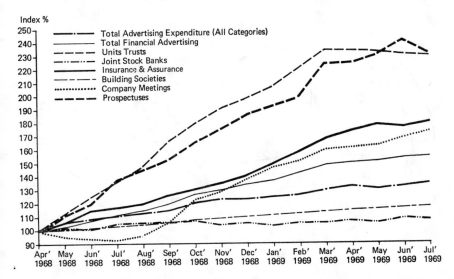

Moving annual totals of advertising expenditure in all media, year ending April 1968=100 (*Advertiser's Weekly*, 3 October 1969)

it took time for them to be sorted and circulated. If they arrived at home, it was usually after they had left to go to the office. This fits Paul Ferris' description in *The City*:

> 'Ewell, Cheam, Woking, Esher, Guildford and a dozen other places provide their morning contingents for the fast electric trains that run, from the counties south of London, the best suburban rail service in Europe. It is further expected of the stockbroker that he shall study the newspapers on his way to the City and have a little gamble . . .'

2.2 Growth of financial advertising

Financial advertising has boomed since the war—another sympton of the business information explosion. And it is still growing. A survey carried out by Research Services for the Advertising Association into advertising expenditure—the first full-scale study in four years—revealed that while display advertising expenditure decreased between 1965 and 1968, expenditure on classified, trade and financial advertising increased proportionately.

Partly this is due to the confusion between the two forms of financial advertising. MEAL, for example, estimate £20·2 million spent on financial advertising on all media between July 1968 and July 1969, an increase of 38 per cent over the preceeding 12 months—and 54 per cent more than in April 1968. Yet it breaks down into unit trusts and prospectuses, the fastest-growing sectors with some 130 per cent increase since April 1968; insurance

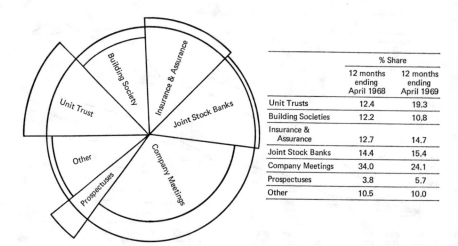

	% Share	
	12 months ending April 1968	12 months ending April 1969
Unit Trusts	12.4	19.3
Building Societies	12.2	10.8
Insurance & Assurance	12.7	14.7
Joint Stock Banks	14.4	15.4
Company Meetings	34.0	24.1
Prospectuses	3.8	5.7
Other	10.5	10.0

Fig. 2. Share of total financial advertising by product group for 12 months ending April 1969 compared with 12 months ending April 1968 (*Advertiser's Weekly*, 3 October 1969)

companies and building societies, up 80 and 34 per cent, respectively, over the same period; company meeting reports at £4·75 million, annually the largest single category in financial advertising; and joint stock banks, whose expenditure actually declined between April and July 1968 (see graph).

The purely financial advertising figures, however, show that while company meetings remain the largest single category, their share of the cake has been declining—while the size of the cake increases (see figure). In April 1968, for example, they rated 34 per cent of the total. Twelve months later they were down to 24·1 per cent. At the same time, prospectuses had reversed the trend. In April 1968 they represented a mere 3·8 per cent of the total. A year later, however, they had jumped to 5·7 per cent.

2.3 Types of financial advertising

Pure financial advertising, therefore, covers five areas:

2.3.1 PROSPECTUSES AND ABRIDGED PARTICULARS OF NEW ISSUES
This is laid down by the Stock Exchange and must cover at least two leading

London daily newspapers. Because of the detail involved, it generally means at least one, sometimes two full pages of copy. In most cases it is left as dull, grey text. Some companies throw in a line-drawing to make it more attractive and more readable. The Caterpillar Tractor Company had the best of both worlds when they arranged for their shares to be quoted on both the London and Scottish Stock Exchanges. They fulfilled the Stock Exchange requirements. Then they took space to present a 'potted version' of the details. Said the hard-hitting first paragraph:

'Caterpillar Tractor Co. is the biggest and best known manufacturer of heavy duty tractors and earthmoving equipment in the world. It also supplies diesel engines to other makes of driven equipment. With nine manufacturing plants in the USA and manufacturing facilities in Britain, Australia, Canada, France, Brazil and Mexico, Caterpillar and its subsidiaries employ a total of 48,000 persons. Affiliated companies have plants at Sagami, Japan, and Bombay, India.'

The copy went on to cover: Caterpillar on world-famous projects; Continuous growth; Record results; Current outlook; Caterpillar in Great Britain and Eire; Saving Dollars; the Caterpillar history in a nutshell; and, of course, Profit Record Summary.

2.3.2 INTERIM REPORTS
Compared with the annual report this is child's play. Albright and Wilson simply produce a small four-page folder giving the necessary figures with a four-paragraph message from the Chairman, Mr O. H. Wansbrough-Jones. Thomas Tilling are a little more ambitious. They produce an eight-page leaflet with a six-page message from the Chairman, Sir Geoffrey Eley. In addition they list—in the case of Thomas Tilling where necessary—the main products and companies within the group. Companies should also, of course, advertise their interim reports in the appropriate media.

2.3.3 THE CHAIRMAN'S STATEMENT, THE ANNUAL REPORT AND REPORTS OF
         COMPANY MEETINGS
There are chairman's statements and chairman's statements. The British Vita Magazine once carried a chairman's statement that included no less than 238 capital letters in just 120 lines. Only 23, however, were used for opening sentences. The remainder were crammed into sentences, such as, 'As you will see, Notwithstanding the Many Problems, both Inside and Outside the Country, our Group ploughs on Steadily, overcoming Whatever Obstacles fall in our Path, and at the same time, continually Breaking New Ground, upon which our Future Security and Wellbeing depends'. Whether the chairman was brought up in Germany or not, it didn't say. A far better approach is adopted by the Industrial and Commercial Finance Corporation Limited. They booked a four-page News-Report which both enlarged and enlivened

their annual report in the *UK Press Gazette* to reach opinion-forming journalists and also in *The Economist* to reach the decision-makers. An effective combination.

2.3.4. INSTITUTIONAL ADVERTISING

S. and W. Berisford Limited, the sugar and produce importers and merchants, took a novel double-page advertisement in full colour in *Investors Chronicle* to announce their move to new head-office premises. It was startling. But it made its point. Everybody who saw the magazine was aware that Berisford, a public company with a £97 million turnover quoted on the Northern Stock Exchange, was moving.

> 'As our headquarters in Manchester were included in a large re-development scheme in the centre of the city, with all the inherent uncertainties ensuing from this, we have built new head office premises adjacent to our existing Holmes Chapel property, into which we hope to move. . . . We are leaving Manchester with a certain amount of nostalgia after being so closely connected with the City for over 100 years but we shall be closer to our canned goods and warehousing interests, and the shortening of our communications will be of considerable benefit. A sales office will, however, remain in Manchester. With the drive and spirit of the Directors, Executives and Staff we can look forward confidently to whatever the future holds for us.'

Thus wrote the Chairman, Anthony Berisford. Underneath was listed their principal subsidiary companies and their trading activities.

That's one example. Another is the straightforward advertisement that simply says—in a whole page in *Management Today*—'N. M. Rothschild and Sons, Merchant Bankers, New Court, St. Swithin's Lane, London, E.C.4.' But few companies could get away with that.

Falconbridge, the Canadian miner, smelter and refiner of nickel, took a full-page colour advertisement in *The Economist* on 29 November 1969 to stress just one word—Expansion.

> 'With Falconbridge, its constant . . . Right now—among various major projects—a £75 million mining and processing installation is under construction in the Dominican Republic for the production of ferronickel. In the ore-rich Sudbury area of central Canada, site of many Falconbridge mines, another mine shaft is being sunk. Lockerby, its called. Next to Falconbridge's Sudbury-area smelter, a new refinery is nearing completion. A complex metallurgical plant, it will turn out iron-nickel pellets. Used in steelmaking, the iron-nickel pellet is a unique breakthrough product of Falconbridge. And, meanwhile, an expanded search for new ore reserves is surging ahead in Canada . . . and elsewhere in the world. Falconbridge . . . big miner and smelter and refiner of nickel.

Nickel that's marketed worldwide. Expansion . . . at Falconbridge, it's constant.'

But expansion is just one reason for launching an institutional advertising campaign. There are a thousand others.

2.3.5 FIRE-BRIGADE ADVERTISING

If a company hits a problem, it may have to advertise to get out—fast. This could mean a takeover bid. Courtauld's fought off ICI in 1962 but the price of independence was high. When victory came on 9 March it had cost them 37½ per cent of Ordinary stock and £361,695 in cash—£112,000 in a fighting institutional advertising campaign. Similarly with the GEC's battle with AEI in November 1967. Advertising was used extensively by both sides.

Or could it mean an identification problem. To the general public the Hargreaves Group were a company dabbling in everything. They didn't have any definite impressions of the company. Hargreaves decided to run a corporate campaign to overcome this position. The theme: 'There's more in Hargreaves Group than meets the eye'.

'Hargreaves would like to drive a tanker right through a popular misconception', said the headline incorporating a line drawing of a giant Smith and Robinson road tanker.

'Although we operate one of the largest road tanker fleets in the country (Smith and Robinson—that's us), a great many people think of Hargreaves as just the coal people. Others know us for quarrying. Or fertilisers. Or vehicle distribution. Or fuel oil distribution. Or vehicle body building. In short each separate kind of customer tends to get a rather narrow view of us. The truth is that the Hargreaves Group is a model of systematic diversification, each arm of its organisation having grown naturally out of one or more of the others. It may be useful to you, at some time or other, to remember that, behind the Hargreaves you are familiar with, there are other Hargreaves companies and people ready to serve you in different ways.'

Clearly, it would also be useful to Hargreaves if people remembered the whole spread of their activities as well.

'Hargreaves would like to blow an old supposition sky-high,' ran another advertisement. This time showing a line drawing of a giant excavator.

'Despite our extensive quarrying operations for limestone, sand and gravel, there are still those who suppose Hargreaves to be just the coal people (they've 90 years experience of us to prove it!) Others swear we are engaged in making fertilisers. Or distributing fuel oils. Or road transport. Or distributing vehicles. Or vehicle body building. What we should like them to know is that we are, in fact, all these things. A highly successful example of systematic diversification. . . .'

D

And so on. But it made its point.

That's financial advertising. Now for the media.

2.4 Planning a campaign

There is only one way to plan any advertising campaign and that's to work to a plan.

2.4.1 DEFINE THE PROBLEM

If it is a prospectus there is no immediate problem. The Stock Exchange rules that it must appear in two national daily newspapers. If, however the company is applying to a provincial Stock Exchange then it should appear in one national newspaper and in one regional newspaper in the area as well.

2.4.2 LIST THE OBJECTIVES

If—like the Hargreaves Group—a company wants to correct either a wrong or a limited impression that it has got with the financial public, then clearly the more newspapers and magazines it appears in the better. Providing, of course, that they are read by the financial public. If the objective is to talk to the financial community proper then the financial press would suffice. Shareholders are another problem. In some cases the only way of contacting shareholders is through direct mail. It is expensive. But its the only way of guaranteeing success. In other cases advertising—in the right media—is again the answer.

2.4.3 DEFINE THE TARGET AUDIENCE

Here it can be shareholders, investment trust, brokers, pension funds, overseas investors or even employees and, of course, customers. Once the target is within sights, virtually everything else falls into place.

2.4.4 DEVELOP THE COPY PLATFORM

This depends on the target. Obviously if the message is aimed at prospective shareholders, the copy must concentrate on the facts and figures of the argument. Nobody ever puts their money into a company because it says please and thank you. If the advertisement is a general prestige shot, the copy can stretch to some colour: 'Caterpillar Tractor Co. is the biggest and best known manufacturer of heavy duty tractors and earthmoving equipment in the world.'

2.4.5 SELECT THE MEDIA

This is the headache. For it means juggling a budget in such a way that it buys the maximum space to make the maximum impact on the maximum number of the selected target audience. It also means mastering the ad-man's mumbo-jumbo.

First the different categories of readers. For the purpose of their regular readership surveys, the Institute of Practitioners in Advertising has established socio-economic definitions:

A CLASS Upper middle class, higher managerial, administrative or professional. About 2 per cent of population.

B CLASS Intermediate managerial, administrative or professional. About 10 per cent of population.

C1 CLASS Supervisory or clerical and junior managerial, administrative or professional. About 18 per cent of population.

C2 CLASS Skilled manual workers. Thirty-seven per cent of population.

D CLASS Semi-skilled and unskilled manual workers.

E CLASS Those at lowest levels of subsistence, state pensioners or widows (no other earner), casual or lowest grade of workers. DE classes combined are 33 per cent of population.

Then there is the question of cost-per-thousand. This entails dividing the advertising rate of a publication by the circulation in thousands to obtain the cost per thousand readers. This is the criterion for judging the value of different publications. Clearly the publication which offers the most target readers for the lowest cost-per-thousand is the best buy.

Discovering the best advertising medium, therefore, involves, essentially, first locating the best publication—or groups of publications—in readership terms and then in cost-per-thousand terms. Take company directors. Market Investigations Limited carried out a survey in 1965 to discover details of newspaper readership among the very highest class of businessman (see Table 2.1). The results showed a win for the *Sunday Times*, followed by the *Financial Times* and *The Times*.

Table 2.1

	Total company directors %	Type of director		Age %	
		Managing or chairman %	Other directors %	under 55	55
The Sunday Times	79	83	76	83	73
The Observer	28	27	28	32	22
Sunday Telegraph	28	31	27	24	33
Financial Times	68	73	65	70	66
The Times	54	58	51	50	58
Daily Telegraph	46	48	45	41	52

Source: *Market Investigations Limited Company Directors Srveuy 1965*

But suppose you didn't want businessmen generally but, says businessmen in the transport equipment industry. A survey carried out among 3,530 businessmen in the industry by Industrial Media Data Limited in 1966 put the *Sunday Express* top of the list followed by *The Sunday Times* and the *Daily Telegraph* (see Table 2.2).

Table 2.2   Readership of newspapers by businessmen in the transport equipment industry. Sample size, 3,530

Financial Times	36%
Daily Telegraph	45%
Daily Express	36%
Daily Mail	22%
The Times	12%
The Guardian	8%
Sunday Express	52%
The Sunday Times	47%
The Observer	23%
Sunday Telegraph	19%

Source: *Industrial Media Data Limited*, 1966

Go a stage further. Which newspapers do chief executives of public companies look at to keep in touch with business trends and developments? This time the answer was a Yes for the *Financial Times*, followed by *The Sunday Times* and the *Daily Telegraph* (see Table 2.3).

Table 2.3   Readership of newspapers for business purposes by chief executives of public companies. Question: Which of the following newspapers do you look at to keep in touch with business trends and developments? Sample size, 1,600

Financial Times	88%
Daily Telegraph	45%
The Times	40%
Daily Mail	20%
Daily Express	20%
The Guardian	12%
The Sunday Times	61%
Sunday Express	34%
The Observer	19%
Sunday Telegraph	19%

Source: *The Financial Times/Research Services*, 1967

Now the cost-per-thousand (see Table 2.4). The *Yorkshire Post* used this argument to prove that their costs compared reasonably with national newspapers. On this basis the *Yorkshire Post* came out at 8s 4d with a 120,774 circulation compared with the 7s 0d cost-per-thousand figure of *The Guardian* with its 292,602 circulation.

Table 2.4

	Circulation	Cost per thousand circulation. SCI (unit trust rates)
Daily Telegraph	1,380,367	3s 9d
The Sunday Times	1,454,079	5s 0d
Yorkshire Post	120,774	8s 4d
The Observer	879,024	6s 1d
The Guardian	292,602	7s 0d
The Times	437,278	4s 9d
Financial Times	172,342	16s 0d

Source: *ABC Figures Jan-Jun '69. Rate effective August '69*

Of course, there are plenty of other factors to take into account such as duplication of readership (*The Sunday Times*, for example, estimate that 37·2 per cent of their readers also read *The Observer*; 31·9 per cent the *Daily Telegraph* and 26·1 per cent the *Sunday Telegraph*); the regional breakdown of readership; the amount of time people spend reading a newspaper; how much they are influenced by what they read and so on.

2.5 Media

The principal media for financial advertising, therefore, is divided among the following categories.

2.5.1 NATIONAL PRESS
A must. The national press can reach more readers with more responsibility than any other advertising medium. That includes everyone from the A-class businessmen with reponsibility for finance to private shareholders.

Two tables from the *Investors Chronicle* survey, *The Professional Investor*, are worth quoting:

'Which of the following daily newspapers do you think most influence private shareholders?'

Daily Mail	70 per cent
Daily Telegraph	52 per cent
Financial Times	30 per cent
Daily Express	27 per cent
The Times (Business News)	23 per cent
The Times (Main Section)	4 per cent

'Which of the following daily newspapers do you regard as having influence in the city?'

Financial Times	95 per cent
The Times (Business News)	57 per cent
Daily Mail	56 per cent
Daily Telegraph	47 per cent
The Times (Main Section)	22 per cent
Daily Express	10 per cent

2.5.2 REGIONAL PRESS

There can be many advantages in using the regional press. For, do not forget, national newspapers do not always have genuine national circulations. The February–December, 1968 JICNARS* figures, for example, show that while 7·1 per cent of *The Sunday Times* circulation is in Scotland only 1·7 per cent of the *Daily Telegraph*'s and just 1 per cent of the *Sunday Telegraph*'s circulation is north of the border. Clearly if a company wanted extensive penetration in Scotland, it would do well to look to the regional press rather than the national press in this case. That is in terms of circulation. In many cases its the same story in terms of readership. The *Yorkshire Evening Post*, for example, was estimated to reach 112,000 people with cheque books and 26,000 with shares out of totals of 359,000 and 83,000, respectively—a powerful argument for any Yorkshire-based company which was out to build a strong local investment base.

2.5.3 SPECIALIST OR TRADE JOURNALS

Almost, by definition, these have important readerships. *The Economist* 'Marplan' Survey, for example, showed that *Management Today* had a 34 per cent penetration of the top A class businessman group, the highest figure obtained by a considerable margin by any weekly or monthly publication. And do not forget the political weeklies. They are read largely by opinion-forming people.

'A manufacturer of, say, an improved form of electrical installation wants to tell his story beyond his immediate contacts with whatever Ministries he deals', says Bernard Gutteridge, free-lance advertising consultant and poet, in *The Listener*, 31 July 1969. 'He wants to be read by specialised correspondents: by MP's who have made the subject their present interest, by civil servants and so on. Read also in the knowledge that the full story is available in its immediate form to the Ministers and their permanent advisers. Where else can he get this universal political awareness than through advertisements (or publicity) in political papers?'

2.5.4 CONSUMER MAGAZINES

Unlikely. But possible. A consumer goods manufacturer could find it necessary to take space in consumer journals to counteract comments on the company in general or the products in particular. This would be fire-brigade

* Joint Industry Committee for National Readership Surveys.

advertising in its true sense. Similarly, a company with a strong consumer investment could find it worth taking space in consumer journals to put their side of a takeover story. And do not forget Russell Cobb's point: an investment analyst is not only influenced by his research department. He can be influenced by his wife. So why not try persuading the wife as well? In some cases, it could work.

2.5.5 TELEVISION
Highly unlikely. Because of costs and the universal nature of television audiences. It's alright selling dog food. Practically everyone watching television buys dog food. But only a relatively small minority, by comparison, are investors and potential investors. The wastage, therefore, would be enormous. One company, ICI, however, have already used television for a corporate advertising campaign. Its possible that the medium could be used for vigorous financial advertising in the future—especially on the regional networks where the costs could be contained.

2.5.6 INTERNATIONAL NEWS MEDIA
Pick up *The Economist*. In practically any issue there will be advertisements booked by Japan's Yawata Steel; America's Crane Co.; Canada's Falconbridge; Sweden's Uddeholm; France's Aquitaine and the UK's Hawker Siddeley Group. They won't be sales advertisements. But institutional advertisements promoting the name of the various companies to an international readership. Similarly British companies took space in overseas publications making their international readerships aware of their existence, their growth and their developments.

2.6 Developments

Nothing stands still. Least of all financial advertising, which is developing rapidly.

First, the presentation of financial advertisements. The over-all standard is still dull and stodgy in spite of the valiant efforts of a handful of companies. 'Chairmanites' reigns supreme. This will change. Professional designers will be invited in. The advertisements will be given a face-lift to appeal to still wider publics. 'Where they can the financial advertising agencies have been applying the more sophisticated techniques of product advertising and pop editorial', says van Ammel (*Financial Times*, 26 June 1967). 'However the pace of change is more likely to be governed by the company chairman than by his agency.'

Second, size. Everything is getting bigger. Smaller companies are becoming national concerns. And national companies are becoming international giants. Both ICI and the British Steel Corporation both stress that the competition they face is not from the shop around the corner but from other international organisations. Investors are also catching on. They are beginning to take more interest in foreign stocks than ever before. The *Financial Times* publishes a whole page on overseas company news and markets every day. As a result, more firms will begin thinking of raising money abroad. And if they do that, they will have to be more concerned with their standing abroad.

Third, business news. A few years ago the press were flirting with business news. Now its the love affair of the century. Sales, training, productivity, recruitment, research, development, every aspect of a company's activities is becoming grist for the journalists mill. As a result, van Ammel believes, 'financial advertising will become more and more involved in all the "Corporate image" facets of client companies. Instead of the once- or twice-a-year announcements of financial results a year-round campaign involving both advertising and public relations will be called for.'

Chapter 3

___

Financial News and Its Media

Drivers on the London-Sydney rally wore them. Crews on the round-Britain power boat race are wearing them. Throwaway paper panties—made by the Goujon (Paper Togs) subsidiary of a company called Bolton Textile Mill. Last night, Bolton revealed that sales of paper panties are running at over one million pairs a week. Profits for the year just ended are estimated at around £350,000 and for the coming 12 months are expected to top £550,000. Since it first went into the throwaway business last year, Bolton's shares have rocketed from the equivalent of 4s 6d to 23s each. They have now come back to a more realistic looking 14s each.
(*Daily Mirror*, 29 July 1969)

That's financial public relations. A good company story told in an interesting way designed to attract millions of readers. It doesn't only promote the company—'profits are expected to top £550,000'—it also publicises the products as well. As far as the company is concerned it is publicity that has not cost a penny. Yet it will help to keep the public informed of the company, its sales and its profits.

Stories like this are appearing every day. They benefit the companies as well as the products. And it is the financial PRO's duty to publicise companies in this way.

3.1 What is financial public relations?

'Basically, it is no more than a branch of business communications', says Maurice Cocking. 'But it is that extremely important branch concerned with relaying information and viewpoints on a company's financial, industrial and commercial activities to those wider audiences termed the financial and investment communities. No Board of directors can suppose that it is acting in the best interest of its shareholders and employees by avoiding publicity with regard to its operations.'

Company law insists on disclosure of company affairs. Advertising is a vital ingredient in over-all marketing. Financial public relations merely builds bridges and carries the good and the bad company news to the outside world of editors, stockbrokers, jobbers, bankers, investment and unit trust managers, pension fund chiefs, accountants, company directors, trade customers and a whole host of potential investors and providers of capital.

'It is thus the important function of the financial public relations man to ensure that both the company's shareholders and the investment public at large get the message', Maurice Cocking adds, 'yet not only get the company's message but the correct message at the right time, in the right place and presented in the right manner. Men and markets alike may then hold the company in true and fair financial focus.'

Financial advertising has been in existence for years. Yet financial PR is still developing. It is still a new skill.

> 'A phone call to GKN brought the reply that the chairman "never talked to the Press". But that was ten years ago. With a new chairman, prestige London headquarters and the Birfield takeover almost turning sour in its hands, GKN appointed a financial PR consultancy in 1966. It now also has a growing PR department of its own under a former Neddy man.'
>
> (*Campaign* 19 September 1969)

Other companies have followed suit, again, usually after a traumatic experience. But they have all realised the value of financial public relations in the long run.

Chairman and founder of Ruder and Finn, one of the top international PR consultancies, David Finn is convinced financial PR is becoming more and more important. As more people become investors, companies become increasingly aware of the need to keep them and, more important, the financial world aware of their plans and developments. In the old days secrecy was the rule. Today its information. In the States, for example, he runs financial PR programmes aimed exclusively at the 12,000 investment analysts, a field that is virgin territory in Britain.

'There are 1,200 investment analysts in this country and I bet not one is receiving any kind of information about a company. This is a field for PR which can be developed and expanded enormously', he says. 'Then there is the press. Very often top executives do not know how to talk to editors. They try to sell them too hard. The financial public relations man should be there to advise and to help. But he should not be a barrier or a buffer. He should be there to help both sides.'

3.2 The start

Yet 10 years ago financial PR was virtually unknown. The City was a closed shop. Companies had barred doors. Businessmen were tight-lipped. In just two weeks, however, the whole system was blown sky-high. This was the famous Aluminium War of Christmas 1958.

The previous year the American Reynolds Metals tried to buy British Aluminium, the only British aluminium company, in order to get their new plant in Quebec. Reynolds were advised by their own banker as well as their London correspondent, Siegmund Warburg, that an American bid would antagonise British nationalism. Instead, they said, Reynolds should operate with a British company. Accordingly they went into partnership with Tube Investments, whose adviser was banker, Lionel Fraser, and through Warburg, Reynolds and TI began buying British Aluminium shares. By October 1958 they had 10 per cent of the shares. TI put in a definite offer for BA shares. BA retorted and claimed they had already reached an agreement with Alcoa, Reynolds' American rivals. TI's chief Sir Ivan Stedeford was furious. He called a press conference and revealed the whole story as well as the terms of his offer to BA shareholders, which were more generous than the Alcoa offer. The press sided with him. The former war-time Chief of Staff, Lord Portal, who was running BA retorted, 'Those familiar with negotiations between great companies will realise that such a course would have been impracticable'. Next, TI sent in a formal bid of 78s for each BA share. BA then announced they would increase the dividend.

On New Year's Eve, however, everything suddenly boiled over. Fourteen financial institutions led by Olaf Hambro and Lord Kindersley wrote to BA shareholders revealing that they were holding two million shares in BA, that they would buy shares at 82s and that the TI offer must be resisted in the 'national interest'. Fraser replied with an interview in the *Evening Standard*. 'How many friends on the other side can say their proposals are in the national interest astound me'.

Reynolds retorted by buying 1,300,000 BA shares in the following two days and slapping in another bid on 5 January. By 9 January together with TI they held 80 per cent of British Aluminium shares. The battle was over. But the scars were deep. Portal resigned. TI nominated their own replacement. And Olaf Hambro wrote to *The Times* on 12 January complaining bitterly that 'it was very unclear why the majority of city editors of the press seemed to be against city opinion and openly wrote in favour of the takeover bid'.

Today it is obvious. As Lionel Fraser wrote afterwards, in *The Sunday Times*, 28 April 1963, 'I believe that the British Aluminium affair provoked a remarkable transformation in the City. Old citadels crumbled, traditional strongholds were invaded, new thought was devoted to City problems, there was a freshness and alertness unknown before, dramatic to watch. Now the merchant bankers are more on their toes; they vie with one another to give a better service to industry and their clients, some even advertise the facilities they can offer; there has been a girding of loins, resulting in more enterprise and competitiveness and less reliance on the "old boy idea". Of course these advances might have taken place anyhow, but I do not believe I am exaggerating when I say that most of them date from the British Aluminium episode and that the effects have spread beyond just banking and have included the whole City.'

Added William Rees-Mogg, now Editor of *The Times*, in *The Director*, June 1962, 'It is, however, clear that in both the Courtauld's and the British Aluminium disputes victory went to the side which gained the greater weight of Press support. In both cases for instance, Lex of the *Financial Times* was arguing in favour of the side that eventually won. In neither case, however, did the eventual winner have predominant support in the City itself. The City establishment tried to defeat Warburg with almost hysterical fervour and in the case of ICI the traditional respect of the City for the quick profit and the big battalions had its influence. In fact it was the professional efficiency of Warburgs' handling of the Press which won the day for them, and Courtaulds were also immensely skilful in exploiting the advantage of having been raided. They represented themselves, quite properly, as the innocent victim.'

The stony façade was beginning to crumble. Two years later, for example, a BBC television camera unit was allowed into the Bank of England—almost an historic event—to film the gold and bank-note vaults containing around £210 million. Yet the suspicion still lingered. Every outsider had to be accompanied by two officials and when the crew left the contents of the vaults had to be counted again just to make sure. Paul Ferris gives another example in his book, *The City*, which illustrates the reaction of businessmen at the time. They didn't mind co-operating with the Press. But it had to be on their terms.

> 'He asked what I might expect from the book and continued without waiting for an answer: "You're writing this presumably as a principal with a royalty, presumably 12½ or 15 per cent. You may be very happy to say: "I acknowledge thanks to Mr X for his help"—you may not even be prepared to say that. On the other hand, if we give you the information, if we're really helpful, you might feel inclined to say: "Well, its only a very small section of the book, so it hardly qualifies for a contribution, any division of—but I should like to do something in recognition of the help given me here. If my book does well, I'll give something to the Blankshire Home for Stray Birds"—which you've never heard of, but which happens to be before me at the moment. What's your reaction?'

But gradually the Press was becoming accepted. Ex-deputy City Editor of the *Daily Express*, Peter Dickenson, who has probably done more than anyone to make the City PR conscious—he runs Hambros public relations—recalls an early occasion when PR helped to win a takeover battle about the same time. This was the British Drug Houses fight against a bid from Glaxo. Hambros were called in—and PR was part of the service. Reporter Dickenson got to work and discovered they were working on a contraceptive tablet.

'We made the point that it was terribly relevant to shareholders—not pie in the sky', he says. 'This was the first news of the British pill. It was also the first time the *Daily Mirror* gave a takeover a big spread.' As a result Hambros won the fight on behalf of BDH.

And today the Stock Exchange news overlaps from the City page on to the show-business pages of the Press.

> 'Life has never been better for Welsh singer, Tom Jones. America loves him ... his fans love him ... even the Stock Exchange loves him. Dealings in the shares of the company which looks after him added a million pounds to the value of the stock on Monday.'
> (*Daily Express*, 12 September 1969)

3.3 Plan

How does a company mount a PR operation? There are three approaches.

3.3.1 FORMAL PR

A company hires a PR consultant or sets up its own PR department. Instead of being a journalist he is probably more experienced in business than publicity.

3.3.2 INFORMAL PR

This is generally the approach an ex-journalist brings to financial PR. He knows the papers intimately. Probably worked on many of them. And, more important, he knows the people involved. He operates less as a company or consultancy PR man and more as a financial journalist based in a company or consultancy. An acute distinction.

3.3.3 THE 'UNORTHODOX APPROACH'. OR THE 'C'M IN. WHAT YOU GONNA HAVE? WHAT CAN I TELL YOU?' METHOD

This is the ultimate. Yet it rarely happens. Because it depends so much on the activities of the company and the personality of its chief executive. When it does it produces tremendous results. A journalist can suddenly become a company fan. He will shadow all its activities, report its progress and quote its chairman or managing director again and again and again. One City Editor, for example, always seems to be referring to Purle Brothers Holdings.

'One share that I am hopeful will make it back to the top is Purle Brothers Holdings. The shares are currently well down on the 1969 high of 48s 6d. But it would not need much to get them going forward again. For this is one of those shares that is never easy to buy in good markets since it has a novelty value—it is the only direct way for investors into the fast-growing industrial waste-disposal industry. What is more, Purle is the recognised world leader, and has a young and lively chairman in Tony Morgan, who is still only thirty-seven,' he wrote on one occasion.

But there is one danger: the John Davies syndrome. As soon as he took over as Director-General of the Confederation of British Industries he set out to woo the Press and TV. And to do this he criticised—constantly. 'Criticism is what is wanted by the public media', he would say. 'I am rarely asked to do anything else except criticise. If you don't make a noise, people don't take any notice of you.' (*The Sunday Times*, 20 July 1969.)

Which is fine if you are John Davies. But fatal if you are running a company in spite of the publicity.

3.4 Communications theory

Financial public relations is one of the key areas of communications for any company. It calls, therefore, for a general understanding of communication.

Essentially communication requires three elements: a source, a message and a receiver. But to activate this process three other principles are necessary: an encoder, to transpose the message into a communicable form; a decoder, to transpose the message back on arrival for the receiver; and feedback, the reaction of the receiver to the message which is indirectly transmitted back to the source, who can then evaluate the response and the interpretation before coming to a value-judgement. Communications theory applied to practical everyday public relations would operate as follows. A company (source) wishes to publicise the chairman's report (message) to the financial press (receivers). The company translates the information in the form of a statement for the press,

> 'XYZ Limited have arranged finance totalling £3,280,000 in connection with the supply of British equipment to a total value of £4,100,000 for a new paper mill to be built at Durban, South Africa, which will come into operation in May 1971 with two paper machines designed to produce 150,000 tons a year of newsprint, magazine papers and fine papers.'

This is the encoding process. It is then transmitted through the message channels. On arrival in the newspaper office it is read and evaluated. This is the decoding process. The reactions of the journalist, reflected in the coverage given to the report, is the feedback to the company.

> 'Finance totalling more than £3 million has just been arranged for a new £4 million paper mill, scheduled to come into operation at Durban, South Africa in May 1971. Its two paper machines will produce 150,000 tons of newsprint, magazine papers and fine papers every year.'

By analysing the communication process in such stage-by-stage detail one can spot the danger points—and realise how to overcome them.

It is vital that the press release is a true and accurate reflection of, for example, the annual report. All the necessary detail must be there. The various facts and figures must be accurate. There should be no opportunity for mis-understanding. The release must be issued at the right time for the receiver. The national newspapers work round the clock. But it is obviously more convenient for them to receive news about a company late morning or eaily afternoon if possible. It is not always possible. But if it is, that company stands to gain more space providing, of course, that the story is news and not a puff released to the press to satisfy the chairman's vanity.

3.5 What is news?

News is information or details of recent events or original reports of opinions or discoveries. Sometimes said to be the information an editor believes will not only interest his readers but help him to gain more readers. Arthur Mac-Ewan, appointed by William Randolph Hearst the first editor of the *San Francisco Examiner*, put it another way: 'News is anything that makes a reader say, Gee whiz!'.

In financial public relations terms, this means financial results, successful orders, appointments, contracts, virtually anything that will give outsiders a better and more accurate view of the activities of a company. This is the kind of information a good financial public relations man can run to earth with no trouble at all. But that's only half the operation. The second half is marketing the information, ensuring the right information is communicated to the right people at the right time—with maximum effectiveness for the company. Many business men and public relations people think this simply means keeping the national press informed. Nothing could be further from the truth. Obviously, the national press is important. But so—from an over-all company point of view—are all the regional, local and specialist press as well. All in all there are 12 financial public relations media.

3.6 Financial public relations media

3.6.1 NATIONAL PRESS
That famous editor of *The Economist*, Walter Bagehot (1826–77), was probably the finest financial journalist of all times. He was consulted by Gladstone so often that he came to look upon himself as a 'supplementary Chancellor of the Exchequer'. Unfortunately many financial journalists think of themselves as Bagehots. Writer, barrister and father of Edward Du Cann, C. G. L. Du Cann, has tried to bring them down to earth.

'The basic question financial journalists should ask themselves is: For what do the Stendhalian few read us? (Vast multitudes of avid newspaper-addicts can't and don't). Not for pleasure—the usual lure. Almost always for profit: profit in the widest sense including instruction and enlightenment. Financial readers are all Benthamites, i.e. utilitarians;

moved by need, greed and hope. From this it follows that sober facts, accurate figures, concrete particularised comments, freed from literary frills and fancies are required. The majority of financial readerships are actual or potential shareowners. Realisation of this fundamental verity is vitally important.'
(*UK Press Gazette*, 14 July 1969)

In other words, the financial public relations adviser's primary objective must be to select the media which would be more effective for his client— rather than the media which would flatter the journalist. It's harsh. But its essential. For there is an enormous range of publications with their individual markets and their particular interests.

One must, therefore, have priorities. Here a survey, *Monitoring of Editorial in National Newspapers* prepared by Tellex Monitors Limited and published July 1969, can help. First they looked at a 1965 Economist/Marplan Survey in which AB businessmen—the top 12 per cent upper middle class intermediate management section of the population—were asked: 'In your working life would you describe yourself as concerned, interested, occasionally interested or not interested in these subjects. . . .' The results, with the scores for 'concerned' and 'interested' added together, were as follows:

British Business and Industry	83 per cent
Labour Relations	80 per cent
Technological Developments	74 per cent
Managerial Studies and Techniques	72 per cent
British Public Affairs	70 per cent
European Business and Industry	58 per cent
Sociological problems concerned with business organisations	49 per cent
US Business and Industry	42 per cent
European politics	42 per cent
Company Law	42 per cent
Stock Markets	40 per cent
Developing Countries	32 per cent
US Public Affairs	26 per cent

Tellex then went a stage further and compared the quantity of editorial coverage of these subjects of key interest in the quality newspapers, the *Financial Times, The Times,* the *Daily Telegraph, The Sunday Times, The Observer* and the *Sunday Telegraph.* A fascinating exercise. The results (see Table 3.1) showed:

Financial Times is a clear leader in the most important categories. For AB businessmen it may devote too much to the stock market and statistics. Political coverage had low priority which in the case of British politics is a significant omission.

The Times offered a very consistent news balance. It did not reach the level of the *Financial Times* on important subjects, scoring best in the less important categories.

The Guardian has a strong penchant for foreign political news and ethical questions, and a low priority for foreign business news. Women's pages were good.

The Daily Telegraph would have scored well in sport if categorised. Foreign business news coverage is very low and foreign political coverage not much greater. Much of its material was not classifiable except as readable trivia.

The Sunday Times, due to its vast size, won the Sunday League, but its coverage on all subjects was not much greater than its rivals. A mere 17·7 per cent of its pages are devoted to these subjects.

The Observer pays little attention to foreign business news and scored well only in less important categories.

The Sunday Telegraph did better with important categories than *The Observer*. Its coverage of British politics was the best of the three Sundays.

Exports got low priority in all papers, apart from the *Financial Times*.

The arts and management studies were well covered by all.

Technological subjects and American political news were probably in excess of the norm, due to the events of the month.

Clearly this establishes the priority among the quality press for a financial public relations programme from the editorial point of view. There is still plenty of scope however among the non-quality or popular press. Although they may not attract the same quality of readership they offer the advantage of quantity. And its at the lowest ends of the socio-economic scale that there is the greatest scope for financial growth.

Daily Mail
Probably the leader of the junior league. The financial staff headed by city editor, Patrick Sergeant, is pioneering the switch to more business news in greater depth. Hence Money Mail, an enormously successful innovation. It beat the fears of the sceptics hands down and now has an extensive following. The opportunities for straight-forward business news stories are limited. Generally it concentrates on a how-to-get-rich approach. But it is possible.

There is plenty of scope, however, in the paper's daily City page. Its three regular sections, The Chairmen Say, Share of the Day and Company News are open to all-comers. The benefit lies in getting into the editorial proper where a story can rate a seven-column heading. The angles, however, might send a shudder down the chairman's spine.

E

Table 3.1

	Financial Times	The Times	The Guardian	Daily Telegraph	The Sunday Times	The Observer	Sunday Telegraph
A. Labour Relations	(6) 4·17*	(7) 3·56	(3) 2·96	(6) 2·49	(8) 0·40*	(7) 0·33	(6) 0·34
B. Tech. Developments	(4) 6·62*	(6) 3·89	(4) 2·92	(7) 2·42	(3) 1·65*	(2) 1·26	(3) 0·84
C. British Business	(3)13·76*	(3) 6·10	(7) 2·56	(5) 3·55	(4) 0·68*	(8) 0·21	(5) 0·52
D. USA Business	(9) 3·10*	(13) 1·58	(15) 0·26	(13) 0·55	(12) 0·16*	(13) 0·004	(14) 0·09
E. European Business	(10) 2·89*	(15) 1·00	(12) 1·02	(14) 0·47	(12) 0·16	(10) 0·12	(12) 0·14
F. Other Business	(5) 4·36*	(12) 1·67	(14) 0·59	(15) 0·21	(11) 0·19*	(14) Nil	(13) 0·10
G. Management Studies	(2)18·80*	(1)10·92	(2) 5·22	(1) 6·62	(2) 2·03*	(3) 1·02	(2) 1·30
H. Exports	(8) 3·75*	(14) 1·12	(13) 0·73	(12) 0·61	(14) 0·09*	(12) 0·04	(15) 0·05
I. British Politics	(11) 1·88	(5) 4·07*	(5) 2·89	(4) 3·87	(10) 0·19	(11) 0·11	(9) 0·23*
J. European Politics	(12) 1·40	(10) 2·63*	(8) 2·33	(10) 1·48	(9) 0·20	(4) 0·59*	(7) 0·34
K. USA Politics	(15) 0·97	(9) 2·92*	(9) 2·04	(8) 2·22	(5) 0·65*	(6) 0·47	(4) 0·59
L. Other Politics	(13) 1·37	(8) 3·03*	(6) 2·82	(9) 1·85	(6) 0·49	(5) 0·56*	(8) 0·33
M. International Bodies	(14) 1·10	(11) 1·77*	(11) 1·33	(11) 0·80	(15) 0·07	(9) 0·21*	(11) 0·16
N. Arts	(7) 3·91	(4) 5·70*	(1) 5·49	(2) 4·67	(1) 2·71*	(1) 1·87	(1) 1·84
O. Statistics	(1)23·15*	(2) 7·88	(10) 1·55	(3) 4·37	(7) 0·45	(14) Nil	(10) 0·18

* Winner in category
(1) = the order of importance
1·0 = 1,000 single-column inches

Source: *Monitoring of Editorial in National Newspapers, Tellex Monitors Limited, July 1969*

'It is bad enough when the banns are called and the bridegroom
the wedding. Hence the furore over Leasco and Pergamon. How dist.
then, when the banns are called, the wedding takes place but the ma.
is not consummated. Consider the happenings at Mecca, the dance
to bingo group.'
(Derek Porter, *Daily Mail*, 23 August 1969)

But it's worth it.

Daily Sketch

The prime market of the Daily Sketch is within the class C2 bracket. As a
result editorial on financial matters—Making Money, the page that sorts
out your financial problems—takes the form of question and answer.

'So I should go for company B shares in preference to company A shares?
Not necessarily—for you must always take into account other factors
such as future prospects, yield, etc. The P/E ratio is a useful guide—but
nothing more than that.'
(*Daily Sketch*, 26 May 1969)

Clearly there is not much opportunity here. But the clue might be their
Share of the Week spot.

'Most children at some time wear clothing bearing a "Ladybird" or
"Chilprufe" label. These garments are made by the expanding Pasolds
group, which has grown at a tremendous rate in recent years. Sales now
exceed £16 million a year compared with under £4 million ten years ago.
Turnover is still increasing, and extra capacity is being added to keep
up with demand, both at home and overseas. The shares are now
around 55s where they show a yearly return of just over £2 10s per cent.
But a bonus of two free shares for each one held is to be made in the near
future, which will have the affect of bringing the share price down to
under 20s and make them more marketable. Now is a good time to pick
up a holding.'
(*Daily Sketch*, 2 June 1969)

An ideal financial story—in an ideal financial spot.

Daily Express

The *Daily Express*, according to the National Readership Survey, February–
June 1968, published by JICNARS, offers three key advantages. It is read
by 33 per cent of adults owning shares, more than any other daily newspaper.
It is read by 31 per cent of adults with cheque books, again more than any
other daily paper. And on top of that it is read by 39 per cent of adults in
key management positions, once more, more than any other daily newspaper.

Daily Mirror

The *Daily Mirror's* famous 'Your Money' column is run by Robert Head. It is probably the liveliest—and certainly the most readable—financial column among the popular press. He has a happy knack of reducing the most complicated financial deals into everyday language. He also manages to make every story interesting and, surprisingly, relevant to his readers. The liveliness, of course, offends some dyed-in-the-wool financial types. But for all that, the *Daily Mirror* and Mr Head are important in the financial news media.

Sun

The *Sun*, however, seems to carry its 'Money' column more out of obligation than interest. The stories are always lively—though, perhaps, tortuous. The tips seem just that. All chance and no background. But an off-beat story with keen interest for the young can still make a big splash with headlines across the page. So it cannot be that bad.

Sunday Express

The *Sunday Express* provides a comprehensive round up for the investor in the street. It generally features at least one major company each week and throws in a number of smaller, slightly off-beat business stories as well. If it can personalise a story, it does so. It also features a lively '£100 to invest' spot which covers good companies down on their luck to rank outsiders.

Sunday Mirror

The *Sunday Mirror* is even more of a child's guide to finance and investment. Generally, City Editor Robert Head tackles a single big subject like house buying, examining it thoroughly in an easy-to-follow question and answer form. Unit trust prices are given. But there is rarely any detail on individual companies and their prospects.

News of the World

By comparison, the *News of the World*, gives a general round-up of the week picking out a handful of shares for special attention. They also give a thumbnail investment sketch of at least one company a week. Sometimes more.

3.6.2 REGIONAL PRESS

There are over 1,200 regional papers in the country. Most of them, however, belong to the big six; the regional newspaper groups. This means problems. Most of the business news will be prepared by the group's city staffs in London. There is little point, therefore, in sending a general business story to the papers direct. Better go straight to the City men in London. The real local stories, however, should still go straight to the local offices.

First, the English regional daily press. If the company is based in the area; if it has a subsidiary or a branch in the area; or even if the company is so big

that it is, by definition, of interest to the regions, the regional daily press are
a key communications medium. Some have their own city and business staffs.
Others rely on their head offices. A few take business news from the various
agencies. Either way there is enormous opportunity for financial news coverage.
Among the most important: London's two evening papers: the *Evening News*
and the *Evening Standard*.

City Editor of the *Evening News*, David Malbert, is a strong critic of bad
financial public relations—'They are light-weight chaps who possess the
minor skill of putting into words some obscure pronunciamento of the board
and distributing it to every publication in the land from the *Grocers Gazette*
to the *Times Literary Supplement* and from *Reveille* to the *New Scientist*'—
and, at the same time, an advocate of a good financial public relations. In
fact, he has done more than probably any other City Editor in recent years
to boost the standards of public relations. His daily City Page is bright, lively
and highly informative.

> 'It's Thanksgiving Day in the United States—and it should be a day of
> thanksgiving in the City, too. For three of our leading companies,
> Imperial Chemical Industries, Great Universal Stores and J. Lyons
> today bring investors tidings of comfort and joy.'
> (27 November 1969)

In addition to straightforward news, the City Page features a weekly
tipster, Pundit, who manages to keep way above the *Financial Times* ordinary
index—no mean achievement.

The *Evening Standard*, by comparison, is more serious, probably more
thorough and certainly more comprehensive. It generally devotes three pages
to City and business news every day. It also carries more financial advertising.
If the *Financial Times* is the City's morning paper, the *Evening Standard* is
probably its evening paper.

The *Bath and Wiltshire Evening Chronicle* gives a solid if slightly dull angle
to financial stories. But they carry a great deal of weight in the area. When
S. Pearson and Son went public in August 1969 they introduced their story
with the dull, flat-foot approach: 'Details of the banking, investment trusts,
publishing, oil and other industrial interests of Viscount Cowdray and the
Pearson family are revealed for the first time in the prospectus for the forthcoming public offer of shares in the family company, S. Pearson and Son,'
they said.

The *Birmingham Evening Mail*, by comparison, is a more lively financial
paper. 'One of Britain's largest private business groups, S. Pearson and Son
is to make a £12,500,000 share offer to the general public next week,' began
their story. Which illustrates as good as anything the difference in their
approach.

The *Birmingham Post* is probably more thorough than both. Ian Richardson, who runs their City section, is a man to watch. He often praises the companies—which helps. But there is generally a strong proviso.

'Hepworth Iron, the big maker of clay pipes for drains, etc. looks set for a considerably better year. Two provisos have to be made, however; that the weather is not too bad and that the construction industry (Hepworth's biggest customer) does not do even worse than it expects to do anyway.'
(18 August 1969).

He went on to analyse the effect of weather on production, the acquisitions and extensions made during the year as well as the rationalisation. His verdict:

'If Hepworth can keep up this sort of performance, the prospective price-earnings ratio on the shares at 13s 9d will be considerably less than the 19 times indicated by last year's results. It could be as low as 13½ times. The yield is 3½ per cent. The shares look worth having on a two-year view.'

Any summing up like this is important for any company. The *Birmingham Post* is worth having on one's side. Its circulation in and around Birmingham is greater than that of any comparable national or provincial paper. In fact surveys have shown that its circulation is greater than all the other quality publications put together. Its readership hits the 229,000 mark—more than four readers per copy. Two out of three are men with 25 per cent in the key ABC1 category.

The *Bolton Evening News* has a Commercial and Financial section which tends to concentrate on the major economic news. If sterling opens with a small gain on the foreign exchange markets, that will be the important news story of the day. If the electronics industry achieves a record £125 million output during the first quarter of the year, it will be dismissed in a single paragraph. The *Bolton Evening News* does, however, cover dealings on the Northern Stock Exchange. Any share quoted on the Northern Stock Exchange stands a fair chance of getting covered.

The 62,000 circulation *Bournemouth Evening Echo*, surprisingly, gives even less coverage to business news. Its daily Stock Exchange section runs to six-inches. Sometimes less. It rarely looks outside Stock Exchange activities for any news.

The *Bradford Telegraph*, circulation 126,000, has the Northern's hard-headed approach to money. Bernard Crean's City Column covers everything. One column alone can range from the effect of French devaluation and possible German revaluation on sterling; equities as a whole and new issues. But Crean not only writes for the *Telegraph*. It is syndicated by the *Investors Chronicle*. A point worth remembering.

The Citizen, Gloucester, runs an 'in the money' feature which covers the world of finance. This is John Roscoe's province. William Lovell writes a weekly spot on company news. Both are valuable outlets for company news. They also tend to react to overseas news probably better than most regional papers. When the French franc was devalued in August 1969 it carried a round-up showing the effect on a number of companies.

> 'Marshall's Universal is a different kettle of fish indeed. It gets a straight and immediate gain from devaluation of the franc and since the shares looked well undervalued before the weekend I consider them worth picking up as a speculative holding.'
> (*The Citizen*, 14 August 1969)

The *Cumberland Evening News* is again the province of R. T. Purvis and his 'Guide to Stocks and Shares'.

Evening Argus, Brighton, is useful if there is a local story. Otherwise not worth the effort. Their City Notes are the same as those of the *Bradford Telegraph*. Both are syndicated by *Investors Chronicle* under the Bernard Crean by-line.

The *Evening Mail*, Slough, is probably one of the brightest regional papers in the business and financial field when it turns its mind to it. It seems to have a knack for treating businessmen as ordinary human beings not the money-grabbing hell-for-leather tycoons that other papers tend to concentrate on. It also manages to tackle business as an interesting subject in itself and so often features a business story on an ordinary news page instead of tucking it away in its own corner.

Express and Star, Wolverhampton, tends to be the same. They give brief but comprehensive news of Stock Exchange dealings. Again local companies stand the best chance of making a splash.

The Cheltenham-based *Gloucestershire Echo* is more ambitious. Their City Notes section by Raymond Painter offers plenty of scope. It tends, however, to appeal to the investor in the street rather than the institutions. Which can be an advantage. Property Growth Assurance Company, the property bond organisation, for example, rated a good three-column spread by Painter in August 1969:

> 'The value of commercial property has risen at a considerable rate in post-war years and there is no reason to believe that it will not do otherwise in the future. One way of being able to get a stake in this field is through property growth bond units, which are linked with life assurance cover to give considerable tax advantage. In addition, under no circumstances do you have to pay capital gains tax, and providing you hold all your units for a year you pay no income tax.'
> (18 August 1969)

He went on to outline the Property Growth Assurance scheme, its shareholders and the man behind the scheme, Peter Hutley, a 42-year-old chartered surveyor and property owner who pioneered decentralised office developments in the late fifties. It was obviously the kind of story to appeal to the business readers of Cheltenham.

The *Huddersfield Daily Examiner* is more detailed and probably more dull. But still effective. R. T. Purvis tends to keep an eye open for the laggards.

> 'The merits of British Match do not seem to be fully appreciated at present. The £1 shares at 56s are still two-thirds of the way down from peak to low, despite a rise of almost 30 per cent to £5·7 million in profits for the year to March. This was also combined with a good improvement in margins. . . . The company clearly seems to have above-average prospects, which are not matched in the share price.'
> (*Huddersfield Daily Examiner*, 18 August 1969)

R. T. Purvis, however, is a syndicated column. A Huddersfield story, say, would not necessarily appeal to such unless there was more general interest. But once a story is accepted, the coverage can be extensive.

The *Hull Daily Mail* provides a solid regional business news service. It follows its local companies like a hawk. If a company's shares jump even sixpence, it usually checks in case there is a takeover in the offing.

The *Ipswich Evening Star* prefers the straight Stock Exchange news. Few real business stories get through.

The *Liverpool Echo*, written by their own men, gives practically a 100 per cent coverage of business news. The London Stock Exchange is fully covered. So is the Northern Exchange. Here there is plenty of opportunity for good business stories.

The *Liverpool Post*, by comparison, runs its own special Business Post section, a comprehensive news service on all aspects of business and finance.

The *Mail* in West Hartlepools is an exciting business paper. It not only covers the news. It polishes the stories with a professional gloss which make them appeal to all readers. Take the S. Pearson and Son story, as an example:

> 'This week one of Britain's wealthiest men—Lord Cowdray—is giving us the chance, for the first time, to buy shares in S. Pearson and Son, one of the largest companies in the country. And everything about it makes this an opportunity not to be missed. It's not often you get the chance to get in right at the beginning of the stock exchange life of one of our biggest corporations.'
> (*Mail*, 15 August 1969)

The *Manchester Evening News* is short, sharp and comprehensive. Their Commercial News section covers everything—even the Manchester fruit and vegetable prices, not to mention Fleetwood fish as well. If there is a chance of featuring a Northern business man, they will do so—and throw in all the details as well:

'Sir Joseph Hunt, who headed the committee which reported on the "grey areas" has been appointed deputy Managing Director of Chloride Electrical Storage of Clifton Junction. An old boy of Farnworth Grammar School, Sir Joseph joined the firm as a junior in the design office. For the last four years he has been mainly concerned with Chloride's fast-expanding lead battery interests and activities overseas. He is also Chairman of Porvair, in which Chloride has a substantial holding.'
(*Manchester Evening News*, 21 August 1969)

The *Morning Telegraph*'s business coverage is adequate. But, again, the important stories are prepared in London. This time by John Heffernan, City Editor of United Newspapers, which runs the *Morning Telegraph*, and Christopher Stone. Local stories—a Sheffield company landing a massive export order—are handled by the paper direct.

The *North-Western Evening Mail*, despite the illustration of a city gent complete with bowler and brolly, runs another syndicated service—Bernard Crean.

The *Northern Echo* is, of course, a power in the North. It provides virtually a national business coverage in a regional setting. Alongside a national story— Is the squeeze starting to grip too hard?—one gets the local business story.

The *Nottingham Guardian Journal* runs a compact Finance and Commerce section. There is nothing bright or lively about its coverage. But it is solid, reliable business news. The opportunities for getting individual companies featured are very slight although the chances are better with a good local-based company.

The *Shields Gazette* is a junior *Northern Echo*. Many of its features—Has the squeeze gone too far?—are also published in the *Echo*. Its business news is not so comprehensive. Certainly not so thorough.

The *Southern Echo* is again Purvis territory.

The *Swindon Advertiser* is dull. It tends to concentrate on the daily stock exchange report without following business news too closely.

The *West Lancashire Evening Gazette*, for all its 76,000 circulation, skirts business and financial affairs. Admittedly it does carry share movements. But very little else.

The *Yorkshire Evening Press* is again Crean territory.

Second, the Welsh regional daily press.

The *South Wales Argus* covers the Welsh business scene. It tends to go for the plain man's how-to-make-money features rather than the more disinterested high-level debate on exchange rates. The John Roscoe by-line is a regular spot.

The *Western Mail* is the national quality newspaper of Wales. It is read by more of the leaders of professions, commerce, industry and public life in Wales than all the London quality morning newspapers put together. It covers commercial and industrial affairs daily and often publishes special reviews on every aspect of Welsh industrial life as well.

Third, the Scottish regional daily press. The Scottish press, of course, is the *Scotsman* and the *Glasgow Herald*.

The *Glasgow Herald*—circulation 83,000—runs a comprehensive Business and Financial section, largely prepared in their Fleet Street offices in London. It has the Scots dour concern for money and, in fact, gives its business staff probably more freedom to range across the whole news scene generally than most regional papers.

The *Scotsman* is the faster-growing quality newspaper in Scotland. It covers business extensively and publishes both the London and Scottish Stock Exchange prices. On Wednesdays this is backed up with its special business section, The *Financial Scotsman*. For companies seeking Scottish investors, its essential.

Fourth, the Irish regional daily press—both North and South.

The *Irish News* (Belfast) is another Purvis paper. While the pink *Belfast Newsletter* is Ireland's answer to the *Financial Times*.

The *Cork Examiner* is a 19th century newspaper. Everything is packed into the pages as tight as possible. Yet it is read and followed by its 77,000 readers. Its editorial approach is somewhat old-fashioned. Witness the start of a story about a company going public:

> 'Buying shares in a company going public is in most cases a profitable operation. There have, of course, been exceptions, but usually the bankers handling the operation try to fix a price which gives the sellers a reasonable deal, but also leaves new investors something to go in for.'
> (*Cork Examiner*, 8 August 1969)

The *Irish Independent*, Dublin's 172,000 circulation daily, covers the British business scene generally. There are probably as many British company stories in an issue as Irish company stories. R. T. Purvis raises his head again with features on the investment scene.

The *Irish Press* has its own financial section, Financial Press, launched 14 October 1969 and edited by Joe Murray, an economics graduate with several years experience of economic and financial journalism. Aimed at the man who knows little of the financial world but would like to know a lot more, it also aims at keeping the financial community in touch with important trends and events in business and the economy.

The *Irish Times*, the *Independent*'s rival with a smaller 52,000 circulation, is a brighter, livelier paper. Its city man, Charles Pritchard, debated the case for buying front rank equities during the depths of the 1969 bear market. The result: The Financial Times Index jumped 12·7 points the same day (admittedly a coincidence). He seems to make no distinction between English and Irish companies. In fact, one can go days without seeing any reference to companies with any Irish interest at all.

3.6.3 WEEKLY PRESS

There is almost as much scope among the weekly press as among the daily press. *The Economist* is probably the most important of all. Its weekly business coverage, broadly divided between Britain, International and Investment subjects, rivals many of the dailies for coverage and expert comment. A feature in *The Economist* on a company is as rare as gold dust and almost as priceless. The other weeklies, such as *The New Statesman* and *The Spectator*, do not discuss business as such although *Time and Tide* runs a regular Investment and Finance column by George R. Thomson, who is a rare mixture of comment, tipping and shrewd business sense. An off-beat—until you think about it—publication carrying a regular Finance and Industry spot is the *Jewish Chronicle*. Their City Editor discusses the Stock Market generally, new ventures by various companies as well as comments made by chairmen presenting their annual reports.

3.6.4 BUSINESS AND FINANCIAL PRESS

Obviously, crucially important. The *Investors Chronicle*, the daddy of them all, has an impressive 89 per cent coverage of the key target groups—the professional investors: bankers, stockbrokers, investment analysts as well as investment, unit trust and pension fund managers. Not only has it a higher percentage readership among this group than any other weekly or Sunday publication, it is also rated top in influencing city opinion among the weekly and Sunday press. The *Investors Guardian* and the *Financial World*, however, are also valuable aids to any financial public relations programme.

On the business front two magazines stand out: *The Director* and *Management Today*. The first, the journal of the Institute of Directors, the latter, the magazine of the British Institute of Management. Both give extensive, in-depth coverage to all aspects of business. Both of vital importance in projecting a company to key areas of the business community.

3.6.5 TRADE MAGAZINES

Many people think that trade journals do nothing but report sales drives, export orders and company appointments. Nothing could be further from the truth. They are key publications for reporting and discussing the financial and business affairs of companies in the industries they are covering. *The Bookseller*, for example, regularly reports annual meetings of publishers. It followed the blow-by-blow developments in the Leasco-Pergamon affair. Similarly, the *British Hosiery Journal*. It carries a special Financial News section, which even goes as far as detailing new companies being launched in the industry. The *Farmer and Stockbreeder* virtually has its own business news section, Money Matters, run by H. R. Lee of the *Investors Chronicle*. While the monthly magazine, *Frozen Foods*, prefers the hot news on the business front of its own industry.

Trade magazines are important as an early-warning system to the financial community. 'The really sophisticated financial analysts are now reading the trade press', says Bob Leaf, head of the giant US consultancy, Burson-Marsteller's European operation. 'They reckon that the trade papers get the stories before the national and business press. They also give them a vital week-by-week guide to what is happening in the industry, who is doing what and who is winning the big contracts.'

There is increasing emphasis being given to business affairs by trade union magazines, a sub-section of trade journalists. Naturally there is a certain bias:

> 'Some 50 direct descendants of the first Lord Cowdray, founder of the gigantic firm of S. Pearson and Son (whose subsidiary S. Pearson Publishers, owns the Westminster Press and *Financial Times*), share a family fortune of over £53 million. This was disclosed when the jealously private S. Pearson company at last went public; its issue of £12,500,000 worth of shares was oversubscribed five times.'
> (*SOGAT Journal*, October 1969)

There are two views about this. One—it's dangerous to let employees and especially trade unionists get their hands on so much information about the way a particular business is run. Two, it's sensible to do so. Employees are entitled to such information as much as shareholders. In any case, it dispells any illusions they might have about a company. Which could be a life-saving thing.

3.6.6 CONSUMER MAGAZINES

These are important for two reasons. Its a further opportunity to contact the investing public in their role as consumers. It is also—do not forget Russell Cobb's dictum—a further opportunity to influence the professional investor. Most consumer magazines carry financial and investment advice columns. A feature in such a context could prove useful in attracting the attention of the small investor or, in the case of *Vogue*'s famous Money column by Sheila Black, perhaps, the medium to large investors as well.

3.6.7 NEWS AGENCIES

These are organisations which gather news for dissemination to newspapers, magazines, radio and television. They range from one- or two-man bands in the provinces to the giant Press Association, which is owned by all the provincial newspapers in the country and which keeps them supplied with a constant stream of news. A story accepted by their City Editor could receive nation-wide publicity. Similarly a story could be picked up by an overseas news agency, or by any of the foreign news agencies based in this country.

More than 6,400 newspapers with a total circulation of 276 million, not to mention 394 million radio receivers and 177 million television sets in 112 countries—these are all available, for example, on a single news agency network, Reuters Economic Services. Founded in 1851 a year after Julius

Reuter began flying Brussels stock exchange prices to Aachen by pigeon. Reuters is now the greatest news-gathering organisation in the world. It specialises in the world-wide distribution of fast information on commodities, finance, trade and industry. Its clients: traders, bankers, brokers, industrialists, governments—and the news media.

A single story about a company telephoned to their London offices, for example, can be flashed around the world in seconds. It can go by computer interrogation, radio teleprinter, permanent line teleprinter, telex, telephone, messenger or even mail according to the demands on the subscribers.

The London staff file over 40,000 words every day. In addition to being sent to the United Kingdom subscribers, sections are sent direct to clients in the Middle East and the United States as well as other regional Reuters offices throughout the world including Brussels which handles their European service. The United States staff, in turn, select items for their Wall Street subscribers and add their own financial American copy in a special 100 words per minute Reuter Ultronic Report. Similarly in Tokyo where Reuter correspondents file 12,000 words of business news every day. And so on round the world.

On top of that come the special services:

COMEURO—a comprehensive world economic service with particular emphasis on commodity prices, market reports and news.

FINEURO—composite of three separate services: Reuters Business Ticker; the International Financial Printer, a fast service for European banks and business men dealing in stocks and exchanges; and the Wall Street Printer mainly for American brokers.

MIDECON—launched November 1966, it is based on Comeuro but includes highlights of Fineuro as well as for exchange details.

COMWESTAF—a cocoa and commodity news service for West Africa.

COMEASTAF—a similar commodity, financial news and prices service beamed at East Africa.

FINMID—a combined financial, industrial and economic news service including the Wall Street Printer service for banks, brokers and financial organisations in Kuwait and Lebanon.

REUTER–AGEFI—a combined Reuters operating with the leading French financial daily paper, *Agence Economique et Financiere*, to distribute financial information throughout France.

But first the story must be accepted by their financial services editor, Philip Kennett. This means it must be worthy and it must be available at the right time for maximum impact. If a board meeting is announcing an important decision, it is no good releasing the details late afternoon. It will be too late for the London evenings. Instead, meetings should be held mid-morning so that the news can be flashed to all subscribers in the United Kingdom—and around the world, if it is important enough. If embargoes must be used, remember Reuter is a round-the-world 24-hour operation. Its no good saying embargo: 24.00 hours. In London that's midnight. In Tokyo, its four o'clock in the afternoon.

Do not forget the implications of a round-the-world service. If a chairman returns from a tour of company installations and depots in three continents, Reuters will be interested in his comments—because it will make a story for their different news services throughout the world. From the company's point-of-view, of course, this can mean world-wide publicity and world-wide interest in their activities.

There are other news agencies, of course, apart from Reuters, which is probably the biggest and the most important. Exchange Telegraph, for example, founded 21 years later in 1872 provides a fast financial, commercial service to newspapers, radio and television networks as well as its own individual subscribers in the United Kingdom.

Other agencies specialise in regional news, either in the United Kingdom or different parts of the world. Some prefer hard news. They also work very closely with the Stock Exchange.

Universal News Services, however, is a news agency with a difference. Whereas the traditional news agencies exist to discover the news and then supply it to its member newspapers, UNS disseminate the news it receives from companies and organisations which pay for the use of its services to the press without making any charge. Its special City service offers the modern company the means of distributing its news to hundreds of newspaper offices by the means of just one telephone call. Its own UNS printers are installed in the City offices of every national newspaper and in the offices of provincial newspapers, financial weeklies and radio and television networks as well. Also through its own subsidiary and associated companies, it reaches the offices of newspapers in many parts of the world. City editors can be alerted to developments, tipped off about timings of a likely story, informed about reactions to events and furnished with comment. But the company pays for the service.

UNS also meets the demands for prompt disclosure of all relevant business information. If a bid defence is being hammered out, if money for the British subsidiary of a foreign part company is being arranged or if a company is coming to market UNS will always carry the news for the company. This will ensure that both shareholders and the business press has the news as soon as possible. It carried the news about the $45 million bond issue for Rio Tinto-Zinc arranged by Rothschilds. It also carried the news about the Imperial Chemical Industries split with Viyella. This, in fact, was a classic UNS operation.

At 19.09 hours on 28 July 1967 UNS received a warning from Viyella that an important business announcement was being made that evening. By 19.10 hours all city editors had been alerted over the UNS teleprinter network: an announcement by Viyella International Limited will be sent you within 30 minutes.

At 19.39 hours UNS began to receive the announcement from Charles Barker and Sons, the advertising agency acting for Viyella.

At 19.46 hours it was on the UNS network and in the hands of business staff.

The following morning it was the main news story of the day. *The Times* Business News gave it page-one treatment with a heading, 'Viyella seeks break with ICI through £16 million shares deal'. The *Daily Mail* said, 'Viyella offer ICI £16 million to go'. And the *Birmingham Post* added 'Viyella wants to be independent of ICI'. Commented Frank Broadway, industrial adviser to Viyella, 'Our statement was necessarily delayed until late evening because of discussions with various people, including ICI. We felt that our shareholders and the press should have the statement at the earliest opportunity and the only practicable way of getting it to city editors at that hour was through UNS'.

3.6.8 SYNDICATION SERVICES

Tucked away, out of the main-stream of a newspaper's editorial operation, are the Syndication Departments. To the papers concerned, they are a useful addition to the paper's services, helping to draw in additional revenue. To companies hoping to establish or even develop their international reputations, they are a god-send. For one story written by one journalist in a single syndication department can mean literally world-wide publicity. A good syndication story can appear in thousands of newspapers throughout the world, each one with perhaps a greater circulation than the original newspaper itself. A story picked up by the giant American United Press International news agency can virtually mean coverage by 1,000 newspapers throughout the United States and maybe even South America as well.

Be warned. Syndication stories are few and far between—especially on the business front—although one company, Management Agency and Music Limited, the go-go Tom Jones company, managed the leap. The *Financial Times* syndication department, the biggest business news syndication organisation in the world, carried a story 'Pop firm is London's market bright spot' on 24 October 1969:

'In a period when prices generally on the London Stock Exchange have been moving downwards, one bright new company has seen its share price trebled. This is Management Agency and Music Limited (MAM), whose shares were offered to the public for the first time earlier this year. The original offer was at 13s 3d (1·59 dollars): the shares later went up to 42s 6d (5·10 dollars) and, although they have fallen back a little they still command a high premium. The company's main asset is the projected future earning power of two singers, Tom Jones and Englebert Humperdinck, and of the man who manages and writes songs for them, Gordon Mills.'

3.6.9 RADIO AND TELEVISION

Seventy-three broadcasting stations in the United Kingdom are yielding an average of 11,000 news or feature items a day. A staggering total. There are 530 new bulletins a week; 220 news feature programmes and a further 1,350 feature programmes. Yet for some wild reason, radio and television are blank spots for most PR practitioners.

'Whether they like it or otherwise, they are determined to remain deaf as well as blind', says Eric Goldschmidt, Director of Tellex Monitors. 'They assume that a 4d handout to Charles Curran at the BBC absolves them from any further action in the field of broadcasting. There is no PR unable to tell me the screen-size of the *Isle of Thanet Gazette*. This is an accepted tool of the trade. Conversely, there are probably only six of the Institute of Public Relations' 3,000 members who could plausibly describe what goes on inside of a television studio.' He cites three reasons for this state of affairs:

'First, the PR profession lacks an inducement to spend time or money in assessing opportunities open to it in broadcasting. Second, technically the PR business is still living in the ice age. Third, as a hang-over from the old Corporation days broadcasting people do not invite co-operation of PR people because they have blotted their copybook too much already.'

Table 3.2

TELEVISION 119	National:	35	News	24
			News features	3
			Features	8
	Regional:	84	News	58
			News features	25
			Features	1
RADIO **126**	National:	22	News	9
			News features	1
			Features	12
	Regional:	104	News	72
			News features	18
			Features	14
TOTAL: **245**				245

Source: *The Petroleum Industry. Tellex Monitors*, 1969

The amount of scope for PR potential, he revealed in a massive report on the petroleum industry, published in 1969. On one night alone, he discovered, there were no less than 60 news stories on the industry. In an average week, they could total 245 items split 126 on radio and 119 on television or geographically, 188 regionally and 57 nationally (see Tables 3.2 and 3.3).

Table 3.3

Broadcast output is grouped under the following seven headings:

A.	Exploration	E.	Product uses
B.	Production	F.	Distribution
C.	Transportation	G.	Marketing and Promotion
D.	Refining		

The following table shows the number of broadcasts in each division:

July	A	B	C	D	E	F	G	Total
18	—	—	10	15	7	4	11	47
19	2	1	5	8	1	1	14	32
20	—	1	—	—	—	—	6	7
21	—	—	7	—	3	4	6	20
22	—	1	10	6	18	11	7	53
23	7	1	10	11	5	1	8	43
24	3	2	12	9	7	4	6	43
All	12	6	54	49	41	25	58	245

Source: *The Petroleum Industry. Tellex Monitors*, 1969

Commented Laurence Sultan, the international public relations manager of Burmah Oil Trading Limited:

'It is a curious fact that while we in PR take the closest account of what the press is writing about our companies and, indeed, about other companies in our field, we tend in general to pay relatively scant attention to what is being said about us in those two other great media of mass communication—radio and television. If I am right about this—and I believe I am—then it is time we woke up to the fact that these media are not only here to stay but, each year, manage to wield a wider and deeper influence on the public; for many of whom they are now the primary sources of news and opinion.'

The opportunities are there—see the accompanying tables—they should be exploited.

There are also opportunities for using closed-circuit television. Stock-brokers, Simon and Coates, for example, scored a first in January 1970 when they gave institutional investors a complete analysis of European

F

Ferries on closed circuit television including recorded interviews with the company Chairman, Mr Roland Wickenden and Managing Director, Mr John Heffron.

3.6.10 INTERNATIONAL NEWS MEDIA

Mose than 700 newspapers, magazine, radio and television correspondents from over 40 countries are based in London. Few are specialists. Most report and interpret the whole British scene. And that includes industrial and financial stories as much as political stories. Between them they command a world-wide audience and provide a valuable link with the international business field.

> 'MISTER CAFETERIA' REMPLIT LE GEORGE–V
> 'Charles Forte, fils d'un émigré italien a construit un fabuleux empire hôtelier: 48 hôtels dans le monde dont 3 des plus luxueux de Paris.'
> (*Paris-Match*, 16 August 1969)

'The great majority of correspondents are interested in good industrial and economic news stories', says the Board of Trade (Overseas Press Correspondents in London 1967) 'but because of the pressure on their time they do need help and co-operation from trade associations and firms.'

The Board of Trade went on to outline five different types of stories of interest to foreign correspondents based in this country:—

1 A prestige news story—an important breakthrough on the scientific or technical front—a wholly new product or a product using a revolutionary technique—a new material—a product which is the biggest, smallest, fastest, cheapest, safest of its kind.
2 A news story of specialised interest to a particular territory—a major contract, a factory installation or a local angle to a new product. For instance, an overseas national may have been associated with its design or a local firm with its developments.
3 An overseas tour by a really senior executive. This may promote requests for interviews or material for personality articles.
4 A press release or feature, angled specifically for one paper, offered exclusively, and written in the appropriate language.
5 A news story, perhaps in itself not a world-beater, accompanied by a striking photograph. The photograph should be fully captioned since it may be reproduced alone.

'There is no substitute in public relations for personal contacts. Companies should try to have personal contacts with leading correspondents, particularly those specialising in industrial and economic reporting. These contacts should not be restricted to the public relations level but should extend to top executives. Many companies derive great benefits from holding occasional lunches for small groups of overseas press people where they have the opportunity to meet top executives informally', adds the Board of Trade.

For British companies, for example, *Le Figaro* could be a powerful weapon for breaking into the French market. It is read by more French businessmen than any other paper. On Saturdays it even publishes a business supplement reviewing not only French but British and world industry and finance as well. Similarly the *Wall Street Journal*, the only national daily paper in the United It is essential reading for the men who influence the decision-taking and purchasing practices of American management.

The Central Office of Information is also worth keeping in touch with. They are regularly bringing top foreign journalists to the United Kingdom, introducing them to businessmen and arranging industrial and commercial tours for them. One party, for example, can consist of:

M. Rene Sedillot—Editor of *La Vie Francaise*, one of the leading economic and financial weeklies in France read by industrialists, business men and executives. Circulation: 125,000.

M. Jean Boissonnat—Redacteur-en-Chef and leading economic and financial commentator of the monthly economic journal, *L'Expansion*. Circulation: 86,000.

M. Regis Paranque—A leading member of the staff of France's leading financial daily, *Les Echos*. Circulation: 45,000.

M. Remy Arnaud—A young writer on the weekly economic journal, *Enterprise*.

All key men to a company trying to break into or consolidate its position in France.

Table 3.5 **Readership of English language publications within leading European companies (excluding UK)**

	Readership by directors of major European companies. Sample size, 352
Financial Times	39%
The Economist	35%
Fortune	29%
Time	28%
Business Week	20%
Newsweek	15%
The Times	14%
International Herald Tribune	13%
Wall Street Journal	10%

Source: *Financial Times*, BMRB 1968

3.6.11 BROKERS AND INVESTMENT ANALYSTS

Financial advertising is a key aspect in promoting a company. So is financial public relations. This covers not only press publicity but the preparation of special newsletters and reports for brokers and investment trusts. Brokers, in turn, prepare their own reports for clients as well as for distribution to the financial press.

> 'Evans Electroselenium is recommended by Argenti and Christopherson. It operates in the growth industry for scientific instruments. Profits rose 36 per cent last year, and the share price more than doubled. By developing more sophisticated products market penetration should be improved and profits could increase by more than 20 per cent per annum.'
> (*Financial Times*, 23 August 1969)

Visits—properly handled—are also of key importance to the broker and the investment analyst. Ten years ago they were dreadful.

'You would ring up and say, "Can I come and visit your company?" and you would get the answer back, "Next thing you'll want to know is how deep are the lavatories". That actually happened', says one analyst. But that is gradually changing although its always important to bear in mind the size of the company involved and the amount of information that is going to be available to the analysts.

Investment analysts are in two minds about company visits.

'There is no point in visiting a big company with a lot of other analysts because they are not going to give you the information you really want and the good analyst is not going to ask the questions they really want answered—because it will mean letting everyone else in on the reply. That's no good at all', says one analyst. 'The best thing is to visit a smaller company. I mean there is no point in visiting just one oil refinery if a company is operating throughout the world. It won't tell you anything about the company. It's much better to visit a company where you can talk to the chairman or the financial director and really find out about the company.'

3.6.12 STATISTICAL SERVICE

Chinese business men in Hong Kong are playing the New York Stock Exchange—with the help of a telephone and a small typewriter-sized electronic gadget called a Stockmaster. At the press of a button they can virtually get the latest stock, share and commodity prices from any exchange in the world. If they want the last traded price, the time of trade, the current bid and asked prices, the continuous high and low for the day, the cumulative volume of shares being traded, ruling dividends and earnings, they can get that as well.

The London Stock Exchange are planning a similar service for brokers and jobbers but on a far more limited scale. It will consist of a television display system with 20 channels, sixteen of which will have 50 share prices on permanent display, again constantly being up-dated by a computer. Another system, SCAN, provides prices according to the official Stock Exchange list. But it absorbs news about balance sheets, profits and losses as well. It has on file nearly 5,000 company records.

Faced with the mass of instant information, it is in a company's interest to make sure that the details being fed out by the statistical services are as up-to-date and comprehensive as possible. Yet the Stockmaster, the London Stock Exchange and SCAN are only the most sophisticated of the statistical services. Moodies, for example, have been producing their special analyses cards for more than 40 years and are as much a part of the business scene as the bowler hat and umbrella. Similarly their *Moodies Review*, which is packed week after week with expert comment on the stock market, individual shares and economic trends generally. EXTEL cards have been going almost as long. Both are indispensable for fact-based decision-making.

3.6.13 DIRECT MAIL
Direct Mail is a major activity. This entails sending the annual and interim reports to shareholders as well as post meeting reports. A number of companies also mail their house journals to shareholders as well. Some even send copies of the speeches made by company directors together with reprints of articles on the company which has appeared in the press.

'There is tremendous potential in direct mail that hasn't been tapped', says Clive Smith, Managing Director of Astral Public Relations. 'In the long-term its much better than advertising for shareholders providing, of course, that the information is correct. Companies should copy insurance companies in this respect—its a logical development.'

Chapter 4

Choosing a Financial Advertising Agency

Do not forget. Advertising is ideas. When you hire an advertising agency you are hiring ideas. It doesn't matter two new pennies whether it is staffed by Guards officer types or earnest Americans with cropped hair. It doesn't matter whether they lunch—or dine—at the Stafford, the Arts Club or the pub around the corner. All that matters is that they provide the advertising know-how and they do it well.

'Advertising agencies are a compound of ballyhoo, calculations and creative energy', says Anthony Sampson. 'In their curious caravan are included accountants, film producers, salesmen, poets, artists, showmen and straightforward businessmen.'

The only problem is finding the right one.

There are 500 advertising agencies in the country, each with a finger in the £500 million spent on advertising every year. They range from giants like J. Walter Thompson and The London Press Exchange, with individual billings near the £20 million mark, to small one- or two-man bands working from first-floor offices above a greengrocer's in Huddersfield. Each has their own special expertise. Each has their satisfied clients who are content to let them handle their advertising for them. The giants look after the giant accounts. The small men work for the smaller companies. In between are the specialists. Some concentrate on industrial advertising. And some concentrate on financial advertising.

These are the city agencies.

'Foster Turner and Benson offer the ideal combination for modern financial advertising and publicity—the long experience and knowledge of leading specialists in financial advertising with a first-class creative department of its own. In addition the resources and experience of S. H. Benson Limited, one of England's biggest agencies, are always available. At Foster Turner and Benson we believe that financial advertising properly done can be as good an investment as any advertising your company does. Goodwill from the investing public and from city institutions can be worth its weight in gold to you at certain times. But you can't just switch it on when you need it. You must build it up over the years. Well presented financial advertising also does a valuable job of public relations to all your friends in the trade—dealers, wholesalers, retailers and your own staff and work people. Remember too, that your advertisement if it is interesting may be read by customers and prospective customers for your product. People prefer to buy products made by companies they have heard about.' (Foster Turner and Benson)

A City agency is not necessarily the best agency to handle a financial account. Some of the giant agencies with their special financial departments can put up a good job. They have handled some important accounts. But it is not their job. A City agency is more likely to handle a financial account. It is their speciality.

'In the 1920's financial advertising meant just advertisement placing', says Mr John Hartley-Smith, Managing Director of Dorland (City) Limited. 'Later advertisements were followed by releases. We used to take prospectuses to City editors under our arm. Now its developed enormously. If the City didn't send out any reports and accounts all the financial papers would be hard pressed to fill.'

'Reputation—your reputation—is our business. Never has reputation and goodwill played a bigger part in business than today. Communications are becoming faster, and the public is becoming increasingly demanding and discerning. It is no longer enough to deserve a good reputation. Goodwill must be actively sought by the skilled techniques of public relations and publicity. This is the area in which we (Charles Barker City) claim to have wide experience. We look upon advice and executive work in public relations and publicity as a specialist service just as important as those provided by, say, the merchant banks and chartered accountants. There are many forms of public relations and advertising. all of which can help a company to project itself. However, unless these activities have the sympathy and support of the board room, they cannot be conducted to the best advantage. We look towards the day when no outward looking company or institution will take a major decision without expert advice, firstly on its likely effect on reputation, and secondly on how best to present it to the various publics concerned.' (Charles Barker City)

In between the two groups, however, are a small band of agencies such as Rupert Chetwynd and Partners, which combine the flair and showmanship of the big West End type agencies with the skill and know-how of the smaller City outfits.

Be warned. Advertising agencies often present a false front. A client, after he has placed the account, is often left to deal with a much more junior person. Then he has to keep on at the agency. Finally, as time goes by, the agency pays him less and less attention. These are some of the criticisms that came to light in a special inquiry into client-agency relations by Research Associates for Pace Advertising of Manchester. It also showed that clients tend to think of advertising men as wanting in honesty and naturalness.

4.1 Savings

Yet hiring a financial advertising agency spells big savings for any company.

4.1.1 IT SAVES STAFF
Most financial campaigns are small compared with consumer campaigns. Its not worth employing the specialist staff. Even the big financial compaigns run by the giant companies only involve a short series of advertisements. Then they only appear for a relatively short time. Financial advertising is growing. But it's not a full-time job for a specialist staff—yet.

4.1.2 IT SAVES MONEY
How much money depends on the size of the budget. For financial agencies, like conventional advertising agencies, live off commissions paid by the media. The client pays as much as if he dealt with these media direct. This means he gets the full agency service for free. The preparation of the campaign, everything from writing the copy to drawing up the media schedule, is free. So are all the contacts with the media, space booking and the proofs. All the client has to pay for is the ancillary production work, finished drawings, type-setting and blocks. If the account is so small, however, that the commission doesn't cover the work involved, then the client can expect a service fee on top of the cost of the space. But it's still cheap at the price.

4.1.3 IT SAVES TIME
City agencies eat, live and sleep financial advertising. They know the Stock Exchange requirements for financial advertising. They are always in contact with solicitors, stockbrokers, issuing houses and accountants. They know the various company and financial requirements. And they are in touch with the advertisement managers of the relevant newspapers and their staffs. If anyone can get a last-minute advertisement into the national press, a City agency can. As a result, they are able to save the client an enormous amount of time—because it is their job.

4.2 What does a City agency do?

It handles all the financial advertising. Give the agency a draft of the chairman's annual report, for example, tell them when the annual meeting takes place and how much money you want to spend on promoting the report and they will handle the operation.

1 They will prepare one advertisement or a series of advertisements, depending on the budget, based on the annual report. The design, the lay-out, whether photographs or line drawings are included or not—these are all the agency's decision.
2 They will also prepare a media schedule listing the size of advertisement space and the number of insertions they recommend in different news-papers and why.
3 These will come back to the client for approval. Once he gives his go-ahead—or the agency has made the amendments he may suggest—the mechanical wing of the agency takes over.
4 The agency books the space in the publications on the approved schedule.
5 A proper design layout together with photographs, cartoons or line drawings are then prepared.
6 The type is then set. And blocks are made of the illustrations.
7 A final proof is taken and submitted to the client for final approval. It is also a last-minute chance to check all the facts and figures. Once this stage is past, it's virtually impossible to make any amendments.
8 The blocks are sent to the printers. A proof is generally submitted by the printer before publication. But it's best not to rely upon it.
9 The advertisement appears. A voucher copy of the relevant publication is sent to the client.

That's the drill for an annual report. It's much the same for interim reports, prospectuses and so on. If, however, a company wants a big corporate adver-tising drive, it will mean an intensive period of indoctrination into the company for the agency. This will take time. But for a corporate campaign to hit home, a company must be prepared to invest time and money into the effort.

'There is no rule for spending money', says Hartley-Smith. 'Only the man who is in control can decide how much. But the money should only be spent according to the needs of the case. That's not cynical. Its true. It depends on the circumstances. I wouldn't try to persuade anyone to spend any money unless I was also convinced of it.'

4.3 How to hire a City agency

Hiring an advertising agency is like getting married. You do not know whether you have made the right choice until you start living together.

'It takes at least one to two years for a new agency to learn all it needs to know about a client, a new product and a new market. It will take you just as long to learn all you need to know about your agency,' said Samuel Thurm,

Vice-President for advertising, Lever Brothers, New York (*Advertising for the Advertiser*, Eric Webster, John Murray, London).' Once an agency acquires an ingrained knowledge of a client's business, it is far easier and far less costly to shift people on the account than to fire the agency.'

Admittedly he was talking about consumer advertising. But the same goes for financial advertising. Perhaps, more so. Consumer advertising is at least dealing with tangibles. Financial advertising deals in intangibles such as public reaction and confidence. It is much easier to study products and markets than public reaction and confidence.

Choosing a consumer-orientated agency, therefore, is a problem. Choosing a financial advertising agency is a headache.

4.3.1 DECIDE WHAT YOU THINK YOU WANT FOR YOUR AGENCY

There is no point in deciding what you want. The agency knows the advertising business. You know your business. Right from the start the relationship must be a partnership. And that can only happen if client and agency work out the problems together.

Forget all the nonsense about jotting down 'what you personally feel to be of major importance in handling your account'. It's like asking an advertising agency to design Concorde. It's not their line of country. Instead look around at all the financial advertising being done by other companies, especially companies in your own industry. Decide why it appeals to you and how such a campaign could be adapted for your own company.

4.3.2 ASK FOR ADVICE

Everyone likes giving advice. Make use of it. Ask your bank. Talk to a merchant bank. Speak to companies already running financial advertising programmes. They will all talk freely. It might take time. But it will save you money in the long run. This is the way you discover the strengths and weaknesses of the financial advertising network. If all this fails there is still the Institute of Practitioners in Advertising to fall back upon. They cannot recommend a particular agency. But they can give you a list to choose from. Some companies make a point of talking to financial journalists in the course of hunting down their agency. If journalists tend to favour an agency, it must be good. They, after all, tend to lead public opinion. In any case, if you accept a journalist's advice and go to a particular agency, its odds on that sometime or other you will come in for a spot of praise in print. Providing you picked the right journalist, of course.

4.3.3 DRAW UP A SHORT LIST

With only a handful of financial agencies to choose from, it will be a short list. That doesn't matter. Get the names and background of all the directors. List the accounts, the size of the billings and—more important—how long they have handled the accounts.

'Finding out who agencies act for is like going to a tailor', says Hartley-Smith. 'You ask him who he makes suits for.'

Then get examples of the campaigns. There is little point in getting worked up about the size and length of a campaign, if you cannot stand the sight of it. It might be an idea to throw in a non-financial agency for luck. Admittedly they cannot all guarantee the same expertise as the 100 per cent City boys. But you might hit lucky. In any case you could get a completely new look financial campaign which would be worth the risk.

4.3.4 WRITE TO THE AGENCIES ON THE SHORT LIST

Make it short and to the point. You are looking for an agency to handle your financial advertising account. The budget, you envisage, will be in the region of so-and-so. Are they interested? If so, will they let you have all the necessary details: size, staff of agency; qualifications and expertise; accounts held, size and for how long; examples of campaigns plus their first thoughts on handling your own account.

4.3.5 ANALYSE THE REPLIES

Some companies go to absurd lengths in assessing agency replies. Peter Youdale, Group Marketing Manager of The Federated Building Group (*The Director*, May 1968) plays schoolmasters and awards marks to agency chairmen who telephone suggesting an early meeting 'on the grounds that they understood the mechanics of selling'. Not content with that he then rates all the replies for their speed of reply; the quality of reply; the warmth and friendliness of the reply and, believe it or not, 'the degree to which the reply showed that the writer understood the reasons for the company asking their questions in the first place'. All this takes time and is not, frankly, worth the effort. Advertising is ideas. And people react to ideas instinctively. They do not pull out a note book and computer and analyse everything into the ground. There is only one way to judge an agency: whether it seems to be talking sense or not. If not, no amount of warmth and friendliness will change the matter.

4.3.6 MAKE YOUR PROVISIONAL DECISION

Youdale, for all his marks and analysis, ended up by visiting no less than 13 different agencies in spite of their original plan to visit only six. This was a shocking waste of time—both for the Federated Building Group and the 13 agencies concerned. Instead decide on one agency. It should not be too difficult. All the time you should see yourself working hand-in-glove with the agency. Are you on the same wavelength? Do you appreciate each other's problems? Are you satisfied with their existing accounts? And so on.

4.3.7 CHECK YOUR PROVISIONAL DECISION

Back to the merchant banks, companies already in the financial advertising business and the journalist. Better safe than sorry. A final word to confirm your decision. Before you were talking in pretty general terms. This time its for real.

4.3.8 TAKE THE PLUNGE. DECIDE

By now you should have a pretty good idea of what financial advertising is all about. If you haven't, you will not be in a position to know whether you have chosen the right agency or not. In any case, a company is not wedded to an agency for life. There are always plenty of others to choose from.

Chapter 5

Choosing a Financial Public Relations Consultancy

Founder of Astral Public Relations and ex-head of group public relations and publicity at Fisons, the chemical giant, Dick Owen was appointed the new group public relations adviser to the Midland Bank in 1969. His salary—£8,000 a year—one of the highest paid staff jobs in PR in the United Kingdom. His role, regarded by the bank as one of 'utmost importance', involved cultivating 'the closest relations with the press'.

Ten years ago this would have been a dream. No staff PRO would have dreamt of getting such money. And certainly no company, let alone the august Midland Bank, would have dreamt of paying such money. Today, its becoming more accepted. Keith Hopkins, Lord Stokes' right-hand PRO, is also in the big league. Others are treading on his heels.

That's a measure of the effect of the business news revolution. Financial advertising is in the wings. In the vanguard are the financial PR men. They are the communications co-ordinators who are the central authorities of communication between their companies and the outside world. They are responsible for co-ordinating the promotion of the company—as a company. Trade promotion and consumer promotion are important. They form the remaining points of the promotional triangle. But the financial public relations man is at the top. Unless he can be sure that every form of communication between the company and the public conforms to strict company principles and standards, any promotion of the company will remain on the ground. This covers everything from print and advertising to annual general meetings.

On the other side of the fence are the PR consultants, businessmen like Roland Freeman, ex-financial chairman of the Greater London Council and a member of the Northampton Development Corporation and journalists like ex-City Editor of *The Times*, George Pulay.

Freeman quit as Managing Director of Public Relations (Industrial) in 1969 and set up his own financial, marketing and PR consultancy, Freeman and Garlick. 'I do not regard annual fixed fees as a sensible basis for organising a publicity campaign designed to increase the sales of a product', he says.

'There should always be some specific reward for success. My new company will only take on major and continuous organisational work for clients if we can share in the benefits which result from it.' A Director of Surinvest unit trusts, Mr Freeman is also Chairman of MM Film Productions and of Cotswold Carpets. In addition he is on the boards of the Festival Ballet, the Elizabethan Theatre Ensemble and Sounds for Industry.

Pulay, by comparison, had been in journalism 20 years before he entered the financial PR stakes. He worked on the *News Chronicle*. Then he spent nine years with the *Daily Telegraph*. In 1962 he moved across to *The Times*. Four years later he was appointed City Editor. Why did he quit? Partly because he had had enough of journalism. Partly because he was becoming fascinated by PR. A combination of the two.

'I had hoped to practice a little of the things I had always been writing about', he says. 'A bit of business running. A bit of helping businesses instead of just writing about them.' Now as one of four managing directors running Charles Barker City, probably the top financial PR operation in the country— they have 50 staff including ten based at their Scottish office—he is in a position to practice what he preached for so long.

PR men, however, continue to have a bad image. 'When I was on *The Times*', says Pulay, 'I was always irritated by badly produced releases and by non-events, trying to make a story out of nothing. One could only recognise a handful of PRO's who had been journalists. That was always the serious side. The other side was a waste of time.'

The Pace Advertising survey into client-agency relationships, undertaken by Research Associates, revealed that while the advertising man was found wanting in honesty and naturalness, the PR man was mainly characterised by deviousness and dishonesty.

Undertake a similar survey among the news media and the PR man becomes the waste-maker. More than 180 tons of useless press releases are mailed to the 1,200 local newspapers in the United Kingdom every year. Labour costs must total £1,500,000. The Post Office breaks its back. And four million separate press releases are tossed straight into the waste bin. Only the salvage industry benefits. Then take into account the trade and technical press. Another five million useless releases there every year. These are not stories the editors cannot use for lack of space. They are stories that have absolutely no relevance to the partner publications at all. And would never in a thousand years warrant even a single line.

Then there is time. PR men are criticised for wasting time.

'It is not every day that the board of one of the three largest banks in the United States chooses to meet in London. Nor is it every day that the members of the financial press are invited to meet Mr George S. Moore, the Chairman of the First National City Bank and other top executives. And one always had reckoned that any public relations

exercise undertaken by Citibank would make a considerable impact. I wonder if I was the only journalist disappointed at the outcome.'
(*Investors Chronicle*, 30 May 1969)

What followed was a tale of junior members of Citibank outnumbering the press; directors refusing to comment on the economic problems of the UK; a two-hour drinks and lunch opening session and journalists meeting Moore as if they were 'going to be ushered into the presence of Caesar'.

'I left the conference before the majority of my colleagues and I must confess I was a little disappointed. I had expected more but the fact was that there was little in the way of hard news and this never makes for a satisfactory press meeting. Perhaps it was a pity that it was left to the day after the press meeting to announce that the National and Grindlays Chairman, Lord Aldington, had been elected to the Board of First National City Corporation, the parent company of Citi-bank. He is the first British citizen to be elected to the board.'

Obviously not the ideal way of cultivating the closest relations with the press.

5.1 Qualifications

There is a lot of huey about qualifications. Hale Nelson, Vice-President of the Illinois Bell Telephone Company has spelled out the 'non-duplicating requirements' of a financial PR:

1 Know economics, political science, sociology, world history, international affairs, finance, cultural anthropology.
2 Naturally some humanities, certainly marketing and industrial relations.
3 Gallop through the present literature on PR to know that it exists.
4 Study social sciences, English, Journalism, art, a minimum of one foreign language, psychology, radio, television, photography.
5 Join the college newspaper.
6 Take business administration, public speaking, advertising, business law, Latin, Greek, logic, ethics, religion, chemistry, physics, debate, maths, publication production, motion picture production.
7 Travel.
8 Get a master's degree. You can't know too much. But above all learn humility.

Another Charles Barker managing director, James Derriman, in his book, *Company-Investor Relations* (University of London Press) has gone a stage further. In addition to the basic skills of his profession, he believes the financial public relations specialist requires:

1 Knowledge of company law, accountancy practice, the practice of the

Stock Exchange and the issuing houses, the mechanics of mergers and bids, and of the Monopolies Commission.

2 An ability to write about financial matters in a way which is at once clear to the reader with little technical knowledge and accurate enough to satisfy the expert (no easy task sometimes).

3 A good working knowledge of the City pages of the national and provincial press, and of the financial press, their editorial policies and their staffs; an understanding of the information requirements of the small shareholder, the press and the investment analysts.

4 Experience of, and affinity for, the ways of the City.

5 The personal qualities to act as a confidential adviser at board level, with the insight to know when (and when not) to press a view which he believes to be right.

'Financial PR is a growth area, certainly', adds Derriman. 'But the pace of active growth is partly controlled by the flow of good people available. We are in fact growing because we have the people available to do it. It would probably be unfair to say that we are growing that rapidly. It's just that we have the good people. Unfortunately there are not many about.'

5.2 Appointing a financial public relations adviser

Such men are few and far between. Which is one reason for the high salaries. Yet there are three ways open to companies eager to engage their services.

5.2.1 THEY CAN HIRE THE MAN DIRECT

Owen and Hopkins are among the highest paid staff PR men in the country. So don't worry. A staff PR man with the necessary background and experience can come a little cheaper. But not much. The old National Provincial Bank, for example, hired Chris Rowlands, who had worked on both the *Financial Times* and the *Daily Express*. When he joined he was put in a room with five people. He didn't even have a typewriter. Now with the NP merged into the new National Westminster he has a staff of 15, senior executive status and responsibility for the promotion of Britain's biggest banking concern with £3,500 million deposits, 49,000 staff, over 4,000 branches and many subsidiary financial interests. In the first six months of 1966 National Provincial were mentioned only 427 times by radio, TV and the press, local, national and specialist. During the first six months after his appointment, the number of references soared to 1,399. For the whole year, he recorded a total of 3,050 references.

'If a story breaks, I believe in getting it and presenting it to the press as soon as possible', he says. 'I have even been down to banks which have been raided to ensure the press get the story and we present all the details.' In addition Rowlands has launched a bi-monthly staff newspaper, Bankground; formed a 13-strong team who lecture women's organisations about family budgeting and banking for women as well as starting a Young Exporters awards scheme.

The advantages of a staff man are obvious. He is always on the spot. He knows the company intimately. He knows the office politics and the lobbying, something few outsiders could hope to discover. And he has no problem over divided loyalties.

The disadvantages could be important. But it depends in the end on the individual and the company. If the staff PR man is an expert, his advice will be just as objective as if he was an outsider—even though this might mean, say, setting the company chairman right on one or two occasions.

'Goodwill is an important asset. To secure it, management seeks objective and experienced advice in handling the outward and inward flow of information between organisations and the various publications with which they deal. In projecting the achievements of the client, it is the task of the consultancy to advise on the use of all means of communication (e.g. printed matter, films, exhibitions) except paid space or time which are the separate province of the advertising agency. Here press relations play a primary role: the consultancy's function is to organise press conferences, to prepare and issue press releases and, where necessary to run a special Information Office for companies, products and services. The emphasis throughout is on presenting a clear picture of the client; it has been well said that "Public relations is concerned with the effect of behaviour on reputation". In dealing with the inward flow of information, the consultancy interprets social trends, economic changes and attitudes to public issues; it reports on developments at Westminster and Whitehall and in local government likely to affect the client.'— Russell Cobb.

5.2.2 THEY CAN HIRE A PUBLIC RELATIONS CONSULTANCY

According to Anthony Sampson, 'They work among chandeliers and marble mantelpieces, telephoning, entertaining, introducing, arranging, conciliating, explaining—lubricating your groaning wheels between corporations and the public. Sometimes they make use of institutional advertising, but their real art consists of unseen promotion—inspiring headlines, television programmes, questions in Parliament, letters to *The Times*. They cultivate an old-fashioned, long-established atmosphere: they wear stiff collars and dark suits and sit in Regency offices. They are the new fixers of British society.'

Almost. But not quite. The PR consultant has to work for his living. If he doesn't work, he doesn't eat. It's as simple as that. Sampson's caricature probably fits West End PR consultants like:

Prince Yurka Galitzine whose clients include the Greek Government—

G

only tourism, of course—Nigeria, his sole political account. One of his lunches can be attended by Will Howie MP; Sir Miles Clifford; J. F. Wilkinson, Head of the BBC's Africa Service; Auberon Waugh of *The Spectator*; the Nigerian Deputy Commissioner, Mr Balewa; the First Political Secretary, Mr Oyesanya; and his partner, David Russell.

E. D. O'Brien, the former President of the Oxford Union, a member of White's and Buck's, the only Director of Information Services ever hired by the Conservative Central Office and probably the most persuasive Irishman ever born.

Michael Rice whose first political account came at the request of the old Commonwealth Relations Office. Since then he has handled the Arab League, Bahrain and Guyana.

The financial PR consultants, mostly based in and around the City, are in a different league:—

Trevor Russell-Cobb, a BA and BSc Economics (London), served in the Welsh Guards during the war. A towering, impressive man, he operates from a tiny, book-lined office high above New Bond Street and prefers not to regard financial public relations as a separate speciality but covers it for his clients as part of the assignment. A former member of the United Nations staff in Geneva, he was responsible for negotiations with European Governments and other international organisations concerning training facilities in economic development and public administration. Previously he had experience in the British Council of government public relations. The author of *Paying the Piper*, the first-ever study of industrial patronage, he is the UK member of the European Liaison Committee set up by the Foundation pour l'Art la Recherche et la Culture, Paris after the first exhibition of industrial patronage held at the Musée des Arts Décoratifs in 1968.

Maurice D. Cocking, ex-City Editor of the *Daily Sketch*, also took a BSc (Economics) at London. Now the Managing Director of Fabus Financial and Business PR Limited, he is widely regarded as among the best financial PR people in London.

James Derriman, Managing Director of Charles Barker City and author of two outstanding public relations books, *Public Relations in Business Management* and *Company-Investor Relations*, has had 10 years' experience of Fleet Street. First he worked at the *Daily Herald* and then Reuters and the *News Chronicle*. A barrister, he joined J. Walter Thompson Company in 1955, worked closely on PR for the Stock Exchange and became an associate director. In 1962 he joined Charles Barker and Sons to form the public relations division, which is now part of Charles Barker City.

Bill Fisher, a quiet American who heads the European operation of the giant US consultancy, Ruder and Finn, is an expert on international financial public relations. Under his lead, Ruder and Finn Europa have:

1 Helped an international tobacco company determine the extent of the European financial community's knowledge of its operation before it launched a major European expansion programme.
2 Master-minded a corporate public relations programme for an international and industrial consumer and industrial company concerned that its multi-divisional structure was generating a fragmented image in Europe.
3 Re-launched a London fashion house after it had experienced a series of well publicised financial setbacks.

Malcolm Henderson, who runs the consultancy founded by his father 24 years ago, the Philip Henderson Company, one of the oldest consultancies in the UK. 'Twenty-two-years ago Philip Henderson wrote: I strongly deplore the threat to old-established family businesses that have played so important a part in our national life and especially would we wish to act for such concerns—for the one reason if for no other, that they offer great scope for creative promotion. The value of good public relations to the reputation of a company in its various communities is incalculable', says son, Malcolm. 'This remains very much the working philosophy of Philip Henderson Company today as it approaches its quarter century.'

Consultants offer two advantages over staff men: objectivity and a wide range of experience. Both, however, depend on the man.

'The consultant is more professional in his approach, taking a broader view and—if he is to do his job properly too—he should be prepared to advise with the utmost frankness', says Frank Jefkins in *Planned Public Relations*, 'Second opinions, outside point of view, constructive criticism—these are invaluable services available from the consultant.'

Admittedly a staff can also have wide experience. But the advantage of a consultant is that he's experienced because he is working for companies in different industries and at different levels, is current and up-to-date. He will also know the present feelings throughout industry generally and, in addition, he will have a wide range of press and media contacts.

'The first duty of any Board of Directors is to its shareholders and to its employees. But no company exists in a vacuum so that if interests of the company (comprising directors, shareholders, and employees) are all very much bound up with the goodwill and service not only of customers and suppliers but also of Bankers, Brokers and all those other specialists, who, more than just rendering their own services, will be shaping their individual viewpoint about the calibre and quality of the Company and its Management. These views will count, for example, when the Company comes to raise capital either privately or on the Stock Market. Provided the company is soundly run, has reasonable prospects had has sensibly and widely communicated itself to the financial and investment communities it will find that it is able to raise funds without difficulty and at the keenest prices. Conversely, those companies which prefer to keep a tight clamp on news about themselves must not be disappointed if they find themselves neglected when either they bring their shares to market, or, if already quoted on the Stock Exchange, they seek to raise additional capital. The City will recognise merit quickly enough but that merit has first to be brought to its attention. It is the experienced Financial Public Relations man who will ensure that this merit is brought to the attention not only of the City but also of the Investment Public at large.'—Maurice D. Cocking, Managing Director, Fabus Financial and Business PR Limited.

5.2.3 THEY CAN HIRE THEIR OWN MAN—AND HIRE A CONSULTANT AS WELL
'Two quite different skills are in fact included in the umbrella term of Public Relations', writes Michael C. Paine in *Advertising: The Marketing Approach* (Crosby Lockwood 1968), probably the best case for this strategy.

'The first, sometimes referred to as Press Relations, covers the dissemination of company news to the public through the medium of the editorial columns of the press and television. The man most suited to this sort of task is someone with previous journalistic experience, who knows how to approach editors. The second, known as Product Publicity, covers the whole organisation of a product promotion, which may require a very detailed plan of action. The PRO may find himself involved in booking hotel rooms, arranging for the reception of a celebrity, entertaining prize-winners, organising transportation, photography, television appearances, refreshments, factory tours, preparation of press hand-outs and other material. This requires administrative ability, which is not necessarily part of a journalist's make-up—in fact it would be a waste of his talents if he were used in this manner.'

The solution: a staff man looks after part one of the operation and a consultant looks after part two.

5.2.4 THEY CAN HIRE A CONSULTANT—AND TURN HIM INTO THEIR OWN MAN
This rarely happens. But when it does, it has a startling effect. Shortly after Carl F. Duerr was appointed Managing Director of Jensen Motors Limited at the beginning of 1968 he launched a vigorous communications policy. He invited the press to attend a works meeting where the parlous financial state

of the company was outlined and the men were told the work force would have to be reduced from 1,200 to a mere 400. He then gave the go-ahead for a press conference with both management and unions. He launched a system of quarterly questionnaires to customers to find out how their Jensen sports cars were behaving. And he appointed Anthony Good, Managing Director of Good Relations Limited to the board of the company. As a result the PR-approach was carried into the board room.

'The PR man has to be where his input can be of greatest influence', says Duerr. 'This is at board level.'

5.3 How to hire a financial public relations consultancy

If hiring a city advertising agency is like getting married, hiring a financial PR consultancy is like having an affair. They never relax. An advertising agency has a job to do. Once it has produced the advertisements, it sits back. A financial PR consultancy is never finished. It deals in news and news reaction. It is a 24-hour service.

Denis Inchbald, Managing Director of Welbeck Public Relations, has estimated (*Financial Times*, 20 June 1966) that there are 450 PR service organisations in the United Kingdom. About 120 are connected with advertising agencies. The remainder are one- or two-man bands. Of 23 consultants listed in the Institute of Public Relations Register with six or more members, 12 were owned by advertising agencies. Among the seven with ten or more members, six belonged to advertising agencies. Total fees ranged from £50,000 to £200,000. Staffs went from 15 to 6. But only a handful are financial public relation consultants. Hiring one, therefore, can be like playing Russian roulette.

Lord Kearton, Chairman of Courtauld's says he wants a PRO who is truthful, presentable and who has a thick skin. Selection Trust, the £160 million mining finance house, however, hired Russell-Cobb for promising them absolutely nothing. 'I told them I could promise nothing—since it's all within the editor's decision. I would try to influence him, however', says Russell-Cobb. Nigel Neilson, who runs Neilson McCarthy, by comparison, virtually chooses his own clients. More than 90 per cent come to him on personal recommendation. 'I always look at their organisation first', he says. 'The worse thing you could do would be to turn the spotlight on a company when it wasn't ready for it.'

There are, however, some guide-lines, similar, in fact, to selecting a financial advertising agency.

5.3.1 DECIDE WHAT YOU THINK YOU WANT

Read all the business newspapers. Tune into radio and television. Make a note of the companies you keep hearing about again and again. If it is a big company, chances are they will have their own staff. If not, they will probably have a consultant. Now analyse the results of their activities and make up your mind whether you would like your company handled the same way. It could mean national press publicity. Or it could mean trade press publicity. If the publicity is as a result of one speech after another to conferences or trade missions, be prepared for that. Nothing comes through standing still.

5.3.2 ASK ADVICE

It's the old problem. Check before taking a decision. Banks, advertising agencies, financial journalists will all have their own ideas about PR and PR men. Unless you have an idea of the kind of PR operation you are looking for you will never get an answer. It might be worth checking with The Institute of Public Relations. They might be able to offer some advice. But, as with all professional groups, it will have to be impartial. The problem is that there are few consultancies which concentrate on financial PR. The vast majority dabble in everything: product PR, export PR, personality stunts as well as the hard-graft of technical and industrial PR. If they do financial PR, they do it on the side. Its not a main activity, just one among many. Some do it well. Others make a hash of the whole operation. Hence the need of advice. Nothing could be worse for a company than launching a financial PR operation only to have to call the whole thing off because the consultancy is still breaking its teeth in the field and causing trouble for the client.

Many consultancies circulate booklets and brochures outlining their services. This is the only way to get round the Institute of Public Relations ban on 'touting or advertising calculated to attract business unfairly'. While some are detailed and reliable, there are a few who are downright misleading. They can't even agree on what is public relations.

> Recognising the news potential of a company 'happening' is the first step—*Rea Publicity.*

> Action to maintain or increase goodwill between a company and every section of the public with which it comes into contact—*Charles Barker.*

> The creation of sympathy towards a client's corporate aims and confidence in his operations—*Brook-Hart Ruder and Finn.*

> PR can support and heighten the effect of advertising, create the right climate of opinion for a new product, new policy or ideas, or correct misapprehension caused by lack of information—*Link.*

> Public Relations is the deliberate attempt to earn goodwill from others—*Galitzine Chant Russell.*

But what about the consultancies? What have they got to offer?

Rea simply refers to the activities undertaken by any PR consultancy. Galitzine examines all the problems of assessing a consultant but ends up by stressing the 'distinct advantages' of hiring a consultancy completely independent of organisations outside the PR field. Charles Barker City admits it is a newcomer to the Charles Barker group. Brook-Hart stresses it is a specialist in both short and long-term programmes. And London Press Exchange stress their world-wide service with offices in Paris and Milan; telex connections with Paris, Hamburg, Dusseldorf, Munich, Rotterdam, Brussels, Zurich, Geneva 'and other cities'; and carefully selected leading public relations consultancies 'elsewhere'.

What does it cost? Here all the booklets hedge. Rea doesn't even mention money. Brook-Hart speak of 'reasonable fees'. Link just refer to 'agreed retainer fee and an agreed expense budget which is not exceeded without the client's advance agreement. LPE and Charles Barker admit fees are based on staff time involved. Astral Public Relations goes further than all the rest—they actually mention figures. For short jobs—up to a week—they charge £50 a day. Anything less is worked out between consultant and client.

5.3.3 DECIDE WHICH KIND OF CONSULTANCY YOU WOULD LIKE
A consultant in public relations, unfortunately, is not a consultant. There are no less than five different types:

1 The one-man freelance.
2 The PR department of an advertising agency.
3 The subsidiary of an agency.
4 The PR consultant proper.
5 There is also a rare breed of PR adviser, who sits and advises while a consultant does all the work.

Too often the decision depends on the luck of the cards. But it deserves serious consideration. To a small company in the provinces just beginning business PR, the one-man freelance might be the answer. It would certainly be a doorstep service. And it would help the company to test the water without committing too much time or money. If the experiment crashed, they wouldn't be committed to huge losses. Only pride, perhaps. The agency PR department is a step up the ladder. It would certainly mean higher fees although it would be worth the extra money. The big danger is whether the agency has the right motive for having a PR department. Some agencies have them because they are vital in supplying a thorough service to clients.

Others have them to try to milk further fees out of the client without putting in too much extra work. This rides on the assumption that the advertising account decides the issue. Make a success of the advertising and the PR account will follow on behind. Or, simply, run a PR department because it gives the agency two opportunities for getting clients and twice as much chance for doubling the service.

PR subsidiaries are more independent and, therefore, probably more reliable. They operate under their own banner. They chase and lose their own accounts. Some are held by the parent agency. Some are not. These mean more freedom and greater objectivity. From the client's point of view it also means more value for money—for they are handling the account for the right reason.

Independent PR consultancies are probably better still. They live or die by their own efforts. If they live, and live comfortably, its obviously the first sign of strength. The first question, therefore, is how strong. Find out about the directors, their background and their experience of PR. Check the accounts they handle and, more important, the fees they charge—if possible. Then make certain which services they can offer and whether there are additional charges or not.

5.3.4 DRAW UP A SHORT LIST

A short list of financial advertising agencies will be short. A short list of financial PR consultancies will be longer. Because there are many more to choose from. There are also many different personalities and types of operation to choose from. Again the only real criteria is personal choice. Despite all the advice, if you feel a partner consultancy can handle your company, go ahead and check. In the end you have to work with the consultancy—not your advisers.

5.3.5 WRITE TO THE CONSULTANCIES ON THE SHORT LIST

Explain the problem. Outline the kind of services you are looking for. If you can give some idea of the money you are prepared to spend, give it. Some consultancies like Russell-Cobb Limited have a minimum fee. In some cases it is £1,500 or £2,000. Russell-Cobb's minimum is £5,000. The Philip Henderson Company, however, reckon on £2,000 minimum. Obviously it is better to start by mentioning the figure otherwise you might waste both your own time and the consultancy's time as well. But don't forget a PR fee is like a piece of string. It depends on the services you are looking for and the experience to back it up. A £1,500 fee might look expensive but if it bought the advice of a top flight man with an infallible financial PR touch, it would be worth every penny. If, however, it bought the time of an ex-*Daily Mirror* junior reporter who had never even looked at a balance sheet, it would be disastrously expensive.

That is not the only problem. There are lots of ways a consultancy can over-charge a client. Some are unfair. Others are absolutely dishonest:

1. CHARGING FOR WORK DONE BY SOMEONE ELSE. The bigger the company the more likely it will generate its own publicity. Not every mention in the press will be as a direct result of PR activity. Some PRO's will admit it. Others will claim the full credit for every single press mention and charge the client.

2. PITCHING THE FEE SO LOW that they beat the competition and land the account. Once they have the account they begin handling all kinds of additional services such as photography, design, print, claiming it is all

part of the service. The client then gets billed for the service with a flat 10 to 15 per cent handling fee slapped on top. If he objects, the consultancy merely collects his additional fee from the supplier instead.

3 DRAWING UP A CONTRACT for a three or five year period. The consultancy will claim this is more economic in the long run. Instead of paying so much per year, the rate is less spread over such a long time because it means the consultancy can programme and plan and so on. The only trouble is that the contract invariably omits a break clause. Half-way through, the client finds he can no longer rely on the consultancy. He wants to break. But the consultancy insists on sticking to the contract— unless the client wants to hand over a remainder of the total fee.

4 JUGGLING WITH THE PRESS CLIPPINGS. Some PR men analyse the press clippings to such an extent that the client feels he is hot news the world over. Which is probably unlikely. If he lets the consultancy get away with it, the client will find the fee and expenses creeping higher and higher in order to maintain the extensive press coverage.

But particularly pay close attention to methods of charging. You have a right to know exactly how your money is going to be spent. In fact, the contract you sign should be given the same amount of attention before you sign it as any other business contract.

Relevant clauses taken from the Institute of Public Relations Code of Professional Conduct.

A member shall conduct his professional activities with respect for the public interest.

A member shall at all times deal fairly and honestly with his client or employers past and present with his fellow members and with the general public.

A member shall not intentionally disseminate false or misleading information, and shall use proper care to avoid doing so. He has a positive duty to maintain truth, accuracy and good taste.

A member shall not engage in any practice which tends to corrupt the integrity of channels of public communication.

A member shall not create or make use of any organisation purporting to serve some announced cause but actually promoting a special or private interest of a member or his client or his employer which is not apparent.

A member shall safeguard the confidences of both present and former clients or employers. He shall not disclose except upon the order of a court of competent jurisdiction any confidential information which he may have obtained in his official capacity without securing and making known the consent of the said client or employer.

A member shall not represent conflicting or competing interests without the express consent of those concerned given after full disclosure of the facts.

A member in performing services for a client or employer shall not accept fees, commissions or any other valuable consideration in connection with those services from anyone other than his client or employer unless such practice is acceptable to the client or employer.

A member shall not propose to a prospective client or employer that his fee or other compensation be contingent on the achievement of certain results; nor shall he enter into any fee agreement to the same effect.

5.3.6 ANALYSE THE REPLIES

Whatever PR people say, they are image merchants. So be warned. A reply from a consultancy is likely to produce a mass of glossy literature, a heap of re-prints of articles by the directors and an invitation to lunch. Study it all. If possible, check what they are saying. See if they list their clients and if so how long they have had them. If they haven't, ask for them. A consultancy can't refuse. If it does, forget it. If a consultancy isn't able to defend its own reputation, it obviously cannot be trusted to defend a client's reputation. Then check and re-check the fee and the services you get for the fee. Carl Byoir, an old-time American PR man, used to charge clients a flat 36,000 dollar fee. 'You now get the right to telephone me', he would say. 'If the answer is right it's worth any sum. If it's wrong, it's worth nothing.' But his advice was so good that he had plenty of takers.

Today organisation and method is taking over. Galitzine and Partners split the year into working hours and charge an hourly rate for the job. The most commonly used system, they say, is to divide the year into 220 working days—or 1,650 working hours, the system generally used by chartered accountants. Salaries are then directly related to the number of hours in a working day. Special factors such as skill, responsibility or priority then vary the figure by a percentage. The minimum calculated cost to the client is then multiplied by three. The first share pays the salaries. The remainder contributes to overheads and profits. Another yardstick, recommended by the Institute of Chartered Accountants, is a daily rate of £1 per cent of annual salary of employees, plus a higher fee for the principal's time.

Clive Smith, Managing Director of Astral Public Relations, a medium-size consultancy with a high reputation, maintains £3 an hour is reasonable for a small-size outfit. Medium-size groups like his own have to charge £5–£6 an hour while the giants, like Lexington International, are forced to charge in the region of £9 to cover costs. The choice must be the client's. A £2,000 fee, for example, can either buy 700 hours at a small consultancy or perhaps only 200 hours at a select Mayfair consultancy packed with electric typewriters and more experienced advisers. Some consultants, however, are against the whole man-hour system. Robert Thorpe, whose consultancy is the biggest in the UK in terms of clients—he has more than 70—maintains, 'You simply can't apply this to every client. The only static thing about our firm's structure and costing is what we are prepared to kick off at.'

There is also a small group of consultants who follow the optician's approach. 'They put the glasses on your nose and say it will cost £10. If you don't blink, then they say ". . . for the frames". Then they say the lens cost 5 gns. Again if you don't blink, they say ". . . each".'

'Are you getting the right kind of publicity? This is a question worth asking. For in most businesses publicity techniques can be substantially improved. And these improvements can produce results out of all proportion to the costs involved. The greatest opportunities for improvement generally lie in the field of public relations activities. For public relations is confused by the majority with advertising. Only minority understand that the two activities follow entirely different patterns. Therefore possibly 85 per cent of UK companies who could use PR profitably overlook a wealth of low cost opportunities. They certainly under use it—to a very substantial extent. The minority who do achieve the most outstanding results and are 'always in the news' and, in the majority of cases, using Public Relations consultants or full-time Public Relations staff. They do not, generally, depend solely on the advertising services of an agency nor on a company executive who has other responsibilities such as advertising, marketing, sales promotion, sales or management. People with other responsibilities seldom achieve the results and economy in costs that specialist PR people can obtain with ease. These specialists—in particular the competent outside consultant with an efficient organisation—can offer the extensive Press contacts and the knowledge gained only through years of specialist training and experience. And they have much to offer, and if their budgeting is right, normally at a price to suit even the smallest company's pocket. Ask yourself a further question: do you know definitely that your company achieves the maximum editorial publicity it deserves—at home and overseas, on radio, television and in the financial press—the kind of editorial publicity obtained by your competitors? If not, then the reason may well be because you do not employ an efficient and experienced public relations team.'—Financial Commercial Industrial PR Limited.

5.3.7 MAKE YOUR PROVISIONAL DECISION

Bring the short list down to two or three. Now read the small print. Check the fees, the services and the time you are buying—if you are buying time. Some consultancies such as Tim Traverse-Healy and Dennis Lyons charge minimum retainers of £3,000 just for 'thinking time'. The nuts and bolts of the operation are done elsewhere. Invite the consultants to your office and grill them. Russell-Cobb believes companies should look for intelligence, independence and the ability to say No—with reasons. He should also be a man who can use words and figures. He should not be aggressive. 'A consultant who is aggressive might tend to get his client involved in some kind of row. That would be wrong. He might also tend to prolong any row that bursts out. Sometimes publicity is controlled as much by what you say as by what you don't say', he says. A company which hired Russell-Cobb would be getting constant availability. They are available day and night seven days a week. They screen all material about the company, checking the references and avoiding howlers. They also give their clients day-to-day advice on the servicing and use of all PR news media.

Leo Cavendish, who runs Financial Press Information Services, believes in the personal touch. 'Ability to get on a personal level is important', he says. 'One of the best ways of choosing a consultancy is by choosing a consultant you can get on with. That's if you want a long, lasting and fruitful relationship. From that point-of-view probably the small consultancies are better than the big ones.'

This will take time. But don't worry. It is your money and your reputation you are discussing. In any case, PR consultants are used to taking their time over landing a new client. With around 1,500 accounts worth around £3 million shuffling between 500-odd consultancies every year, its worth the effort. The London headquarters of Carl Byoir and Associates reckon on a 12-month gestation period between initial contact and the signing-on ceremony. And they are probably the biggest PR operators in the world with around three million dollars a year billings and 250 consultants in five different countries. But when they land an account, it generally stays. Fourteen clients have stayed for ten years or more. Six others have been on their books for five to ten years. That's only in the United Kingdom. Head of the London office for the last eight years, Henry McNulty, spent a year talking to the giant Borg-Warner Corporation before they finally said Yes. He began in 1965. Carl Byoir in the United States signed up the Borg-Warner account for America. But they left out their 23 foreign subsidiaries.

McNulty spotted the deficiency. As Borg-Warner were developing its sophisticated engineering operation throughout the world, it was vital they developed their corporate image in Europe as well. Byoir's Chicago man, Harry Schaden, made contact with Borg-Warner in America. At the same time McNulty approached some of the European-based companies. As a result he was called to Chicago to give a PR presentation to 30 of the organisation's top salesmen. He emphasised the necessity of establishing a corporate image of Borg-Warner throughout Europe and the tremendous benefits this would mean in their marketing operation. From there he flew to Washington, West Virginia, to discuss the PR problems being faced by the corporation's Marbon Chemical Division. He then returned to London. The hard work then began.

There were further talks, telephone conversations, letters, proposals and reports to and from the US. After nearly 12 months came a call from the Borg-Warner PR chief, Doug Mueller. He had sold the idea of a European PR operation to the president, James F. Beré. McNulty flew to Chicago. The budget was approved. He had finally landed the account for Britain, France, Germany, Holland and Italy.

Landing the Cummins Engine account, by comparison, only took ex-*Newsweek* journalist, McNulty, ten days.

Forget the bragging. Few consultants land a PR account over Matelote à la Bourguignonne at the Coq au Vin.

5.3.8 ASK FOR THE PUBLIC RELATIONS PROPOSALS

This is an integral part of the PR legend. 'Without a programme we don't think there is any hope of success', says Finn. But be careful, some proposals run to 130 pages. It is best to check at the start whether the consultancy will be charging for them or not. In most cases, however, proposals run to around six pages.

> 'Our brief was to assess whether Public Relations could be of benefit to XYZ Limited and, if so, in what ways such activity should be pursued. In making our proposals we have borne in mind that the firm's objective, in general terms, is "to increase all types of profitable business without any lowering of the standards of professional efficiency on which the firm's high reputation in the City is based and at the right moment to expand overseas".'

This was the start of a set of proposals submitted by Financial Press Information Services which went on to analyse the company concerned, its growth and its reputation:

> 'The aim of Public Relations, therefore, must be increased general awareness of the firm's size, strengths and reputation in what can be termed "development areas". Basically there are two points to be made:
>
> The firm's history, current organisation and continued progress.
> The firm's investment expertise.'

Then came the proposals, divided into three categories. First, lunches. City editors get around. They answer reader's letters. They decide what goes in the paper. They should be invited to the company together with commercial attachés from countries in which the firm is interested. Similarly, journalists who write the market reports and London-based City correspondents working for foreign newspapers.

Second, literature. The firm already had a good recruitment brochure. A companion volume should be prepared concentrating on the company services, skills and structure. Other company publications should be mailed to the press as they appear.

Third, general strategy. Executives should take part in seminars and conferences. They should be ready to comment on radio and television whenever the media took a particular interest in their industry. And so on.

> 'We believe that XYZ Limited can benefit from PR and that the initial programme should cover the essentials outlined above. We also believe that a PR consultancy's prime function is to keep up a flow of ideas and then implement those which prove acceptable. We are perfectly prepared to have some of our suggestions turned down. The best PR results are obtained by a constant dialogue between client and consultancy. Any worthwhile programme must not be fixed and rigid, it must be capable of continuous development.'

Paul Winner, who launched Paul Winner Marketing Communications, by comparison, began his proposals for a campaign to the financial and business community on behalf of an insurance company by stressing two points:

> 'It is important to create a wider understanding of the investment merits of a company's shares and to help bring their investment rating more into line with status and prospects. If this is not important immediately to facilitate capital raising in the near future it is important in the context of mergers and takeover bids.

> 'It is worthwhile to contribute to increased understanding by the general investing public about the industry's shares in general and help remove them from the "specialist only" category to which they have been consigned by many financial journalists, accountants and the vast majority of investment analysts.'

He went on to stress that 'a willingness to explain oneself and express a view is the very essence of good public relations, and should be encouraged'. Who better to explain this and justify insurance than the very people who work in it? An organisation with 65 main branches, 250 local offices and 10,000 staff had much to gain from handling enquiries from the press.

> 'Financial public relations breaks down into two main areas of activity:

> 1 That concerning investment status.
> 2 That concerning production, i.e. insurance requirements and how they are met by policies.

The financial press is interested editorially in both these main areas and is the most influential medium of communications here. Investment analysts and stockbrokers are a relatively tiny but crucially important audience for (1). The insurance trade press is interested in both (1) and (2) but primarily the latter. The daily press is frequently interested in (2) for general news and feature material but this will usually be handled by or under the direction of the city editor. Similarly the trade press in most industries and trades is concerned about aspects of insurance from time to time. Radio and television, national and local, are also interested in material and information usually concerning (2).'

Proposals submitted by another consultancy could run to 100 pages or more. This is not important. What is important is that the client can see whether the consultancy is geared to running a first-class financial public relations operation or not.

5.3.9 CHECK YOUR PROVISIONAL DECISION
Better safe than sorry. Check with the merchant bank, the financial journalists and other companies with PR consultancies of their own. A wrong appointment could be disastrous. It could sour a company's relationship with the news media for a long time. Do not be frightened of calling other companies handled by the consultancy to check whether the actual service they are offering is as good as they say.

5.3.10 TAKE THE PLUNGE
Go ahead. After all the consultation, checking and double checking, you should have an idea by now. The only real way to discover is to hire the consultancy and give them a chance.

5.4 Hiring a staff public relations man is much the same

'The supreme advantage of the staff PRO and his internal unit is that he is an accepted member of the organisation, sharing the confidence of colleagues and possessing loyalties which extend beyond time sheets and fee limitations', says Frank Jefkins (*Planned Public Relations*). "Career opportunities within the organisation depend on a degree of enthusiasm which will never quite touch the hired outside help, however proficient he may be. This is not meant to imply criticism of consultants, but for anything less than £10,000–£12,000 the consultant obviously cannot give undivided attention as the staff PRO can.'

The staff PR man, however, must be a journalist first and a company man second. He must judge everything with the eyes of an outsider. For unless he looks at everything as an outsider he won't be in a position to assess outside reaction to company plans and policies. This is obviously difficult. Its hard for a man planning a career with a company to slash his chairman's annual report to shreds. But it is necessary. The best company PR operations come when the man at the top appreciates the value of PR and goes out to promote himself and his company. Lord Robens, Sir Miles Thomas, Henry Ford, Lord Thomson and Charles Forte have all hired PR people to project themselves and their organisations. And it has had tremendous results because the top men have been sympathetic and eager for active PR policies.

But a company must learn to trust its financial public relations people. They must be allowed to visit all the offices and factories, meet everyone from directors to the ordinary man on the shop-floor and have complete freedom to discuss every aspect of the company's affairs. The more they understand the company and the staff, the better they will be able to promote the company. They will be able to discover more stories and angles as well as photographic subjects. Unless this happens they will not be able to operate effectively.

Oscar M. Beveridge tells the story of two PR consultants interviewing a company treasurer about the forthcoming release of the quarterly figures.

> 'The public relations men had been advised by the president, before he left on a business trip out of town, to see the treasurer for the figures. After half-an-hour of shadow-boxing, the treasurer said, "I know that you know the figures are ready and that I have them. I also know that I am supposed to give them to you. But after more than 20 years in this job, all of which have been spent in keeping such information confidential, I just can't bring myself to divulge them!". And he didn't.'

This is obviously absurd. And wildly uneconomic. If a company is going to hire financial public relations experts, they must give them their head. In many cases that means working not with middle-managers but with the directors themselves. 'We hate working with a particular strata of managers', says Cavendish. 'We want access to every single level. We want to work with managing directors as well. If PR is not going hand-in-hand with the top man, it won't be as effective as it could be with a better relationship. It won't be so happy.' Even if the financial public relations advisers work with the directors, there will be no sudden, overnight results. Changing attitudes and boosting reputations is a long, slow process. And, of course, in the end it all comes down on the basic strengths of the company itself. Says Clive Smith, Director and group public relations controller of Astral Public Relations:

> 'You don't think you can make purses out of sow's ears. Companies should have PRO's to make them attractive to investors to buy. But the PRO can't make it attractive when the company, the basic goods, are unattractive. PR should not manipulate at all. It's just a great ear trumpet. It's perhaps all right in industrial public relations to suppress some sounds and to amplify others—this is not for financial public relations. These are not the qualities that should be looked for, applied in any way in this delicate matter of company finance, company public relations.'

Part three

Financial Advertising and Public Relations in Action

H

Chapter 6

Going Public

In 1927 W. R. Morris, later Lord Nuffield, floated preference shares in Morris Motors at a nominal 5s instead of £1. The excitement was so great that a stockbroker collapsed on the floor on the house. Commented Sir Miles Thomas, who stayed with Morris for 25 years, rising to vice-chairman, 'That created something of a record for a new issue'.

Although not all new issues are as exciting as that, it can still be a hair-raising experience. One day a man is virtually an unknown businessman. The next day he and his company are thrust upon the public platform and expected to behave as if they had both been brought up under arc lights.

'To ensure the success of any company's Stock Market floatation, it is important that as wide a public as possible be reached and reached on a national scale', says Maurice Cocking.

Clive Smith, Astral Public Relations Managing Director, estimates that, from the public relations point of view, it takes at least two years to 'pre-position' a company before it is ready to go to market. 'A company should have a consistent profit record for four to five years', he says. 'During that time it should be seen in the business columns. It takes at least two years to really pre-position a company. This means getting the company mentioned in not just the financial columns but the general columns as well. If you do a good job on the first, it's easier to interest City editors at the time when you approach them about going public. The success of going public depends on firm public relations all along the line.'

A company should begin drawing up its plans for going public the first day it opens for business. If it does this, nothing will go wrong. Nothing will be left to the last minute. Nothing will be forgotten. A good reputation, regardless of how much it is deserved cannot—repeat, cannot—be built up overnight. It takes time. It takes money. And it takes effort. Leave it to the last minute. Launch a massive financial public relations operation. Spend a fortune. It will be no good. It might be thrown back in your face. It could even leave you open to charges of share-pushing. There is no alternative. Begin planning right from the start.

Rentokil, the international pest control and wood preservation company, for example, prepared for their market day by sending out more than 400 press releases in the 12 months before going public. This resulted in 1,900 cuttings, including 100 features and 400 photos, totalling no less than 12,000 column inches, not to mention 25 radio and television mentions. Acrow, by comparison, took every possible contract they could find in the City of London prior to going public—and swathed whole buildings in scaffolding with the name prominently displayed. Itoh, a leading Japanese company, launched a full series of advertisements in *The Economist* before their international launch.

Every company should also have an open-door policy. It should be frank with its employees. It should keep them informed of the demand and orders for their product or service. Some form of employee communications programme such as house magazines or newspapers should be in operation. There should be regular informative meetings between management and staff. The last place Disraeli's two nations should be allowed to gain a foothold is the shop—or office—floor.

Similarly with suppliers and customers—or clients. Representatives should be invited to the company to meet the management and the staff. Production schedules should be explained and any particular benefits outlined. If a customer places a big order with the company, an informal 'signing ceremony' could take place. Some companies even prepare special company publications especially for suppliers and customers to cement the relationship—and also, of course, to keep the orders rolling in.

'Creditable references to the company in the press, and on radio and TV; the readiness with which its name is dropped into everyday conversation and the confidence shown by the City in its financial stability, trading position and future growth, all these are factors which influence the attitudes of employees and shareholders towards a company. These two groups of people, whose interests are inseparably linked with the firm, look for continual reassurance that they are working for and supporting the right kind of company. It is, therefore, a sound investment to try and win for the company some public recognition of its work and achievements in a specific field and this is where PR can help even if it is not supported by advertising', says Paul I. Slee Smith, Publicity Manager of the Plastics Division of ICI for 20 years, *Industrial Public Relations* (Business Publications, London, 1967).

An active advertising and public relations operation is vital. Industrial and consumer advertising and public relations is necessary for any company. A company builds its industrial reputation by establishing itself in the industry. This means keeping the industrial press informed of their activities, their orders and their plans. A parallel financial advertising and public relations operation will establish the company in those important financial circles.

'A private company which fails to realise the importance of public relations until the eve of going public is in a poor position to do anything about it', says Derriman (*Company-Investor Relations*).

This means a company must exploit the financial public relations media.

6.1 The media

6.1.1 THE NATIONAL PRESS

The second largest manufacturer of knitting machinery in the UK, G. Stibbe of Leicester, was planning to launch its Ordinary shares on the Stock Exchange before the end of 1969. The valuation: more than £4 million. A fairly small old-established family business—three-quarters of its shares controlled by the Stibbe, Polito and Whitehead families—it was competing against Bentley Engineering, the leading knitting machine manufacturer, a subsidiary of Charles Clore's Sears Holdings and a highly efficient group six times its size. Yet it had some trump cards. Knitting was booming. It was one of the few glamour sectors in textiles. By going public, Stibbe would be giving investors a share in the spoils. It had a sizeable stake in world markets. Over 60 per cent of its machinery was exported. Profits were good. They were running 150 per cent higher over the past 10 years with a pre-tax return of nearly 9 per cent on sales. Management was young and dynamic. Orders had been pouring in so much so that business was actually being turned away.

All this made a tremendous impact in a special *Sunday Times* report complete with photograph of vice-chairman, Paul Stibbe.

> 'The company is no stranger to the Stock Exchange—most of its preference shares are already quoted. And it is likely to make more friends among investors in its plans to grow bigger with its customers. The issue, when it comes, will be one to watch for', said Graham Searjeant.

6.1.2 THE REGIONAL PRESS

London, do not forget, is a region complete with its regional press. The two evening newspapers both cover business and financial news.

> 'One of the biggest property development and estate agent groups in Kent, familiar to thousands of commuters, plans to go public. Mr Fred Couchman, Chairman and Managing Director of the Martin Couchman group, tells me today that he plans to market his organisation on the Stock Exchange "within two years". As the first step in the go-public scheme, a new company called Martin Couchman Group has been registered with a capital of £1 million. The company has been named after 48-year-old Mr Couchman's son, as he thinks Martin sounds better than Fred. This is the vehicle that will bring the organisation to market. It will act as a holding company for the two main operating subsidiaries, Martin Couchman (Properties) and Martin Couchman (Development).'

This was immensely valuable publicity for the company. Property specialists in the City as well as property investors will be watching the group more and more as it comes near to market day. The story could have stopped there. But Couchman was able to make some bull points as well.

> 'The estate agent side operates nine branches throughout Kent. Last year, this side of the business notched up £120,000 in commissions giving it a profit of £32,000. But it is the property development interests that provide the major portion of profits. Mr Couchman tells me that there are plenty of sites ready for development. His group has just bought 3½ acres of the Vickers Sports Ground at Crayford for housing developments. A similar site has been acquired at Sidcup, too. Profits for the whole group in the financial year to 30 June, Mr Couchman puts at "just over £100,000". During 1969 profits of the order of £170,000 are the hoped-for target. And the fact that Mr Couchman doesn't plan to bring his group to the market for a couple of years should ensure that the situation as far as finance, mortgages and the other problems facing the industry generally should be somewhat sorted out.'

6.1.3 THE WEEKLY PRESS
Here there is an enormous opportunity for a company to establish itself in its community and to begin building its reputation from the grass-roots. Weekly papers are not so conscious of the need for hard news as the national and regional press. They prefer stories about local people and local businesses. What could be better?

6.1.4 BUSINESS AND FINANCIAL PRESS
This is the heart of the operation. If a company is featured in the business and financial press it is launching its financial public relations attack head on. It is a valuable opportunity and should be exploited to the full.

Mothercare, that fast-growing new retail chain—sailes up from £675,000 to £8·5 million in six years—featured in a four-page article in *Management Today* in June 1969. The creation of a new retail chain from scratch was 'a rare event, even more so when it is simultaneously creating a new retail speciality'. The Mothercare history, itself, was also 'a clear marketing success', wrote Doina Thomas. She explained how managing director, Selim Zilkha, a 42-year-old banker, had adopted his ideas from the French firm Prenatal in 1961, how the company had boomed and how they were planning to go international, not only before any of the giants but before its domestic plans were even at the half-way stage in their development.

'After losses in 1963 and 1964, the company made some increasingly satisfactory profits. Although the going was harder last year, with the ratio of after-tax profit to turnover as low as 3½ per cent, the chain has been showing phenomenal returns on capital—as high as 27 per cent net in the 1968 financial year. Stores are by nature high-return operations, but Mothercare's apparent profitability has another explanation. The capital-employed figure is brought down sharply by a very large overdraft (£600,000 at end-1968). With this loan element included, Mothercare's return becomes much less spectacular, and the true nature of its build-up is more clearly revealed', said Miss Thomas.

Although Zilkha has said he is 'in no hurry' to go public (*The Times*, June 1969), features like this can do no harm.

6.1.5 TRADE MAGAZINES

Every industry has its trade press. Accountants and secretaries, for example, have 23. There are 40 aeronautical journals; 20 automation; 83 building; and 59 electronic publications. Engineers with over 150, probably have more than any other industry. They are a valuable source of communication within the industry. They are also the back-door to the national press. Most are hard-pressed for staff—and news. As a result any company cultivating its relevant trade press, keeping it informed of its activities and its plans can easily make a name for itself and establish a following in the industry.

KMPH, the radical, creative, rip-roaring advertising agency which went public with a bang in July 1969 cultivated the advertising press right from the beginning. When Brian Palmer quit the board of Young and Rubicam in May 1964, it was a trade paper story. So was David Kingsley's decision to leave Benton and Bowles to join him the following week. And, again, when John Cuff, the Benton and Bowles chairman who left the previous year, emerged from the shadows to become chairman. When the agency celebrated their third birthday, it was another opportunity for publicity. There in the advertising trade papers were photographs of the directors holding a giant birthday cake shaped like the figure 3—and a photograph of them all as three-year-old children.

'Three years old last week, the KMP Partnership whose directors, David Kingsley, Michael Manton, Brian Palmer, Len Heath and John Cuff are shown at the appropriate age. The picture is from a giant montage dreamed up by the KMP creative group as a birthday surprise. Wives and mothers were conscripted to search family albums for baby snaps. A cake and layouts were smuggled in and out of Thorn House, agency headquarters. Photographers, studios, everyone was sworn to secrecy. The first the directors knew was when they arrived for work last Friday morning to find cake and montage dominating their communal office. Said Kingsley, "It's moments like this that make you very glad you started an advertising agency".'
(*Advertisers Weekly*, 9 June 1967)

6.1.6 CONSUMER MAGAZINES

This is more different—because not every company automatically falls within the scope of a group of consumer magazines. Companies which are consumer-orientated, however, have every opportunity. It should be seized for the consumer is not just a customer or client. He is also a potential investor.

6.1.7 NEWS AGENCIES
News agencies are just as interested in news as newspapers and magazines. They are worth cultivating. For a story picked up and carried by a news agency can bring tremendous publicity in its wake.

6.1.8 SYNDICATION SERVICES
Similarly with syndication stories. A good syndication story can create international publicity for a company about to go public. Good syndication stories, however, are few and far between. But it is worth the effort.

6.1.9 INTERNATIONAL NEWS MEDIA
Again, it depends on the company involved and the story. But London-based foreign correspondents can produce enormous international publicity for the right company with the right story. 'Finding it harder to make contacts, they are proportionately more grateful for help', says Leo Cavendish.

6.1.10 RADIO AND TELEVISION
Do not forget the 73 broadcasting stations in the UK and the 11,000 news items they prepare every day. There are plenty of opportunities for slipping in a mention about a particular company.

6.1.11 BROKERS AND INVESTMENT TRUSTS
The prudent company will be talking to brokers and investment trusts a long time before it goes public. The nearer 'market day' comes, however, the more it should increase the pace. Special visits should be laid on to the company's headquarters and centres. Directors should be on hand to answer their questions and forecast their future development.

6.1.12 STATISTICAL SERVICES
A number of statistical services have special sections devoted to unquoted companies. Obviously it is in a company's interests, especially one coming to market, to ensure that the information being distributed is both as accurate and as comprehensive as possible. They should also make certain that the switch for unquoted to quoted status is immediately reflected in the distribution service.

6.1.13 MISCELLANEOUS
The national press, radio and television, even syndication services are conventional financial public relations media. Some companies, however, aided and abetted by their public relations advisers, break new ground, develop new financial media of their own and create enormous publicity in the process. Take, for example, the Silexine Bus, which went into service in London on

14 August 1969. On the face of it, a superb promotional stunt by London-based Silexine Paints, one of the fastest growing marketing-oriented paint companies in the UK. Silexine went to five London art colleges and asked them for designs for repainting a London bus as a 'Welcome' to the capital's five million visitors every year.

The winning entry by David Tuhill, which covers the entire bus, captures guardsmen marching past traditional views of London. When the bus went into operation for the first time, after being entirely re-painted in a three-week session at London Transport's overhaul works at Aldernham, it gained enormous publicity. Everybody was talking about the Silexine Bus. Which is the clue to the whole operation. For Silexine is a private company. Hence the decision to paint a bus for the number 11, Shepherds Bush to Liverpool Street route, which happens to run through, not only Fleet Street, but the City as well, and past even the merchant bank which acts for the company.

'This was deliberate policy', says Leo Cavendish, head of Financial Press Information Services, which master-minded the whole promotion. 'It ties in well with the company's long-term objectives. It creates consumer interest and City interest as well.'

Covering anything between 64 (off-peak) and 195·5 (full-peak) miles daily, the multi-coloured bus must be seen by thousands of investors and stock-brokers every day. There will be little trouble, therefore, making people aware of the name Silexine, if—or when—it comes to market.

6.2 Below ground

That's the surface operation. Below ground equally important work should also be in hand. Business newspapers, magazines and news agencies have been given background information on the company, its history, its products or services as well as on its staff and financial record. Many companies go further still and provide newspaper libraries with detailed biographies and up-to-date photographs of directors and managers. This will prove a boom to the company on market day.

S. Pearson went a stage further. They had a complete dress rehearsal for their market day, the largest floatation of any company in London Stock Exchange history, a year before they went public. A company prospectus was prepared drawing together for the first time details of the 150-odd subsidiary companies in the Pearson empire spread in countries from the Mediterranean to North America. Directors were referred to by initials. Companies were given pseudonyms. But the figures were real.

6.3 Market comes closer

The company decides to go public—definitely. They approach an issuing house or broker. Accountants and solicitors begin to pour over company's affairs to ensure they meet the demands of the Stock Exchange, the issuing house itself, and, of course, the mass of company laws. They then decide how the launch will take place.

1 BY PROSPECTUS. This is virtually an open invitation to the public to buy up its shares, the method usually adopted by companies coming to the market for the first time or companies launching a brand new security.

2 BY PLACING. Instead of throwing open the invitation to the public, it is thrown open to only the issuing house or broker who can then buy the shares or securities to re-sell later to their own clients. These are general pension funds, insurance companies and institutional investors. The Stock Exchange, however, insists that at least 25 per cent of the placing in the case of equities and at least 20 per cent in the case of other securities are offered to other brokers' clients in the market as well.

3 BY OFFER FOR SALE. This is similar. But in this case the issuing house or bank buys the whole block of securities either to re-sell in whole or in part to the public at a later date.

4 BY OFFER FOR TENDER. Instead of buying the shares at a definite price, here the public have to virtually bid for them. Its almost a cross between Russian roulette and a public auction. The securities are not offered at a definite price. So the public have to name the price they are prepared to buy them at. The issuing house then takes the average of all the prices offered. Those who were prepared to buy at that price or above can do so—at the average price. Those who bid too low cannot.

5 BY INTRODUCTION. No capital is raised. The securities are merely brought on to the market either because they are already quoted on another Stock Exchange or because they are already so widely held that there are probably a number of potential purchasers around.

The company decides. As a condition of quotation, incidentally, it then has to sign a 'General Undertaking', a kind of public relations or information rule book backed by the Stock Exchange, which insists that the company (among other things):

1 Informs the Stock Exchange of board meetings when declarations or recommendations of dividends will be considered.
2 Releases decisions on dividends or bonuses to the Stock Exchange immediately following the meetings. Similarly with preliminary profit figures for both the year and half-year; proposed issues of new capital or any changes in capital structure as well as 'any other information necessary to enable the shareholders to appraise the position of the company and to avoid the establishment of a false market in the securities'.

3 Informs The Stock Exchange at once of takeovers, realisations of assets, board changes, plans to alter the nature of the company's business.
4 Publishes half-yearly reports as well as yearly reports and accounts together with details of their operations, subsidiaries and trading pattern. Substantial holdings must also be declared.
5 Obtains Stock Exchange approval for shareholder circulars and any documents issued by holders of securities as well as notices of meetings apart from the routine annual session.
6 Releases to the press the basis of any allotment of securities.

The Investors and Shareholders Association suggested the following might have been the Prospectus for Management Agency and Music, when 1,750,000 Ordinary Shares at 13s 3d were offered to the public during 1969 (to the tune of Englebert Humperdinck's 'Please release me').

> Please believe me, I'm quite skint,
> By the time the tax man takes his stint,
> So now I'll share it all with you
> Helped by Tom, and maybe Mary too!
> Tom's green green grass was getting brown,
> But Bulls and Bears won't let him down.
> Mary thinks her days will never end
> If Stags are waiting round the bend. . . .

The prospectus, of course, is the key link in the whole going-public operation. Most companies see it as a straightforward legal document hedged around by the requirements of the Companies Act, 1948, Stock Exchange regulations and the Licensed Dealers (Conduct of Business) Rules 1960.

'For the professionals, this is part of their crucifixion', says Leo Cavendish. 'From the public's point of view they are a bit tedious, a bit of a bore.' He suggests tidying the document up a little, making it more understandable and more readable for the general public. Other financial advisers disagree. 'There is no real advantage in jazzing it up', says Hartley-Smith, Managing Director of Dorlands (City). 'It's only a legal document which must be published.'

Derriman takes the middle course. 'The prospectus should contain whatever is necessary to establish the company among the investing public in the best light consistent with the facts', he says (CIR). But he goes on to make three PR points.

First, no relevant information should be omitted although it is not necessarily laid down by the Stock Exchange.

Second, the document should be drafted as concisely, clearly and attractively as possible.

Third, it should be typographically as attractive as possible.

The fear, of course, at the backs of people's minds is that a 'jazzy' prospectus would leave them open to share-pushing. Which seems impossible when you consider the amount of information that must be featured in a prospectus and the number of regulations governing that publication.

1 PRELIMINARIES. The name of the company together with a description of its activities if it is not already a household word. Rentokil, for example, referred to themselves as 'Specialists in Timber Preservation, Pest Control, Damp Proofing and Thermal Insulation'. Then details of the offer and how the applications will be handled. Finally, the names of directors as well as the company's various bankers, brokers, solicitors, auditors, accountants, registrars and transfer office and secretary and registered office.

2 HISTORY AND BUSINESS. This is the meat of the prospectus. It must refer to the launch of the company, the ideas behind it, how it has grown and developed. If a company can list its clients, it should do so. It should also detail its home and overseas business.

3 MANAGEMENT AND STAFF. The directors must be listed together with their career biographies. Other senior staff should be included. The total number of staff must also be listed followed by a comment on the state of employee-management relations—which always seem to be 'excellent'.

4 PREMISES. The full address of the different properties held by the company must be given together with a description, approximate floor area and details of tenure. Some companies give full information about premises in the UK but only list the centres overseas. Some go into even more detail and spell out the service charges they incur as well.

5 WORKING CAPITAL. This cannot help but be a general comment such as: 'Having regard to the proceeds of such issue and to the bank facilities available, the Directors are of the opinion that the company has adequate working capital for its present requirements'. But that is sufficient.

6 PROFITS, PROSPECTS AND DIVIDENDS. This is generally read in conjunction with the Accountants Report. If any figures show a lag following a steep rise in profits, for example, its best to explain the position in full. Similarly if losses have been substantially reduced.

7 ACCOUNTANTS REPORT. Profits, assets, dividends—it's all here. Some prospectuses just give a mass of figures. Others pick out the more important figures and devote separate notes to them. Either way, there is little room for manoeuvre—except on the typographical front.

8 STATUTORY AND GENERAL INFORMATION. This covers Articles of Association; Capital Changes in the company; subsidiaries; material contracts;

director's interests; and any other information the company feels relevant. KMPH Limited as befits a top advertising agency, struck the happy medium in their prospectus, published 25 July 1969. They gave all the necessary details, admittedly in a clear, attractive fashion, and there in a right-hand column were some current and recent examples of the best of KMP advertising. Some go further. One prospectus, offering 5,600,000 Common shares, was handsomely printed in blue. 'The sexiest new issue for many a long year', commented *Daily Mail* city editor, Patrick Sergeant (10 September 1969).

Before the prospectus is published, proofs must be submitted to the Stock Exchange for approval. Once they have given the go-ahead it must appear in at least two leading London daily newspapers as well as being sent to Exchange Telegraph and Moodies. In the case of provincial quotations, local newspapers are accepted as substitutes. Advance proofs should also be sent to the financial public relations media.

S. Pearson and Son called a press conference to discuss their prospectus. Other companies have been more ambitious. Freeman's, the £31 million Clapham-based mail-order house had a special press visit to their head-quarters when they were going public in 1964. It worked wonders. They gained enormous coverage, helped, of course, by the fact their Lavender Hill location made them a natural 'Lavender Hill mob'.

Rentokil went even further. They hired a special train to carry news agency reporters, financial journalists as well as jobbers and stockbrokers from London Bridge to their Lingfield headquarters on 5 March 1969—two days before they went public. Each was given a copy of the prospectus together with a press kit, giving full information about the group, its markets and its potential together with biographical notes on all the directors. The group marketing director outlined the company to them on arrival before they toured the whole centre in five parties, each led by a director. The follow-ing day details of the offer and information about the Group went out to 250 newspapers and trade journals. As a result every national newspaper and major provincial paper carried the story and comment on the issue:

Rats + cockroaches + woodworm = dry-rot = £20 million
(*The Sunday Times*).

A Pied Piper Worth A Following
(*Glasgow Herald*).

A meeting was then held for the financial institutions in the City to give them an opportunity to question the Board on the company's policy, prospects and performance. A special shareholders booklet was also prepared and subsequently sent to all new shareholders.

These are not mere press junkets. They are immensely valuable for the company.

'I, personally, like to have the opportunity of meeting the directors, or at least the active members of the board, when a new company comes to market', says P. J. Naish, former secretary of the Association of Unit Trust Managers (*Law Guardian*, February, 1966) 'Apart from giving life to the record of the company, a face-to-face meeting with the men who are responsible for it is a great help in the judgement of the character of the issue as well as the character of the directors.'

6.4 The company goes public

As soon as everything has been agreed, the news can be released. Until then its best to keep everything under wraps. If a problem crops up, its better to be able to withdraw or delay without attracting a mass of publicity. It also means that when the news is released for the first time, the company stands to make a bigger impact than if they had been talking about the move openly for months. This, however, depends on the size and importance of the company.

Investors Overseas Services were big news in August 1969 weeks before they came to market. In fact they were so hot that people in Europe's international money market, were actually dealing in the shares before they had even been issued; before IOS had even fixed a price and in spite of a warning from the company that anyone dealing in the 'when issued' market would not get a look in at the real underwriting.

The release, therefore, should stress the plan to go to the market, the type of issue, the date the prospectus will be published, the date of the issue itself as well as full details on the company, its business, the directors and so on. That should also include the name of the issuing house and the name of the brokers. Handled correctly, with the right timing and the right background information, this can result in wide publicity.

'Dalton Barton Securities has chosen the perfect moment to go public. With the equity market still showing withdrawal symptoms, and new issues floundering like sea birds in polluted water, this may appear to be a rash statement, but it is easily justified. The company is a merchant bank which was formed in 1963 by Mr Jack Dellal, a former textile merchant. Also on the board is Mr Stanley van Gelder, a chartered accountant associated with another highly rated share, Bolton Textile Mill. The Offer for Sale is by Joseph Sebag, and application lists for the 700,000 shares open and close on Thursday, July 10th. In the five years since it started, Dalton has virtually doubled its profits annually. In 1963 the pre-tax figure was £17,000; for the year ending December 1968, it was £254,000; and for the current year, which is now half over, the board are forecasting pre-tax profits of "not less than £600,000".'
(Stewart Fleming, *The Guardian*, 7 July 1969)

John Davis, *The Observer*'s City Editor, was even more enthusiastic:

> 'This Thursday's public offer for sale of 700,000 ordinary shares at 42s
> each in the West End bank Dalton Barton Securities looks like being
> an even bigger sell-out than I predicted when this marketing was forecast
> here three weeks ago. All the signs are that the "stags" who have not
> had too good a time of it lately, will be weighing in with lumpy applica-
> tions for the prospects of a premium look good. Only a collapse in the
> market between now and the start of dealings on July 15th would stand
> in the way of this, and that seems like a 50–1 chance winning the Derby.'
> (*The Observer*, 6 July)

That's just the nationals. Do not forget the other media. KMPH, for
example, made a big splash in the advertising trade press. On 22 July 1969
came the first break. 'Bankers Glyn Mills are bringing to the market just over
a third of the equity in the KMPH advertising agency via an offer for sale',
said the *Financial Times*. 'The shares in Ordinary 2s form will probably be
priced at around 14s, putting the company on a capitalisation of approaching
£700,000. Full details will be published on Friday, July 25th.' And on Friday
not only was the prospectus published but full background stories appeared
in the trade press, *Advertisers Weekly* and *Campaign*.

> 'London's new radical agency is now five-years old and this week's look
> to the City and stock market for a public quotation means the radicals
> have turned a complete circle into establishment. The four lots of £2,500
> that each of the founders mortgaged themselves to the hilt to put in the
> bank in 1964 is now worth £750,000. KMP went "radical" at the right
> time. But after five-years of squeezing, freezing and taxation burdens
> rebels aren't welcome any more. Sound financial advice and management
> expertise are. So KMP have timed it right again.'
> (*Advertisers Weekly*, 25 July 1969)

Campaign gave the story a different angle. Equally flattering. Equally effective.

> 'KMP goes public next week with its sights firmly set on expansion.
> Its main priority is to buy an agency of roughly the same size, with a
> billing of about £4 million. Director, David Kingsley said, "We are only
> interested in majority interests. We have been looking at certain com-
> panies for some time and know exactly the sort of people we want to
> approach".'
> (*Campaign*, 25 July 1969)

A giant like S. Pearson and Son could expect enormous attention. Not
only from the national press in the UK but from the international business
press as well. If any company could scoop the financial public relations
media, it was S. Pearson. The news had been out for four months. Background
stories had appeared in virtually every national newspaper. Even *Punch*

profiled Lord Cowdray. Stories were also appearing in the press announcing that the prospectus was being issued. 'Further details of the issue will be published today', ran a front-page story on 7 August in the *Financial Times*, for example. 'The prospectus will be advertised on Monday and application lists open and close next Thursday. Brokers to the company are Cazenoves.'

When the prospectus was issued on 7 August, the press went wild with enthusiasm. Partly because everyone enjoys examining the financial secrets of an empire that had been under wraps for years. Partly because background information, including a fact-packed four-page briefing, was specially prepared for the press. And partly because the issue was obviously going to be such a fantastic success.

'Unless my gloomy friends are right, this issue should go like a bomb', said Robert Head in the *Daily Mirror*. The *Financial Times*, 51·6 per cent owned by S. Pearson Publishers, devoted a front-page story to the issue. Further details were published on an inside page across four columns complete with photograph of the press conference to mark the issue. Another national followed suit. 'Cowdray's empire is worth £72 million', said Charles Lloyd in the *Sun*. 'It's a £110 million family', said the *Evening Standard*.

LAZARD BROTHERS & CO., LIMITED
Strictly embargoed until 3.30 pm Thursday, 7 August 1969

6 August 1969

NOTES FOR CITY EDITORS

1 As you will see from the Prospectus, S.P. & S. is a broadly based group with a wide spread of interests in the UK and North America which have been built up from the base of the assets originally acquired and developed by the first Lord Cowdray.

2 The company's policy over the years has been to give as much consideration to capital growth and to long term opportunities as to immediate increase of income. It has concentrated on those areas in which it has had experience and where the application of specialised skills and the concentration of resources has enabled it to take advantage of opportunities for future growth. This policy is reflected in the pattern of the Group's development. Over the ten years 1959 to 1968, the profit record shows that pre-tax profits attributable to the company's shareholders (i.e. after deducting minority interests) have risen from £3 million to £7 million. While it is not possible to establish a truly comparable valuation of the Group in earlier years, the asset values of the Group (again after deducting minority interests) have increased from about £34 million in 1959 to £106 million as valued at June 30th last. (£116 million less £10 million of new money).

3 Main interests. The main areas in which the Group's resources are concentrated provide a balance between merchant banking, portfolio

investments, oil and industrial and commercial interests which is probably unique among UK companies. More than one-third in value of the Group's interests are overseas, most of these being in the USA and Canada.

(The notes went on to give details of each of the main areas. They then tackled the question of Valuation; the decision to go public and the timing.)

After the Offer for Sale approximately 20 per cent of the equity capital will be in hands other than those of the Pearson family or the family Trusts.

The change from a private to a public company will, of course, result in some change of techniques, but it is intended, as far as possible, to retain the advantages of a family business—quick decisions, the minimum of overheads and supervisory staff, and continuation of authority, whilst at the same time seeking advantage from having quoted shares and a public interest in the group.

L. B. & Co. Ltd.,
6.8.1969.

The regional press were more staid. 'Pearson announce offer terms', said the *Glasgow Herald*. 'S. Pearson has market value of £72 million', said the *Western Morning News*. *The Guardian Journal* of Nottingham were a little more excited. 'Shares offer gives Cowdray empire a £72 million price tag', said their heading. The weekly press, the business and financial press—'S. Pearson arrives', said the *Investors Chronicle*—the trade press, the international press and all the financial public relations media threw their hats in the air and gave the prospectus enormous coverage.

'Patrick Hutber, City Editor of the *Sunday Telegraph*, hit the nail on the head (as usual) when he called the offer of shares in S. Pearson and Son "the most interesting issue since the war". It is all this for a number of reasons. It brings to the Stock Market one of the few remaining family companies of any size left in the country or, in fact, in the world. . . . It is a share which big investors will regard as a must for their portfolios. . . . It is a share which will prove a delight to clever analysts and a headache to the sliderule bodgers, of which the City has more than its share. If you like to read, Pearson . . . publishes the best financial paper of the lot, the *Financial Times*. Also in publishing it owns Westminster Press and Longmans. If you like to drink, Pearson controls the Château Latour vineyard in the Medoc. Like animals? Well Standard Industrial Group, controlled by Pearson, owns Chessington Zoo. For the financial wizards among the Pearsons control Lazards, one of the City's best merchant banks. Among the firm's other interests are a big investment

I

trust, oil, property, glass, pottery, and a stake in various activities in Greece. Put them all together and we get the daddy of all conglomerates.'
(*Advertisers Weekly*, 15 August 1969)

At last. The company is now a public company. When Mario and Franco Restaurants went public they placed a special note on all the tables in their restaurants reminding customers they were now a public company. They also suggested they might like to try the other four restaurants in the group. Staff were also reminded. Going public was important for the company and the staff, said the note.

The big story, of course, is the number of times a company is oversubscribed.

'Advertising agents KMPH has been well received by the market. Its offer for sale of 358,000 Ordinary 2s shares through Glyn Mills and Company at 14s each was nearly eight times oversubscribed. Applicants for up to 800 shares will go to a ballot for 100 shares and all other applicants will receive allotments of about 12 per cent of shares applied for. The chances of receiving an allotment in the ballot are proportional to the number of shares applied for.'
(*Daily Telegraph*, 31 July 1969)

Admittedly, this could mean the initial price should have been higher to enable the company to raise an even larger sum. But given the fact an offer is oversubscribed, there is no harm in making the fact known. Then there is the question of allotments. S. Pearson received over 21,000 applications for some 49·2 million shares. This meant scaling down the requests. Again a legitimate news story. But the company must be careful how they scale the requests down. It is tempting to forget the small man and plump for the big investors—but dangerous. A company must maintain its goodwill with the investing public. This means a fair allotment.

Pearsons, for example, found that they received applications from employees for 700,000 shares when they had only reserved 500,000 for them. As a result they decided to honour the requests for shares up to and including 1,000 shares in full. Requests for more, were scaled down to 1,000. Ballots were then held for applications for up to and including 500 shares. Successful applicants in the ballots as well as applicants wanting more than 500 received their shares as follows:

Application	Allotment
100–200	100
300–500	200
600–2,000	30 per cent with a minimum of 200
2,100–40,000	20 per cent with a minimum of 600
41,000 and over	15 per cent with a minimum of 8,000 shares

Any ballot means some win, some lose. Yet everyone was confident enough to back the company with their own money. The letters announcing the results of the ballot should, therefore, bear this in mind.

> 'Instead of: On the instructions of the directors . . . we have to inform you that it has not been possible . . . etc., why not something like: We are sorry to tell you that it has not been possible . . . Nevertheless the directors have asked us to thank you for your interest . . . ?' says Derriman (*Company Investor Relations*).

Of course, some companies go public without being quoted. The opportunities for publicity, therefore, are less. But they are still there. James Burrough of Beefeater gin fame, for example, attracted press attention when they announced their plan to go public—but unquoted.

> 'As a private company we are limited to 50 shareholders and we already have 46', chairman, Alan Burrough, told *The Times* (30 July 1969). 'Being a family company, shares become dispersed wider and wider as members pass theirs on to their children, and it would be unfair to restrict this'.

The Times added:

> 'Family control is all important to the Burroughs and Tedburys, descendents of the first chairman who hold the shares. According to Alan Burrough the company will wait as long as possible before putting shares on the market, and would never consider accepting any of the bids it "frequently" receives. But there is a gap in the defences. Alan Burrough, one of the third generation of the family in the company, is in his early 50's. The oldest male member of the fourth generation is only 15.'

6.5 Share certificates

It is amazing that a company can be so reputation conscious that it looks at every aspect of its organisation and activity, impressing the public generally with its image and reputation, yet it still overlooks its share certificates. The Fordham Investment Group, a young, dynamic, thrusting company run by 24-year-old David Rowlands has a dull, flat-footed share certificate. It could be a certificate from any one of a 1,000 companies. Nothing of the fire and reputation of the company comes across. B. & R. Leyland by comparison, is a gem of financial art nouveau. Its flowing script, elegant half-moon headings and elegant decorative logo comes from another world. It gives the impression the company is in the church furnishing business, not industry.

At the very least, therefore, companies should ensure that the certificate conforms to their house style. The wording is laid down by the Stock Exchange. That does not mean the company logo or symbol also be included.

Life as a public company has only begun. The promotion doesn't end there. It is only beginning. Says Beveridge:

'After the concern underwent its public sale, the active head of the business, the president, steadfastly refused to make speeches or appear before groups of analysts or the press. Radio and television appearances were mentioned only once by his public relations counsel. The reaction was so violently negative that the subject was never brought up again. The president even postponed the annual meeting twice for no apparent reason, since his report was ready and the accountants had finished up their work in good time. At the meeting he appeared haggard and stumbled badly in reading his speech. At one point he dropped a sheet of paper on the floor and had difficulty finding his place when he picked it up. Finally, the Secretary of the company spoke up and asked for a recess which the president gratefully granted. When he had once more got his papers in order and had somewhat regained his composure, the meeting proceeded to adjournment. One can only imagine the limited degree of competence with which stockholders were willing to credit him after this debacle.'

6.6 Statutory meeting

The company is now a public company. Within the next two to three months it must call its first general meeting. This is the Statutory meeting when the directors names are taken, the number of shares allotted and other details are completed. Two weeks before, however, all the details must be sent to shareholders in a special Statutory Report. Most of the information covers the well-trodden ground of the prospectus. The likelihood of attracting the attention of the business news media yet again is, therefore, pretty minimal.

6.7 Share listing

A public company must keep in touch with its public. That means, above all, its shares must be listed. For share listing is both vital and effective. It can mean, for example, greater distribution and easier marketability of stock. 'A corporation generally acquires new stature when its shares are listed', says Beveridge, 'because the action serves as evidence that the company has met the size and financial soundness requirements imposed by the nation's stock exchanges'. Leo Cavendish agrees. 'Listings are important', he says. 'It is essential. It is certainly a company's duty to tell its shareholders what the price is.'

Share listing in America means far more than it does in the UK. The New York Stock Exchange, for example, maintains that one of the 'most important and fundamental purposes and intents' of listing 'is to assure that adequate and timely publicity is given to matters concerning listed companies of significance to the investing public'. Research has also shown that listed corporations can complete their common stock financing at nearly half the cost for similar unlisted companies. The cost of selling stock is lower. Rights issues are more successful. Convertibility is greater. And the value in relation to assets and earnings is better.

In the United Kingdom, share listing is hardly recognised as such. Companies generally list their shares in the *Financial Times*, perhaps, in another newspaper as well. They rarely list their shares in the regional press and hardly ever in the trade press. Here, of course, the trade press is partly to blame. For most of them feel they are giving a comprehensive news coverage of an industry without referring to the state of the companies in the market at all. There are a few exceptions. Some of the newsagent papers feature publishers while *Advertisers Weekly* runs a City news column on advertising and publishing. Even Derriman fails to mention the real advantages to be gained by share listing in his book, *Company-Investor Relations*.

6.8 Reasons

Yet there are ten reasons why a public company should adopt a realistic share listing programme.

6.8.1 BECAUSE OF INVESTORS
At the lowest level, people have invested their money in the company. They have a right to know how that company is doing. That means following the share price movement day by day. The democratisation of shareholding makes this even more important. With more shareholders from more sectors of society investing on the stock market, it is in a company's interests to give them up to date information on the company.

6.8.2 BECAUSE OF POTENTIAL INVESTORS
Share listings do not just provide a service to existing shareholders. They also attract the attention of potential shareholders as well. If the shares are listed, outsiders will be able to follow the company's fortunes from day to day.

6.8.3 BECAUSE OF THE PRESS
The press have tremendous influence in financial affairs. This has been shown in a number of surveys. Do not forget, for example, the British Market Research Bureau investigation into the factors which influenced institutional investors, stockholders and private shareholders during the GEC–AEI battle. Press comment rated 69 points compared with 97 for company circulars and 95 for stockbrokers. Not forgetting that the stockbrokers themselves admitted being influenced by the press as well. If a share is quoted in the press, it will be studied by the journalists. They will watch out for any steep rise or fall. Then they will find the reason why. This can be a tremendous advantage to a company.

'As Fordham Investment Group slipped another 2s 9d to 14s yesterday, rumours started going the rounds. Fordham must be in trouble was the

opinion around some quarters of the City, perhaps from going too far, too fast. This is not the case and Fordham is still going great guns. The reason for this steep decline in the share price, which has brought it down from 18s over the past week, is, I hear, a large and badly handled selling order. This is thought to be the result of a forced liquidation of a loan account. . . . Now the share price looks set for some recovery and the feeling in some sectors of the market is that had the dealing been better handled, the price need never have tumbled so steeply. So if you are in the shares, sit tight.'
(*Guardian*, 17 July 1969)

Similarly journalists examine the shares of a whole industry. If they are rising steadily, it can mean a story which will draw readers attention to the trend. Again it benefits the companies concerned.

6.8.4 BECAUSE IT BOOSTS THE MARKETABILITY OF THE SHARES
By listing its shares, a company ensures that it gains a following in the market. This is helped all the more if the share listing is accompanied by other facts and figures which show the company in comparison with others in the same industry.

6.8.5 BECAUSE IT HELPS GAIN THE ATTENTION OF THE INSTITUTIONAL INVESTOR
There are two principle reasons for share listing. First, to ensure existing shareholders can follow the progress of the company. Second, to try and attract new shareholders, individual and institutional, to change the shareholder profile of the organisation. This share listing can achieve. There are many institutional investors in Europe, for example, who refuse to invest in a company unless its shares are listed in a leading share information service.

6.8.6 BECAUSE IT CATEGORISES A COMPANY
Take an entertainment company. Should it be listed under straightforward Industrials or under Hotels and Catering? The decision could be important. Because if the entertainment business, generally, was going through a rough patch while Industrials were on the up and up, that company would show up very badly in the Industrials section. If, however, it was under Hotels and Catering all along, the difference and, therefore, the effect on its shares, would not be so striking. Correct share listing ensures, therefore, that if a company is going to be compared with others, it is at least compared with those companies the company itself feels it is in competition with—not complete strangers.

6.8.7 BECAUSE IT OFFERS GREATER MANOEUVRABILITY
If a company is listed, it means that its price is given day-by-day. This, in turn, means that investors and especially the institutions, can move in and out of a share much quicker and with greater freedom of manoeuvre than otherwise.

6.8.8 BECAUSE ITS THE BEST INSTANT CREDIT RATING A COMPANY CAN GET
It might sound strange but there are companies which check out a potential supplier by studying their share listing before, say, finally signing contracts for a major order. Everyone wants to be assured the company you are dealing with is not going broke. A share listing can give that instant credit rating.

6.8.9 BECAUSE IT ENSURES A COMPANY IS A RECOGNISED PART OF THEIR INDUSTRY
Any part of a share listing service is a ready-made profile of a particular industry. As such it is useful to everyone ranging from a market research company studying the industry to an outside company drawing up a list of companies to invite for tender. One building contractor, for example, recently went public just to join the share listing for his industry in order to get on to the tender lists. And it worked. He landed some big contracts as well.

6.8.10 FINALLY, BECAUSE A SHARE LISTING PROVIDES THE COMPANY ITSELF
        WITH A GREAT DEAL OF INFORMATION IT COULD NOT GET OTHERWISE
Without a share listing, how many companies would know the closing price of their stock without a constant stream of telephone calls to their jobber? Not to mention the cover and the P/E ratio as well. Forget the other nine reasons, a share listing is worth it for that alone.

> 'The price of natural rubber has been steadily rising and is now at a nine-year peak—to the dismay of many industrial users. Strong buying from Russia and China, in particular, is behind the almost monotonous increase in rubber prices this year, while record imports by the US are playing their part in forcing up the demand for synthetic. Against this background, it is not surprising that rubber shares now command third place in the *Financial Times* leaders and laggards table for this year. Share prices in this sector are looking far healthier than many others. Much of the future is therefore being discounted. But estimates suggest that there is no sign of any falling off in demand which indicates that investors may still have something to go for in buying rubber shares.'
> (Charles Lloyd, *Sun*, 4 August 1969)

6.9 Types of share listing

There is share listing and share listing. The *Financial Times*, for example, in addition to carrying the daily Stock Exchange dealings from the official list details 2,000-odd companies in its Share Information Service. Not only is the closing price given but the highs and lows for the year; the change over the previous day; the Dividend percentage or amount; the times the price is covered; the gross yield and the P/E ratio as well. *The Times*, by comparison, lists less than 2,000 companies as well as all the information given by the *Financial Times*—except for giving the number of times the price is covered.

The *Daily Telegraph* lists around 1,600 companies and gives only the high and low for the year and the change on the day. *The Guardian*'s Closing Prices is just that. Admittedly 1,500 companies are listed including 48 from the Birmingham and Northern Exchange but the only detail given is the closing price and the change from the previous day. Among the more popular papers, the *Daily Mail* provides the more comprehensive service. It lists around 1,000 different companies every day, followed by the *Daily Express* with about 800 and the other papers trailing behind.

6.10 How to decide

To decide the most effective sites, the company must answer three questions.

6.10.1 WHO ARE THE SHAREHOLDERS?
If the shareholders are all big institutional investors, clearly it would be absurd to have the shares listed in national and regional papers all over the country. If they were all based in London, a listing in the *Financial Times* would probably be sufficient. If some were based, say, in Bristol, it might be good tactics to list the shares in the local regional newspaper as well. But if there is a wide spread of investors, large and small, living throughout the country, a different approach is needed. A national company in investment if not in activities deserves national exposure. Its shares should be listed in the major business newspapers. If it has a lot of active small shareholders, perhaps, it should be listed in some of the popular papers as well. Similarly, if there is any heavy concentration of investors, say in Manchester, the shares should also be listed in either *The Guardian* or the *Manchester Evening News*.

6.10.2 SHOULD THE INVESTOR PROFILE BE CHANGED?
Some companies want more institutional investors. Others want more smaller investors. The location of the share listing can help by blazing a trail. If a smaller company wants the institutions to take a greater interest in its activities, it should ensure that its shares are listed in the serious financial publications. The *Financial Times* and the *Investors Chronicle*, for example, would be a must. Its financial PR operation would then concentrate its activities in the same direction as well. Similarly, if a major company wanted a wider spread of investors. Here the *Financial Times* and the *Investors Chronicle* would have to be supplemented by the more popular newspapers. If the company has various centres throughout the country, the shares could also be listed in the principal newspapers covering the regions.

6.10.3 WHAT ABOUT THE TRADE NEWSPAPERS?
Some trade papers run city columns, some do not. Check. If a trade paper runs a city column, every company in that industry should have their shares listed in the publication. It will not necessarily boost the number of investors.

6.11 Timing

Theodore Roosevelt always insisted on making his most important announcements on a Sunday. Not because it was the first day of the week. But because he recognised the importance of timing. Sunday, he knew, was a slow news day. There was little major news over the weekend. As a result, any comment from the Press would make headlines Monday morning. Companies have to make a similar decision when they first decide their financial year. Or, as the Americans say, the natural business year. It would be absurd to have every company reporting at the same time. There would be an enormous stampede for attention. Many important companies would get ignored in the rush. There would be no time to make a rational assessment of the companies and their progress. And, most important of all, it would be unfair on the majority of companies. For, in the vast majority of cases, the calendar year bears absolutely no relationship with a company's business year.

'There is much to be said for companies selecting the financial year-end best suited to their business instead of keeping slavishly to either the calendar year or the fiscal year', says Jones. He gives five reasons:

1 Stocks should be assessed when they are at their lowest point. Not their highest.
2 The balance sheet should reflect the company in its most liquid position. Not its most illiquid.
3 The balance sheet should reflect a complete cycle of operation. Not the end of one cycle and the start of another.
4 Auditors give a better service if clients demands are spread over the whole year. Instead of concentrated into a few months.
5 It could be advantageous for income tax if the year-end date fell early in the fiscal year. But it depends. . . .

The year-end decided, the next decision is publication day for the annual report. The Finance Act, 1948, insists that the profit and loss account should be published up to nine months before the annual meeting. If a company has interests overseas, the deadline extends to 12 months. Any exceptions have to have Board of Trade approval. Most companies recognise that this is far too long to give any meaningful guide to their activities. As a result, most companies tend to publish their annual report around six months after the end of their business year. Three months would be a more realistic period.

In the US, of course, many companies are ready with their annual report the first day of the new financial year. The Chesapeake and Ohio, for example, mail a one-page report complete with key operating figures and comments, to their 92,000 stockholders as soon as one year is completed. The Continental Illinois National Bank and Trust Company of Chicago have completed and mailed the full annual report by the fifth—yes, fifth—day of the new financial year.

Chapter 7

Interim Statements

Snap! is the half-time message Baxters (Butchers) sends its shareholders today. Profits come out at £411,000 for the first six-months—exactly the same as in the equivalent period last year. Identical, too, is the interim dividend, which is held at last year's rate of 4 per cent.
(*Evening Standard*, 12 November 1969)

Interim reports are prospectuses in action. Directors can no longer operate in a haze of brandy and cigar smoke from one year to another. Companies are no longer private empires. They must report progress. 'No company has the right to allow itself to be unexplained, misunderstood or publicly distrusted', said the President of the New York Stock Exchange. Interim reports are the latest shot in the campaign to ensure companies are explained, understood and trusted.

It all started with the Wall Street crash in 1929. The American Institute of Accountants convinced the New York Stock Exchange that companies should reveal enough facts and figures to assure their published accounts were not misleading. The Securities and Exchange Commission backed the idea. They insisted that not only should companies publish annual statistics but that they should be filed with the Securities and Exchange Commission as well. Interim reports came next. In 1955 the Securities and Exchange Commission proposed that companies listed on United States stock exchanges should file details of their financial progress 45 days after the end of the financial half year. Other countries followed suit. More than 70 per cent of companies listed on the Melbourne stock exchange in Australia, for example, publish interim statements. It's the same in Canada.

Progress in the United Kingdom has been slow. One or two companies began issuing interim figures in the 1940's. Most were against the idea. Ten years ago, for example, less than 400 companies quoted on the London Stock Exchange were issuing half-yearly figures. Only 15 were producing quarterly figures although quarterly reports were compulsory in France for companies over a certain size. In 1964 the chairman of the Second British Assets Trust, which had been releasing quarterly figures for nine years, discovered that only three companies were publishing quarterly and only 21 half-yearly profit statements out of 101 British companies in which the Trust held shares. But the breakthrough came the same year. Every company which has won a Stock Exchange quotation since then has been forced to publish a half-yearly report to shareholders.

Giants like ICI, Shell, Great Universal Stores, Courtaulds and Dunlop now issue interim statements as well. Associated Fisheries, Borax (Holdings) and Unilever have gone a stage further. They also issue quarterly figures.

7.1 Against interim reports

Of course, there are objections.

7.1.1 IT TAKES TOO MUCH TIME

Companies with out-of-date stock-control systems maintain its not worth the effort. It takes too much time and energy to assess the financial value of the stock. Although other companies like Purle Brothers Holdings, for example, can publish its interim figures for six months to 31 May by mid-July. Mechanical book-keeping is, of course, unheard of. So are running balances and so on. The *Financial Times* had the last word on the subject. If companies pleaded progress statements were impossible it 'would amount simply to a confession of the inadequacy of their accounting system', said a leading article on the subject.

7.1.2 IT TAKES TOO MUCH MONEY

The cost of printing and distributing the interim statements is prohibitive. A fair point. Other companies, however, manage it. In any case, companies only have to circularise the final results to shareholders not the interim. If they cannot afford the cost, they can still meet the Stock Exchange requirements by advertising the interim figures in the press, and then sending out confirmation to shareholders afterwards if it was still thought necessary.

7.1.3 THE FIGURES COULD BE MISLEADING

This was Sir Leonard Lord's point. When he was chairman of the old British Motor Corporation in 1957, he stressed the knocks the British motor industry had suffered over Suez. Output for the first quarter was 51,407 units, he said. By the last quarter, however, production had shot up to 123,341 units. The difference in the figures, he maintained, proved that interim statements were undesirable for the motor industry.

7.1.4 THE FIGURES COULD BE UNRELIABLE

Interim statements were often unaudited. This could be dangerous and misleading. On top of that, it was not always possible to discover how much money was tied up in work in progress.

7.1.5 THE REPORT WOULD BE GIVING AWAY INFORMATION TO COMPETITORS

By releasing figures regularly, a competitor could discover the progress of the company and adjust its own operations accordingly. For a company with a single-product line, perhaps, this is fair comment. But companies in America, Canada and Australia have been releasing similar figures at regular intervals for years without any noticeable harm. Says City Editor of the *Evening News*, David Malbert, 'In short, give all the relevant information that can be released without endangering the company. And I venture to suggest that at least 90 per cent of what is held back on security grounds is already well known to competitors.'

7.1.6 THERE IS NO LAW ABOUT IT

True. There is no law that says companies must publish interim statements— except companies quoted since 1964. The Jenkins Committee, however, welcomed the idea. So does Jones. 'This assertion implies that the shareholder has no interest either in the progress of the company from one year-end to another or in the market price of his shares, a contention which is, of course, untenable since, apart from other considerations, the shareholder at some stage may desire to dispose of his holding', he says.

7.2 For interim reports

There are, however, immense advantages to be gained by publishing interim reports. 'From the public relations approach, interim reporting is quite clearly a valuable practice in principle', says Derriman, 'and financial experts who have championed the cause of fuller information for the investor support it from their point-of-view'. Cavendish is even more enthusiastic. 'Interim reports could be made to be even more important than they are now', he says. 'Most of them are not accompanied by too much flesh and blood. But if you're going to give any information you might as well do it well.'

7.2.1 IT ENSURES A SOUNDLY BASED SHARE PRICE

Twelve months is a long time for an investor to go without getting any report of a company's activities. Anything can happen. The company could be riding the crest of a wave. Or it could be plummeting to the depths. The investor has a right to know. Regular flow of information will also ensure that a company is not subjected to wild speculation or depressing rumour. A year is in many cases too long, says Harold Rose (*Disclosure in Company Accounts,* Institute of Economic Affairs 1963), for 'investors to be without information as to the progress of their company, especially in a situation in which trading conditions are changing. The absence of an interim report tips the balance of advantage sharply in favour of the "insider". . . . The growth of the practice in Britain indicates an awareness of their importance.' Rose goes on to deliver a heavy rebuke to the old Lord school.

'The argument that interim profit statements might be misleading—that all too common declaration against self-education—is a particularly weak one. For in nine cases out of ten it is the absence of information that is potentially most deceptive, and where an interim figure was distorted by special items one would expect a responsible board to indicate this. Seasonal influences are easily identified.'

This is backed up to the hilt by the Institute of Directors. 'Directors should assure themselves that their reasons for rejecting the issue of such reports are genuinely based on their belief that shareholders would be misled. The wise board will not look for excuses for keeping shareholders uninformed, but rather for opportunities to increase their knowledge of the company', they said.

7.2.2 IT ENSURES A SOUNDLY BASED ASSESSMENT
The financial analyst, the institutional investors, the press and all the other financial PR media—all those who are not direct investors—can reach a realistic conclusion about the company. Slater Walker Securities, for example, faced growing 'bear' talk early August 1969. The shares already almost 40 per cent off its adjusted peak fell to 37s 6d before recovering to 40s. Chartists were even talking of a further slump to as low as 30s. But none of this was based on a proper assessment of the company. Slater announced that he would bring forward the announcement of his interim results. He did so, revealing among other things, a surge in half-time profits from £1·6 million to £4·53 million before tax and an interim payment, effectively unchanged, at 5·2 per cent. The bear raid petered out.

Mecca faced similar problems the following month. After a board room row, there was growing talk about profits. Faces were glum and hopes were low. Yet Mecca fought back by publishing its interim figures and raising the interim dividend by a point. Once again, it helped to guarantee that investors judged the company by a soundly-based assessment.

7.2.3 IT ENSURES CONTINUED INTEREST IN THE COMPANY
If 12 months is a long time for investors to wait without getting any clues about the progress of the company, it is also a long time to maintain interest in the company among the PR media. 'Up-to-date information is welcomed by institutional investors, the financial press, brokers and investors generally and the practice is encouraged by the stock exchange', says Jones.

7.3 Interim reports

Imperial Chemical Industries, S. Pearson Publishers, Keizer Venesta, Cunard, British Enkalon, Mecca, The Brooke-Harrison Group (all of them, incidentally, appeared on the same page of the *Financial Times* on 5 September 1969) and hundreds of other companies have all realised the advantages to be gained by publishing interim statements. Yet each statement has its own style. Each statement bears the imprint of the company's personality.

ICI gave seven sets of figures: group sales to external customers; group profit before tax and investment grants; depreciation; taxation after deducting proportion of investment grants; group profit after taxation; profit applicable to minority stockholders of subsidiaries and total group profit after taxation. These were detailed across three columns: first-half 1968, year 1968 and first-half 1969. Underneath came 350 words of further detail and comment.

S. Pearson Publishers gave trading profits (less depreciation) of all three companies of the group, the *Financial Times*, Westminster Press and Longman; investment income; interest payable; taxation; minority interests, preference dividends and net profit for equity. These were detailed across two columns, half-year to 30.6.69 and half-year to 30.6.68. Underneath came half the ICI copy, about 150 words.

Keizer Venesta began by describing their activities: 'Importers and distributors of plywood and manufacturers of plywood containers', a good move because obviously they are neither as well known as ICI nor is the name of the company as self-explanatory as S. Pearson Publishers. Four sets of figures, for the six-months to 30.6.69 and 30.9.68 and the 12 months to 31.12.68, were given for merchanting and manufacturing sales as well as merchanting and manufacturing profit before tax. They also gave more copy than either of the others: 400 words of accompanying text.

Cunard were different again. They gave group turnover; profit on operations; interest less other income (net); depreciation and profit before tax for the half-years to 30 June 1968 and 1969 as well as the figures for the whole of 1968. The copy was headed. 'Extracts from Statement by the Chairman, Sir Basil Smallpeice'—the only sign of a personality in all seven reports. This was followed by five numbered paragraphs covering everything from the longshoremen's strike and the sale of the former *Queen Elizabeth*.

The Brooke-Harrison Group, unlike Keizer Venesta, failed to give a thumb-nail sketch of themselves. There were no clues either in the copy. Only two sets of figures—sales and group profit (or loss) before taxation—were given. These were, in turn, tabled for the 26 weeks to 28 March 1969 and the 52 weeks to 27 September 1968. Only 200 words of copy followed.

British Enkalon gave more figures and less copy than the other six. Sales; trading profit less provision for contingencies; less interest; profit before tax; less Corporation Tax at 45 per cent (42½ per cent);

profit after tax and depreciation charged in arriving at the trading profit were all given. This covered the three six-month periods to 30 June 1968 and 1969 and the six-months to 31 December 1968. The copy merely said: 'The satisfactory trading profit for the first half of 1969 reflects a continuation of the increased demand for our products experienced during the second half of last year. Sales in general remain buoyant and we expect a satisfactory year.'

Mecca, much the most publicity-conscious of all the companies, produced—inconsistently—a sober looking statement. They gave 13 different sets of figures; group trading profit (excluding minority interests); interest received; leasehold amortisation; depreciation; interest on debenture and long-term loans; interest on bank and short-term loans; directors emoluments; net profit before taxation; corporation tax at both 45 and 42½ per cent for 1968; net profit after taxation; dividends paid or proposed on preference share capital and on ordinary share capital. The accompanying copy, divided into three notes, stretched to 80 words.

7.4 Stock Exchange requirements

The Stock Exchange, therefore, insists on half-yearly reports to shareholders for companies quoted since 1964. But it does not lay down too many hard-and-fast rules. The 'General Undertaking (Cos)' simply says that half-yearly reports should contain 'similar information to that required by the Council for preliminary announcements'.

First, the ground rules. Every public company must keep the Stock Exchange immediately informed of:

1 The date of a board meeting when the proposed interim or final dividend will be discussed.
2 The decision of the board on the interim or final dividend. If its a final dividend, then a profit statement is also necessary.

This is straightforward. The company secretary simply writes to the Quotations Department of the Stock Exchange giving the date of the meeting, usually four to six weeks after the end of the half-year period. This is posted on the floor of the Exchange. A copy of the note should also be sent to the major financial public relations media, such as the national financial press, especially the *Financial Times* which lists such information in its Financial Diary every Monday. There is little point in informing the other sectors for the press and news agency will see the Stock Exchange notice in any case. Then the contents of the interim statement itself. The Stock Exchange insists (as a condition of quotation from 1 September 1966) it covers:

1 Trading profit or loss before tax.

2 Tax.
3 Special credits or debits.
4 Dividends.

In each case corresponding figures for the preceeding year should also be given together with any additional information necessary to judge the figures in their true light. If, for example, a company is badly hit by a six-month strike, losing valuable orders as a result, it should say so. Similarly if the company gets an enormous boost through realising assets, it must say so as well.

'Owing to the late delivery of the *Queen Elizabeth 2* the earnings of several planned voyages were completely lost. Also, because of continuing uncertainty about delivery date, forward selling was brought to a standstill until the actual hand-over on April 18. Nevertheless *Queen Elizabeth 2* made a profit of £383,000 in May and June combined. This profit covers $2\frac{1}{2}$ times the interest of £150,000 payable for those two months on the full Government loan.'
(Cunard interim report, 30 June 1969)

Gradually, however, interim reports tail away into bromides:

All units have contributed to this improvement and the figures reflect the growing confidence on the company. Demand continues strong and is reaching record levels.

The directors confidently anticipate that the group will be operating more profitably during the second half of the year. Each company is now trading on a much sounder basis and the prospects are good.

The satisfactory trading profit for the first half reflects a continuation of the increased demand for our products experienced during the second half of the year.

That is the minimum for new companies which have gained their quotation in the last two years. Other companies, not subject to the letter of the rule, however, are also following suit for they realise the benefits to be gained. Many, in fact, are going a stage further and releasing other figures as well. Cunard, for example, release their group turnover. Mecca give details on leasehold amortisation, depreciation, interest—both debenture and long-term and bank and short-term. ICI split their group profit into profit applicable to ICI and profit applicable to minority stockholders of subsidiaries. They also release their volume of exports for the period as well. Follow Rio Tinto-Zinc, however, and you will not go far wrong. Their half-yearly report for the six months ended 30 June 1969 was a model of precision and clarity. First they give all the necessary figures: sales to group customers; operating profit; income from investment; gross interest receivable; gross interest payable; profit before tax; tax; amortisation of goodwill; profit attributable to outside shareholders. But then they gave an accompanying 850-word report covering group sales, revenue, operating profits—'The considerable increases in the operating profits of Hamersley and Palabora have been partly offset by the decreases in the operating profits of Borax and of the lead and zinc mining and smelting operations, and disappointing results at Avonmouth' —investment income, interest receivable, interest payable, tax, net profit and forecast and dividends.

Rio Tinto became Rio Grande for the press.

'Sir Val Duncan who heads the world-wide mining complex of Rio Tinto Zinc, today announces sparkling six-month profit figures. Earnings before tax are nearly £4 million higher. Largely because of the higher output from the group's iron ore complex at Hamersley in Australia assets for the period have risen from £145 million to £158 million. Higher copper prices for sales from the Palabora mine in South Africa also helped swell the sales total.'
(*Evening Standard*, 17 September 1969)

'Given that the historic price/earnings is still 28·2, it may still be hard to reckon that RTZ is cheap in its current, "gently rising" phase of earnings growth. However, RTZ is not being bought for this decade, but for the 70's when it has the real benefit of Hamersley iron, Bouganville and the aluminium and lead/zinc refining complexes to look forward to.'
(*Financial Times*, 18 September 1969)

British Oxygen, however, contented themselves with eleven sets of figures in their interim report for nine months on 30 June 1969 and the bald comment, 'It has been decided that in future the quarterly figures will be issued without explanatory notes unless such are called for'.

7.5 Preparation

An interim statement should be prepared in draft form a week before the necessary board meeting. It should then be discussed with the financial advertising agency and the financial public relations consultants. Between them they should decide the following.

7.5.1 WHAT NEWS VALUE THERE IS IN THE STATEMENT?

A company could lose £1 million in a strike. This could effect profits dramatically. The company could say how it happened and why. Similarly a company could boost profits enormously. Again it must give the reason. It is up to the advisers to alert the company to the likely response from the financial public relations media. Chairman of Reckitt and Colman, Mr B. N. Reckitt, for

K

example, pointed out in his statement in the six months to 5 July 1969 that United Kingdom profits for the first half of 1968 were abnormally favourable and the United Kingdom advertising and promotional expenditure in the first six-months of the year had been disproportionately high.

7.5.2 WHAT POINTS ARE OF MAJOR INTEREST?

A company could have made a sudden switch from losses to profits as a result of a merger. There could have been intense interest in the merger at the time. It is the company's duty to illustrate how the amalgamation is working out. Again the advisers should anticipate the reaction and be prepared to suggest the best way of releasing the news. A simple release might be the answer. Or it might be necessary to call a full-scale press conference.

7.5.3 HOW THE STATEMENT SHOULD BE RELEASED

On the advertising front, this involves decisions on media, size and design. Some companies advertise their statements in the major financial media. Others prefer just two national daily newspapers, the Stock Exchange minimum substitute for direct distribution to shareholders. Similarly size. ICI, for example, seem to prefer booking a space, $8\frac{1}{2}$-inches across three columns, for their interim statement. Mecca, on the other hand, go for a small black-border box, 4-inches across three columns. Then design. Some companies prefer to make their statements consistent with their over-all design policy. Others treat them as entirely separate. Keizer Venesta incorporated their logo into their statement. The Brooke-Harrison Group simply played it straight. These are all matters for the agency to advise on. The PR people, however, will be tackling the question of releasing the information, ensuring it is published as quickly as possible to all the relevant news media and undertaking to handle any resulting questions. Unilever's interim figures, for example, are always simultaneously released at 1.16 pm in both London and Rotterdam. Reuters, Extel and the evening papers get priority. Both the agency and the consultant—or staff man—then swing into action.

7.6 Interim statement day arrives

The board meets and approves the statement. The whole statement should then be released to the Stock Exchange at once. The go-ahead should be given for the advertisements to appear definitely in the selected media. And a press release should be distributed to the press—and the Stock Exchange— as quickly as possible. This is handled by either the advertising agency or the PR consultant. Some companies—not many—go a stage further and prepare more comprehensive detailed figures especially for the serious financial press. This can cover profits, losses, turnover and so on on separate subsidiary companies or divisions. Again, its information which will help outsiders gain a soundly based assessment of the company and its position in the market.

PRESS RELEASE IMMEDIATE   *7 August 1969*
RENTOKIL INTERIM REPORT

The first report of Rentokil Group Limited since the Company went Public in March shows that profits for the first-half of 1969 increased by 24·9 per cent compared with the corresponding period of 1968.

For the six months to June 30th, 1969 Group turnover was £5,911,000 (£3,937,000) and Group profit before tax was £858,000 (£687,000). Exports during this period increased substantially to £390,000 (£129,000). The profits of the Group's overseas subsidiaries for the six months ended 31st March, 1969 showed a significant increase at £189,000 (£58,000).

Because of seasonal factors, the Group's results are better in the second-half of each year. The Interim Report states that prospects for the second-half of this year are good and the Board remains confident of achieving the profit forecast made at the time of the Offer for Sale, which was not less than £1,900,000, for the full year.

Since March, Rentokil has acquired Rashbrooke Chemical Products Limited, a company offering a hygiene service to industry and Damp-course Insertions (Sales) Limited. Overseas Companies have been incorporated in Switzerland, Indonesia and the West Indian Island of Grenada.

The Board has declared an Interim Dividend for 1969 at the rate of 15 per cent, less tax, payable on November 19th.

'Some of the leading stocks took heart when Dunlop issued their report of an excellent first-half export achievement. This spurred Dunlop up to 33s 1½d for a net gain of 9d after they had opened with a small fall, and inspired a number of the other blue chips to similar performances.' (*Scotsman*, 30 July 1969)

'Crane Freuhauf's interim figures are hardly likely to do anything to dent the cheering impression created by last week's announcement of the £3 million (potentially £15 million) container order placed by the American group Seatrain Lines. Turnover in the six months to 30 June soared by 47·5 per cent to £6·35 million, producing pre-tax profits of 63·7 per cent to the good at £779,000. The tax charge remains virtually unchanged at 45 per cent leaving attributable profits of £429,000 against £262,000.' (*Daily Telegraph*, 14 September 1969)

But the press is only one of the financial PR media. Shareholders are another. The Beaumont Property Trust, for example, simply print their interim report in the form of a letter and mail it direct to shareholders. Other companies go a stage further and produce a special card, big enough to fit a foolscap envelope—for ease of mailing, cost, etc. Albright and Wilson mail a small

'Christmas card' statement with the necessary figures and a message from the chairman. 'Predictions are always difficult', wrote Mr O. H. Wansbrough-Jones on the 30 June 1968 interim statement, 'but given reasonably stable trading conditions our earnings should show a modest improvement although interest charges covering our expansion programme are an increasingly important item'.

Similarly Baker Perkins Holdings Limited. Chairman Mr A. I. Baker's 300-word review for the first-half of 1969 covered profits, the state of various loan stocks, the appointment of a new managing director for their Australian subsidiary, the plan to reduce the disparity between the interim and final dividends and the prospects for the future. On the back of the card, it lists the various group products, its subsidiaries, branches and associates. Rentokil go one step further. Their card has two folds. It also has a message from the chairman. But in addition it gives the directors names, the secretary and registered office of the company as well as the registrars. Thomas Tilling use a foolscap-sized card with three folds and four sheets. The cover lists the directors, the secretary and the registered office. Page two and three are given over to the unaudited results, which—novel point—include the group cash flow. The next two pages contain the directors interim report signed by the chairman, Geoffrey Eley. Pages six and seven list the main products and companies of the group. And the last page is blank.

Lex Garages go the whole hog and virtually produce a mini-annual report and accounts. Their 12-page booklet gives all the directors names and details about auditors, bankers and so on. Joint chairmen, Mr Norman Chinn and Mr Rosser Chinn, give a full 1,000-word interim report. There is a Consolidated Profit and Loss Account as well as a complete Balance Sheet not to mention full progress reports on their six Divisions. Obviously a case of leading by the Chinn.

7.7 Other company statements

But, of course, interim statements are not the only form of progress report a company can make. Companies can—and should—keep the financial public relations media regularly informed of their activities and progress through a series of announcements or circulars. Instead of sitting back until they are hit by a takeover bid, which then sets them firing off special circulars in all directions. 'A board which seeks to ensure good public relations in the financial field should actively watch for opportunities to provide information of help to the investor', says Derriman.

Major orders, big selling drives, success stories, technical break-throughs, any major development can be the subject of a special circular. Similarly, strikes, disasters, cut-backs should also be the basis of a special communications drive. Investors and the financial public relations media want to know the latest developments—or setbacks—of a company. By keeping them informed all the time, it ensures that they always have a realistic idea of the company's progress.

Drafts of any circular to shareholders, however, must be approved by the Stock Exchange. They will have to give their consent to both the contents and the timing of the operation. Rupert Murdoch, Chairman of the News of the World Organisation, for example, issued a special statement on 17 September 1969 warning that 'serious' problems created by a strike at the key Eric Bemrose printing subsidiary were 'bound to affect our forecast profits'. It was picked up and carried by the press.

Chairman and Chief Executive of BSA, Eric Turner, made a similar move the same week. Within three years he had rebuilt the company and boosted sales to the United States by 50 per cent in one year alone. Profits rose. Shares flourished. From a 11s 7d low in 1962 they hit 47s 3d by 1969. Then suddenly the rumours started. The company was short of cash. The shares plunged and speculators made a killing. With the shares down as low as 6s 6d at one time Turner decided to fight back. He booked advertising space in a number of national newspapers to give the facts. There was a crisis. From a £3·3 million profit in 1968, the group would make only £750,000 for 1969, the lowest for over ten years.

> 'The Board of Birmingham Small Arms appears very sensibly to be taking the line that attack is the best means of defence. BSA shares have become vulnerable to the rumour-mongers and bear raiders because of the lean times on which the company has fallen. Ahead of the annual report due in November, the Board has given an assessment of the picture as they see it. The statement should help to steady the share price.'
> (*Financial Times*, 13 September 1969)

Turner also wrote to shareholders and gave them the facts. He hinted at better utilisation of assets, a closer look at raw material costs and stock control. Again the information was released to the press. The result? Both *The Sunday Times* and *The Observer* looked at the company on 14 September. They charted its troubles, the fight it was putting up against low-powered cheap Japanese machines as well as the knocks it was taking in the key United States market. Yet, in the end, both papers were hopeful.

'The BSA package stands a fair chance of pulling the motor-cycle business around in two or three years. Returns on assets should go up but mainly as a result of liberating a large part of the capital presently employed in the business. Total sales will probably stay at about the current £25 million mark. Containing costs will thus be first priority for improving earnings', said *The Sunday Times*. *The Observer* commented, 'Turner has warned that it is going to be a long haul, and it may well be some time before BSA shares are popular again in the market. Anyone buying them now must be prepared to sit it out.'

Harsh words. Yet Turner was able to plug the dyke. The assessment of BSA shares was at least based on a realistic appraisal of their situation.

Chapter 8

Annual Statements

Gussies still great. Great Universal Stores, almost a unit trust in retailing, with 2,000 shops, stores, multiples and our biggest outfit in mail order are keeping the squeeze at bay. In the year to last March their profits before tax rose £2,883,005 to £48,419,971 and the dividend is to be 38¾ per cent against 37½ per cent.
(Daily Mail, 18 July 1969)

Fine Fare (Holdings), Europe's biggest supermarket group, boosted profits by just over £1 million last year, announces Chairman Mr James Gulliver today. In the 12 months to end-March, they totalled £4,756,000 compared with £3,750,000 the previous year. Commenting on his results, Mr Gulliver says, 'We are delighted with the Fine Fare results, which represent an increase in pre-tax profits of 27-per-cent.'
(Evening Standard, 21 July 1969)

The annual report, described by Chairman of the London Stock Exchange, Sir Martin Wilkinson as 'the most important document published by a quoted company' (*The Accountant* annual awards, 8 May 1968), is the highlight of the company year. It is the greatest opportunity a company has to further relations with the investing public, the City and the Press.

'Nuclear power, synthetic materials, automation, supermarkets and other modern developments will all require finance on a substantial scale, while the colossal capital commitments of the nationalised industries will add to that demand', says Jones. 'All these factors make it desirable to educate the public in matters of company finance and probably the most obvious way of achieving this objective is to prepare the annual accounts of companies in a more attractive and comprehensible form.'

Financial public relations experts are even more emphatic. 'Because the annual report and accounts is not only the history book of the last financial year but also the prospectus for the current and possibly subsequent years this document is the company's most important publication', says Cocking.

8.1 Annual reports, however, are still all things to all businessmen . . .

8.1.1 THEY ARE A PROGRESS REPORT

The Australian Estates Company, Limited, for example, were able to report a novel form of progress in their annual statement for 1969. Chairman, Sir Denys Lowson, revealed that a Brahman cow sold by their Rockhampton Branch at Belmont in October 1968 had fetched $13,000—the highest price paid for a cow of any breed sold in Australia.

8.1.2 THEY ARE AN OPPORTUNITY TO ATTACK

Brewers seem to use their reports as an opportunity to attack the government. 'It might be thought that the brewing industry, which serves its public so well with one hand and must use the other for the government's benefit as revenue collectors, might reasonably expect some praise or acknowledgement from the chief beneficiary. Instead we have received more critical attention and surveillance than any other industry', said Mr John Young in his annual statement as Chairman of Young and Co's Brewery in 1969. 'Not content with subjecting us to a futile investigation by Mr Aubrey Jones and his Prices and Incomes Board whose report proved so ill-informed, the government then hastened to submit us to a further misinterpretation with a two-and-a-half-year investigation by the Monopolies Commission. Their time-consuming, laborious and costly report produced an even more futile commentary upon our affairs.'

Colonel W. H. Whitbread, Chairman of Whitbread, the United Kingdom's third largest brewery, blamed the government for 'interference' in his annual statement the same year. But probably the most outspoken political attack to appear in an annual statement came from Sir Reginald Wilson, Chairman of the Transport Holding Company in 1969. The efficiency and financial viability of the State-owned rail and road undertakings would improve if there were less political intervention in their affairs, he said. Thirteen of the last 21 years had been spent waiting for major Transport Acts or reorganising after them. At the same time, government intervention and controls had been steadily increasing. And a further upheaval seemed possible when the Conservatives were returned to power. The *Financial Times* picked up the report and discussed it in a leader on 24 July 1969. 'It is time that the parties reached a sensible compromise on this issue and that public transport ceased to be a political football', they said.

8.1.3 THEY ARE AN OPPORTUNITY TO DEFEND

The Industrial Reorganisation Corporation's 1969 report and accounts was a superb example of aggressive defence. Faced with a number of hostile critics including Mr Iain Macleod who had made no bones about the fact that the IRC was expendable, Managing Director Charles Villiers had obviously decided to hit back. In two-and-a-half years they had invested £13·5 million in equities and £52·5 million in Loan Funds, £5 million of which had already been repaid. The IRC, therefore, had been responsible for just over 1 per cent of total public sector expenditure in 1967. Hardly the reckless giant. The report then claimed that in the present economic climate, the national interest could be best served by boosting productivity and by improving the balance of payments. Manufacturing industry accounted for a third of the GNP, employed a third of the national labour force and was responsible for two-thirds of foreign trade. Yet 13 years ago imports rated £35 to every £100 of manufactured exports. Today they were as high as £72 per £100 of exports. Change was vital. And a government-sponsored agency was actively aiding and abetting change. If it was not for the IRC change might come too late— or not at all.

'It is not just that the report is excellently presented and forthrightly, not to say, racily written, but rather that it is, in effect, an apologia', said the *Investors Chronicle*, 27 June 1969, 'Throughout, the IRC is carrying the fight to its critics and going out to justify its existence'. If a government agency can earn that kind of praise, there is no reason why public companies should not follow suit.

8.2 In the beginning

'The ———— Company makes no reports and furnishes no statements', snapped an American company when the New York Stock Exchange asked for a copy of their annual report in 1866. It was a little better in 1900 when the American Sugar Refining Company, one of the biggest publicly owned corporations of the day, published their balance sheet. Only four items were listed under assets and three under liabilities. There was no statement of income at all. The breakthrough, however, came in 1903. United States Steel published a 60-page annual report including 36 pages of facts and figures and 22 pages of photographs. 'Probably the most complete and circumstantial report ever issued by a great American corporation', commented the *Scientific American*.

By 1926, 339 companies out of the 957 on the New York Stock Exchange were issuing reports. But the figures were not always reliable. Some companies were tossing in almost any figures which came to mind. As a result the New York Stock Exchange insisted in 1932 that reports be passed by an independent auditor. The Securities and Exchange Commission went a stage further. Two years later they insisted that even the financial report would have to be 'consistent with recognised and accepted principles of accounting'.

In the United Kingdom annual reports continued to be dull, dreary and dreadful. They looked like writs drawn up by accountants. They stuck to the letter of the law. They ignored the demand for facts and figures. And they ignored the cries for understanding from investors who couldn't make head nor tail of them. It took a world war to make British companies realise the importance of annual reports. From 1939 to 1945 more and more companies realised that because investors found it impossible to attend annual meetings and keep up-to-date with company affairs, they had better take the initiative and try to keep the investors informed. In 1948 the Cohen Committee played the trump card. No less than 41·4 per cent of shareholders of ten prominent companies were holding less than 100 shares, they said.

Businessmen realised the implications. They also saw the professional analyst on the horizon together with a vigorous Stock Exchange Council behind the scenes. Others saw not only a wave of takeover bids all around them but the threat of nationalisation hanging over their heads as well. The more discerning businessmen would also have spotted the first hesitant steps of modern financial public relations in the wings. The Companies Act, 1948, however, took the decision out of their hands. From then on companies had to present the annual general meeting with:

1 A profit and loss account.
2 A balance sheet.
3 An auditors report.
4 A directors report.

The arguments were over. The annual report had arrived.

The Accountant awards for the best produced company accounts stimulated more companies to produce reports for the layman. It also focussed greater attention on the design and clear-headed presentation of the report. 'What is superb this year may well be surpassed next year', said editor-in-chief Percy F. Hughes, 'This business of striving for perfection in the presentation of accounts is not a static thing. I believe it to be something that must grow and be adapted to changing industrial conditions and thought.'

The Companies Act, 1967, went even further. Accounts would have to include:

1 The identities and places of incorporation of subsidiaries and particulars of their shareholdings.
2 The identities and places of incorporation of companies—not subsidiaries—whose shares it holds as well as details of those shares.
3 The name and place of incorporation of a subsidiary's holding company.
4 Directors salaries.
5 Any rights to salary or commission waived by a director.
6 Details of employees receiving more than £10,000 a year.

The directors report attached to the balance sheet must also include:

1 The principal activities of the company and its subsidiaries during the year as well as any significant changes of activities that occurred during the period.
2 The names of directors

3 Any significant changes in the fixed assets of the company or any of its subsidiaries.
4 Details of any share issue as well as the reasons for making it.
5 Information about any contract with the company in which a director had, either directly or indirectly, an interest.
6 Any arrangements that had been made to enable directors to acquire shares or debentures.
7 The number of shares and debentures in the company and its subsidiaries held by directors.
8 The turnover and profitability or otherwise of different businesses where there are different businesses involved.
9 The average number of employees and their wages total for the year.
10 Political or charitable contributions.
11 Exports—for certain companies.
12 Any other details essential for the understanding of the company—unless it would harm the business.

But that's not all. The General Undertaking, signed by companies seeking a Stock Exchange quotation, also insists on the directors report or audited accounts including:

1 A geographical analysis of any overseas trading operations.
2 Details of any interests held by directors' families in the company.

Finally, a technical point, the Stock Exchange insists on:

1 A statement by the company whether it is a close company—as defined by the Finance Act, 1965—or not.

A formidable list. Yet handled correctly the annual report is probably the great weapon in the management's financial public relations armoury. 'When the annual report is developed to its full effectiveness it is the greatest sales tool, persuader, goodwill builder, and educational device in management's public relations kit', says Beveridge. A well prepared and well documented annual report is a superb weapon to aim at the financial public relations media. With a good annual report, a company can come out with its guns blazing.

But that's not all. A well prepared annual report will also interest other groups as well.

8.2.1 IT WILL INTEREST EMPLOYEES

More and more companies see employees—especially middle management— as a key audience for the annual report. Many publish a special layman's guide to the annual report. Others prepare a more simplified version of the report itself. Either way employees are entitled to financial information about the company in which they have invested their life. They might also, of course, be able to invest their money as well.

8.2.2 IT WILL INTEREST WHOLESALERS

This follows the old line: The more they know about you, the better they like you. Dealers can almost make or break a company. The better the company treats a dealer, the better for the company.

8.2.3 IT WILL INTEREST CUSTOMERS

Many companies realise this. Hence the glossy photographs of products scattered throughout the report. One chairman of an electronics company always maintained that he landed more contracts through the oh-so-soft sell of his annual report than through any other form of promotion. An ICI survey of their stockholders has revealed that 36 per cent often make a point of buying ICI products while another 36 per cent sometimes buy ICI goods.

8.3 Planning the report

The first thing a company should do is to call in the experts. The public relations adviser—'I put the verbs into the chairman's speeches'—a lay-out artist and a photographer should sit down and analyse the previous annual report. What was the objective? Did it work? If there was any feedback from shareholders, the press or City institutions, it should be considered. If not, the experts should try and discover why not? Between them, they should draw up their proposals for the next annual report.

'Different companies call for different treatment', says John Hartley-Smith, Chairman of Dorlands (City). 'It depends on the product'.

The size of the pages, the quality and the number needed for the report, must all be examined. Most annual reports, for example, are now produced on A4 size paper. The quality ranges from a straightforward gloss paper to the more extravagant art paper of Dorland Advertising Holdings. The number of pages can be anything between the 16 pages of the Leyland and Birmingham Rubber Company and the 52 pages of the Rio Tinto-Zinc Corporation. The lay-out artist and the photographer estimate how many illustrations should be included, whether they will be line drawings or photographs and in how many colours. Selection Trust Limited, for example, have glossy cover, seven pages of full colour and a mass of charts. The Thomson Organisation just have a glossy cover and black-and-white prints while Unilever have a photograph on the cover and a mass of charts inside.

Girard Trust Corn Exchange Bank of Philadelphia, by comparison, tend to live up to their name. Starting in 1948 they have included cartoons in between the facts and figures in their annual reports 'to try to attract attention by poking a little gentle humour at ourselves and the banking business generally'. But, generally, its not a risk worth taking. If a company can utilise their report to sell themselves and their products, they should do so. Paper and printing companies such as Eucalyptus Pulp Mills, for example, are in an ideal position. They can print their reports on company paper of their own making.

But beware. The financial public relations media are not impressed with 'flashy reports'. They tend to consider them a waste of money. There is also the danger of making the wrong approach. At a seminar on financial public relations, chartered accountant, J. Darrel Nightingale, outlined the mistakes to avoid, 'Treating the shareholder as an enlightened simpleton; having no theme or personality; having no flow—the result of too many writers; being an absolute mixture of director's report, chairman's speech, notice to attend, accounts, etc.'

These problems decided, the designers will have to discuss the kind of type, the printing process—this largely depends on the numbers involved—lay-outs, the type of printer for the job and so on. They will then have to draw up a budget and a time-table. The budget is important. A major company with thousands of shareholders must be prepared to spend £100,000 if necessary. This seems expensive. But worked out on a cost-per-issue basis, it could be as cheap as 2s–3s for a 40-page booklet. ICI, for example, publish a 42-page annual report in two columns—black and red—on white paper. No illustrations. No photographs. Because of the cost. With 650,000 stockholders, it is prohibitive. Yet at a unit cost of 2s plus 9d postage the bill still comes to £90,000. On the other hand a smaller company with fewer shareholders might find they are spending a similar amount. On a cost-per-issue basis, however, this could work out at the astronomical sum of 6s each. An annual report is a major event in the company's year. But that is no reason for allowing the costs to soar through the roof.

Next the time-table. It's absurd. But it is best to allow anything between three and four months from the moment the budget, a rough design and time-table are prepared to the actual publication, especially if the report is going to be translated into French, German and perhaps, Dutch, as some reports of international companies are nowadays. Said Sir Geoffrey Eley, Chairman of Thomas Tilling Limited (at the 1965 *Accountant* awards ceremony):

> 'What we are after is, first of all, clearly and simply to inform a lay shareholder of what is going on and what he owns; secondly, we aim to provide what is needed for the professional shareholder, the financial paper analyst or the institutional backroom adviser. We believe that the more publicity, the more knowledge we let in, the better it is for us and our shareholders and the whole economic society of which we form a part.'

8.4 The annual report itself

'It must be attractive to look at. I think that's terribly important', says Clive Smith of Astral. 'You've got to have something that is eye-catching, interesting, that people will want to pick up and read.' But attractiveness is not enough. The report must also be comprehensive, objective and—more than anything—factual. It was this lack of detail that was criticised by the

1964 panel who judged the *Accountant* award scheme. The six most common faults, they claimed, were:

1 Lack of information about the nature of the business.
2 Lack of names and details about subsidiaries.
3 Lack of information about trade investments.
4 Lack of detail about the basis of assets included in the accounts as well as the basis of valuation of stock-in-trade.
5 Lack of a statistical summary covering not less than five years.
6 Lack of cross-references between the accounts and the notes.

Director-General of the NEDO, Mr Fred Catherwood, attacked the limitations of balance sheets from a different angle on 16 October 1969. Instead of looking into the future they continually looked back to the past, he said. Thus giving a heavy bias in the wrong direction. It was like the works manager who boasted his factory was making splendid profits because all its plant was so old that it had been written off whereas another factory was doing badly because it was burdened with modern plant.

Bear this in mind when examining the bones of the annual report.

8.4.1 COVER

'The cover designs adopted by a few large companies today are not only attractive and in excellent taste, but are calculated to invite even those most allergic to accounts to open the booklet and inspect its contents', says Jones.

Alfred Herbert, Reed Group and the International Publishing Corporation, seem to prefer plain white high-gloss card. The British Printing Corporation like grey covers with huge reverse white-on-grey lettering. United Biscuits fill the front cover of their report with their linked U to B logo—full of different packets of biscuits. Pasolds, the Ladybird children's clothes with—unbelievably—quaint fairy-tale pictures of busy ladybirds weaving cloth with the help of a flower; washing wool in a mountain stream and even operating abacus-based computers. While Thomas Tilling seem happy forever with that spring photograph of their Crewe House, Curzon Street, London W1, headquarters.

8.4.2 CONTENTS PAGE

Some do. Some don't. International Publishing Corporation, for example, only list five headings: Chairman's Statement; Director's Report and Accounts; IPC Divisions; IPC Subsidiaries and Trade Investments; and IPC Publications. Rio Tinto-Zinc list 30 items ranging from their list of directors to a page on the Finance Act, 1965, Capital Gains Tax. Guest, Keen and Nettlefolds throw in their financial calendar as well. While Fisons, John Harvey and Sons, Reckitt and Colman and the Reed Group do not bother with contents at all. They go straight into the report. A contents page, however, is useful. First, because it will alert the professional to the amount of material in the report. Second, because it will help the ordinary shareholder find his way around the document. There are no set rules but a contents page should include:

1 Notice of meeting and Notes.
2 Salient features.
3 Chairman's statement.
4 Directors report.
5 Auditors report.
6 Accounts for the year.
7 Profit and loss account.

It is possible to extract various items of information from the different sections, of course, and give them headings in their own right. The contents page could then look like:

1 Financial calendar.
2 Notice of meeting and Notes.
3 Directors and senior executives.
4 The Company.
5 Salient features.
6 Directors report.
7 Trading results.
8 Finance—dividends, etc.
9 Donations,
10 Auditors report.
11 Accounts for the year.
12 Balance sheet.
13 Profit and loss account.
14 Financial record.
15 Principal subsidiary companies.

8.4.3 NOTICE OF MEETING

Some companies are quite pompous. 'Notice is hereby given that the seventy-second Annual General Meeting . . . will be held . . .' says Thomas Tilling. Metal Industries Ltd are far more sensible. 'The 26th Annual General Meeting will be held at . . .'. Then there are all the other additions. 'To receive the Report of the Directors together with the Accounts for the year ended . . . and the Report of the Auditors thereon'. And of course the company secretary always insists on signing the report 'By order of the Board'.

This is all splendid stuff. Very pompous. And very business-like. Yet, in fact, quite unnecessary. The Companies Act, 1948, only stresses the need for special business to be listed in the Notice. Everything else is superfluous. This doesn't mean companies should forget about an agenda altogether. Shareholders attending the annual meeting are entitled to know what is planned before they get there. It does mean that companies should forget their pomposity and list the agenda in everyday English.

8.4.4 NOTES

These must cover four points.

1 PROXY VOTING. Any shareholder entitled to attend and vote at the meeting is entitled to have one or more proxies attend and vote in his place. This is laid down in the 1948 Act.

2 NOTIFICATION OF PROXIES. The company must give shareholders a deadline for informing them of any arrangements being made for a proxy.

3 VOTING RIGHTS. Only holders of certain types of security are allowed to attend and vote at annual meetings. Holders of $5\frac{1}{2}$ and $6\frac{1}{2}$ per cent cumulative preference shares of £1 each, for example, are not entitled to attend or vote at Thomas Tilling annual meetings. The company must, therefore, remind investors who can and who cannot vote.

4 INSPECTION OF COMPANY DOCUMENTS. This is the invitation to inspect. Companies must give shareholders a chance to inspect the annual state-ment, all transactions of directors as well as their family interests in the equity share capital of the company and its subsidiaries both before and during the annual meeting. Most companies reckon the documents would be available for inspection at their head office from the day the Notice of Meeting is mailed until the annual meeting itself. And then most companies have the documents at the meeting as well.

Some companies incorporate these points in the Notice of Meeting. Some list them underneath. A few, like ICI, mix them up. Their 1968 report, for example, listed the proxy details in the actual Notice signed by the company secretary and then gave the time and place for inspecting the documents underneath. They also made two other points; the time of posting the report itself to stockholders and the fact that the chairman's speech at the annual meeting would be available to stockholders on request. This is also the place in the report where it is convenient to mention whether the company is or is not a close company within the meaning of the Finance Act, 1965.

8.4.5 SALIENT FEATURES

Annual reports, do not forget, are not only going to those who know the company but to those who do not. It would seem prudent, therefore, to spell out very briefly the history of the company, its growth and its present opera-tions. ICI, for example, manage this in five paragraphs.

'Imperial Chemical Industries Limited was incorporated on 7 December 1926 to amalgamate four leading chemical companies, namely Brunner, Mond and Co. Ltd., Nobel Industries Ltd, The United Alkali Co. Ltd, and British Dyestuffs Corporation Ltd. Today it is Europe's largest chemical manufacturer and one of the largest industrial organisations in the world. The Group comprises the Company and over 350 subsidiaries in the United Kingdom and overseas . . .'.

It goes on, crisply and concisely to describe how the product range has expanded; its best-known trade marks; its operations in the United Kingdom employing 139,000 people; its overseas interests in 45 countries together with its selling agents in many others. Then come the 'Group results in brief' which at the same time services the professional in a hurry and the amateur looking for advice.

ICI, Rio Tinto-Zinc, Albright and Wilson all extract the most important figures of the year. Rentokil call this section 'The Year at a Glance'. GKN merely say, '1968 in brief'. Courtaulds are more formal with their 'Summary of Results', which even includes a classification of their world sales as well as an analysis of their profit: how much came from fibres, textiles and related activities; how much from paint and from packaging less, of course, their central expenses. Unilever go a stage further. In addition to their Salient figures, they include a three paragraph summary, 'The year in brief':

'Combined sales to third parties rose by about 14 per cent over 1967 to £2,306 million, combined profit before taxation by about 20 per cent to £170 million. Rates of taxation were higher in many countries. The profit accruing to ordinary capital increased by over 7 per cent following the increase of 35 per cent for 1967 when the effect of a sterling devaluation was taken up for the full year.

'Higher sales were achieved in most product groups, notably in foods, detergents and toilet preparations, and paper, printing, packaging, plastics and chemicals.

'All the main product groups except animal feeds contributed to the increase in profits.'

It's all there. At a glance. With 74,267 ordinary and 1,456 preferential shareholders together with a further 116,681 debenture and unsecured stockholders in Unilever Limited not to mention the holders of Unilever N.V. share and loan capital, it is clearly important for Unilever to hammer the message home. But the method would seem to offer many advantages for the much smaller company as well.

8.4.6 CHAIRMAN'S STATEMENT

There is no law that says the chairman must make a personal statement to shareholders at all. He is under no legal obligation. He virtually does it because he wants to. Not because he has to. The custom grew up before the war. Chairmen being chairmen, they take to getting up during the annual

The four-language financial advertising campaign launched by the Reed Group in the principal European financial media in 1969 prior to raising money by means of European Units of Account.

What do you know about the Reed Paper Group?

To start with, the word "paper" is misleading. Certainly we make paper, lots of it.

But we manufacture and market many other things, too.

● Which of these do you think Reed are involved with?

stationery	retail shops
boats	drainage systems
computer tapes	paint
printing papers	ceramic tiles
newsprint	lithography
paint brushes	chemicals
cartons	plastics
teleprinter tapes	injection moulding
refuse sacks	paper merchanting
wallpaper	building materials
furnishing fabrics	corrugated cases

ANSWER: All of them! And many others.

● In which year was the Reed Paper Group founded?

ANSWER: 1903.

● In how many different countries does the Reed Paper Group have interests?

(a) 15 (b) 21 (c) 36 (d) 40

ANSWER: Over 40

● In which of these countries does the Reed Paper Group *not* currently have interests?

(a) Great Britain	(h) Kenya
(b) Singapore	(i) Netherlands
(c) Norway	(j) Ireland
(d) Canada	(k) U.S.A.
(e) Australia	(l) Germany
(f) Belgium	(m) New Zealand
(g) France	

ANSWER: None. Reed has interests in all these countries, and thirty more!

● How many people are employed worldwide by the Reed Paper Group?

(a) 10,000 (b) 17,000 (c) 28,000 (d) 52,000

ANSWER: 52,000 people.

● Last year's trading profit before depreciation was:

(a) £6,700,000 (b) £17,800,000 (c) £21,400,000 (d) £28,900,000.

ANSWER: £28,900,000.

● Which was the first company in Britain to receive a loan from the U.K. Government's Industrial Reorganisation Corporation for development of one of the company's new industrial techniques?

ANSWER: The Reed Paper Group (received a loan of £1.5 million).

● In 1967-68 the Reed Paper Group's sales were:

(a) £12,000,000 (b) £80,700,000 (c) £159,600,000 (d) £249,500,000.

ANSWER: £249,500,000.

Well, how much did you know about us? If you'd like to learn even more, why not send for a free copy of the Reed Paper Group Limited Annual Report for the year ended 31 March, 1968. It gives the full financial facts about one of the world's biggest, soundest and fastest-growing companies.

Que savez-vous à propos du Reed Paper Group?

Tout d'abord, le mot "Paper" (papier) peut vous induire en erreur. Certes nous faisons du papier, et même des tas.

Mais, nous fabriquons et vendons aussi bien d'autres choses.

● Quel sont, à votre avis, les secteurs d'activité de Reed?

papeterie	magasins de vente
bateaux	systèmes de drainage
bandes d'ordinateur	peinture
papiers d'imprimerie	carreaux de céramique
papier journal	lithographie
pinceaux	produits chimiques
cartonnages	plastiques
bandes de télétype	moulage par injection
sacs à ordures	papier en gros
papier peint	matériaux de construction
tissus d'ameublement	boîtes de carton ondulé

RÉPONSE: Ceux-ci et plusieurs autres

● En quelle année a été fondé le Reed Paper Group?

RÉPONSE: En 1903.

● Dans combien de pays a-t-il des intérêts?
(a) 15 (b) 21 (c) 36 (d) 40

RÉPONSE: plus de 40

● Parmi les pays cités ci-dessous quels sont ceux où le Reed Paper Group n'a pas d'intérêts?

(a) Grande-Bretagne	(h) Kenya
(b) Singapour	(i) Pays-Bas
(c) Norvège	(j) Irlande
(d) Canada	(k) États-Unis
(e) Australie	(l) Allemagne
(f) Belgique	(m) Nouvelle-Zélande
(g) France	

RÉPONSE: Aucun. Reed a des intérêts dans chacun de ces pays, et même dans trente autres.

● Combien de personnes le Reed Paper Group emploie-t-il dans le monde?
(a) 10.000 (b) 17.000 (c) 28.000 (d) 52.000

RÉPONSE: 52.000

● Le bénéfice d'exploitation de l'an dernier avant amortissement était de:
(a) £6.700.000 (b) £17.800.000 (c) £21.400.000 (d) £28.900.000.

RÉPONSE: £28.900.000.

● Quelle a été, en Grande-Bretagne, la première compagnie à recevoir de la Société gouvernementale pour la Réorganisation Industrielle un prêt en vue du développement de l'une de ses nouvelles techniques?

RÉPONSE: Le Reed Paper Group (qui a reçu la somme de £13.5 million).

En 1967-68, les ventes du Reed Paper Group ont atteint:
(a) £12.000.000 (b) £80.700.000 (c) £159.600.000 (d) £249.500.000.

RÉPONSE: £249.500.000.

Alors, en saviez-vous beaucoup sur nous? Si vous voulez en savoir encore plus, pourquoi ne pas vous faire envoyer un exemplaire du rapport annuel du Reed Paper Group Limited pour l'année se terminant le 31 mars 1968. Il vous apporte toutes les informations financières sur l'une des Sociétés les plus grandes, les plus prospères et à l'expansion la plus rapide du monde.

Auriez-vous l'obligeance de m'envoyer un exemplaire de votre rapport annuel.

Nom:

Situation:

Adresse:

Adressé à:
**Reed Paper Group Ltd.
Reed House, 82 Piccadilly,
London, W1A 1EJ
Angleterre**

Reed
PAPER GROUP

Quiz:

Che cosa sapete del Reed Paper Group?

Prima di tutto la parola "Paper" (carta) è troppo limitativa. Naturalmente fabbrichiamo carta, moltissima per la verità, ma fabbrichiamo e vendiamo anche moltissimi altri articoli.

● In quali di questi settori pensate che il Gruppo Reed operi?

carta per corrispondenza	negozi al dettaglio
imbarcazioni	impianti di drenaggio
nastri per calcolatori	vernici
carta da stampa	piastrelle di ceramica
carta da giornali	litografia
pennelli	prodotti chimici
cartoni	materie plastiche
nastri per telescriventi	stampi a iniezione
sacchi per rifiuti	vendita carta
carta da parati	materiali da costruzioni
tessuti d'arredamento	scatoloni di cartone ondulato

RISPOSTA: In tutti ed anche in molti altri

● In quale anno fu fondato il Reed Paper Group?

RISPOSTA: nel 1903

● In quanti Paesi opera il Reed Paper Group?
(a) 15 (b) 21 (c) 36 (d) 40

RISPOSTA: oltre 40

● In quali di questi Paesi il Reed Paper Group non svolge nessuna attività?

(a) Gran Bretagna	(h) Kenia
(b) Singapore	(i) Paesi Bassi
(c) Norvegia	(j) Irlanda
(d) Canada	(k) Stati Uniti
(e) Australia	(l) Germania
(f) Belgio	(m) Nuova Zelanda
(g) Francia	

RISPOSTA: In nessuno. Il Reed opera in tutti questi Paesi ed in altri trenta!

● Quanti dipendenti ha nel mondo il Reed Paper Group?
(a) 10.000 (b) 17.000 (c) 28.000 (d) 52.000

RISPOSTA: 52.000

● Gli utili commerciali realizzati l'anno scorso prima dell'ammortamento furono di:
(a) Lgs 6.700.000 (b) Lgs 17.800.000
(c) Lgs 21.400.000 (d) Lgs 28.900.000

RISPOSTA: Lgs 28.900.000

● Quale fu, in Gran Bretagna, la prima società a cui l'Ente per la Riorganizzazione Industriale del Governo Britannico accordò un prestito che le permettesse di sviluppare uno dei suoi nuovi procedimenti industriali?

RISPOSTA: Il Reed Paper Group, che ottenne un prestito di Lgs 1,6 milione.

● Nell'anno 1967-68 il fatturato del Reed Paper Group fu di:
(a) Lgs 12.000.000 (b) Lgs 80.700.000
(c) Lgs 159.600.000 (d) Lgs 249.500.000

RISPOSTA: Lgs 249.500.000

Eravate al corrente di tutto questo?
Nel caso desideraste avere informazioni piu dettagliate, richiedete una copia gratuita della Relazione annuale al 31 marzo 1968 del Reed Paper Group. Vi troverete il completo quadro finanziario di una delle società piú grandi, solide ed in rapido sviluppo del mondo.

Spett. Reed,
Prego inviarmi copia della Vs. Relazione annuale.

Nome _____

Titolo _____

Indirizzo _____

Spedire a:
Reed Paper Group Limited,
Reed House, 82 Piccadilly,
London, W.I.A 1EJ, Inghilterra.

Reed

Quizz:

Was wissen Sie über die Reed Paper Group?

Gleich zu Anfang: das Wort "Paper" (Papier) ist irreführend.

Selbstverständlich stellen wir Papier her, sogar eine ganze Menge.

Aber außerdem produzieren und verkaufen wir auch noch vieles andere.

● Mit welchen dieser Dinge hat Reed ihrer Meinung nach etwas zu tun?

Mit

Schreib- und Papierwaren	Einzelhandelsläden
Booten	Entwässerungsanlagen
Computer-Bändern	Farben
Kopierpapier	Keramik-Kacheln
Zeitungspapier	Lithografie
Pinseln	Chemikalien
Karton	Kunststoffen
Fernschreibbändern	Spritzguß
Müllbeuteln	Papierhandel
Tapeten	Baumaterial
Einrichtungsstoffen	Wellblechbehältern

ANTWORT: Mit allen! Und noch mit vielen mehr.

● In welchem Jahr wurde die Reed Paper Group gegründet?

ANTWORT: 1903

● In wieviel verschiedenen Ländern hat die Reed Paper Group Interessenten?
(a) 15 (b) 21 (c) 36 (d) 40

ANTWORT: Uber: 40

● In welchen dieser Länder hat die Reed Paper Group augenblicklich *keine* Interessenten?

(a)	Großbritannien	(h)	Kenia
(b)	Singapur	(i)	Niederlande
(c)	Norwegen	(j)	Irland
(d)	Kanada	(k)	USA
(e)	Australien	(l)	Deutschland
(f)	Belgien	(m)	Neuseeland
(g)	Frankreich		

ANTWORT: In allen diesen Ländern und drei ihr wicteren hat sie Interessenten.

● Wieviele Leute sind in der ganzen Welt bei der Reed Paper Group beschäftigt?
(a) 10.000 (b) 17.000 (c) 28.000 (d) 52.000

ANTWORT: 52.000

● Der Handelsprofit letztes Jahr vor der Entwertung betrug:
(a) £6.700.000 (b) £17.800.000 (c) £21.400.000 (d) £28.900.000

ANTWORT: £25.900.000.

● Welche war die erste Firma in Großbritannien, die von der Industriellen Reorganisations-Korporation der britischen Regierung eine Anleihe erhielt, mit der die Firma eine ihrer neuen industriellen Techniken entwickeln konnte?

ANTWORT: Die Reed Paper Group (Sie erhielt eine Anleihe von £1,5 Millionen).

● Der Umsatz der Reed Paper Group betrug 1967-68:
(a) £12.000.000 (b) £80.700.000 (c) £159.600.000 (d) £249.500.000

ANTWORT: £249.500.000

Nun, wieviel wußten Sie über uns? Für den Fall, daß Sie mehr über uns wissen wollen, lassen Sie sich doch ein kostenloses Exemplar des Jahresberichts der Reed Paper Group Limited, schicken der mit dem 31. März 1968 endet. Er informiert Sie ausführlich über die finanziellen Daten einer der größten, leistungsfähigsten und am schnellsten wachsenden Firmen in der Welt.

Sehr geehrte Herren!
bitte schicken Sie mir ein Exemplar ihres Jahresberichts.

Mein Name _____

Beruf _____

Adresse _____

_____

_____

Reed

An: Reed Paper Group Limited,
Reed House, 82 Piccadilly,
London, W1A 1EJ England

A London bus—a brand-new financial advertising and public relations medium, dreamt up by the Financial Press Information Services for their client, Silexine Paints, with tremendous success.

A copy of this Prospectus, having attached thereto the documents specified herein, has been delivered to the Registrar of Companies for registration.

THE ASTON VILLA FOOTBALL CLUB LIMITED

(Incorporated under the Companies Act 1862)

(A member of The Football Association, Limited)

BUY SHARES IN ASTON VILLA AT £5 EACH TO HELP THE

CLUB REGAIN ITS FORMER GLORY

AS A SHAREHOLDER YOU WILL

● Be a part of Aston Villa

● Share in the Club's success

● Have a say in the Club's affairs

● Be entitled to a Season Ticket at 5% discount

● Be able to speak and vote at meetings

DO NOT DELAY

COMPLETE THE APPLICATION FORM BELOW AND POST IT

TODAY

BECOME A SHAREHOLDER AND JOIN MR DOCHERTY IN HAVING A SAY IN ASTON VILLA'S AFFAIRS

Probably the first time a cartoon has appeared on a prospectus—the going public document produced by Aston Villa Football Club in March 1969.

The one-and-a-half page prospectus for **KMPH Limited**, which was the first to include visual references to a company's activities. Like most of KMPH's activities, it proved yet another pace-setter.

KMPH Limited Continued

Accountants' Report

Date fixed for hearing on pharmaceuticals

FINANCIAL TIMES REPORTER

Non-ethical

Special group to tackle metric legal tangles

BY HAROLD BOLTER

ANNUAL STATEMENTS—Continued

BIBBY & BARON (HOLDINGS) LIMITED

INCREASED PROFITS AND TURNOVER

MR. H. CECIL WILD ON THE PAPER AND PACKAGING TRADES

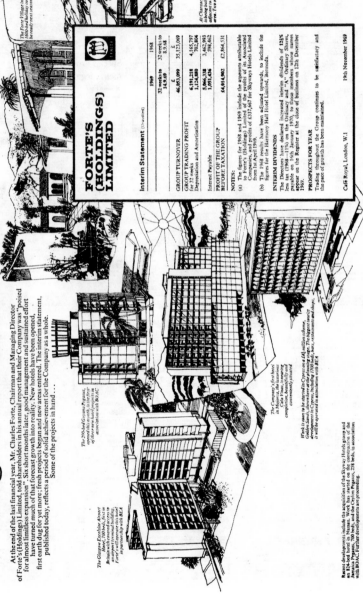

Our Chairman tells a tasty story

Phillip Kaye, Chairman of the Golden Egg Group serves up his tasty Report and Accounts at today's AGM. A delicious £517,000 profit including a beefy contribution from the Angus Steak Houses Ltd. The taste of things to come from an expanding hotels division. A profitable froth from the Shorts pub developments and a spicy tale from the speciality restaurants. A Golden Egg share has just about trebled in value since issue in 1964. The Chairman wishes shareholders, customers, suppliers and staff a Happy and Golden New Year.

THE GOLDEN EGG GROUP LTD. Streamline Hotels Limited, Shorts Limited, Angus Steak Houses Limited, The Golden Egg Restaurants Limited, Tennessee Pancake Houses Limited, La Dolce Vita Limited, Mumtaz Indian Restaurants Limited. Copies of the Report and Accounts are available on request from the Secretary. Victory House, Leicester Square, WC2.

WARNER HOLIDAYS

The Chairman reports profits for the year ended March 31st, 1969

1968	1969
£270,000	£430,000

"We are opening our new overseas hotel in Majorca for June 1970. We hope to see you there."

WARNER
HOLIDAYS
LTD.
51 Havant,
Hants.

Please send your
MAJORCA BROCHURE

Mr/Mrs/Miss..................................

Address ....

....

ME HOLDINGS
IMITED
June, 1969

Sex in financial advertising. Warner Holidays multi-purpose Chairman's Statement, hotel launch and brochure request advertisement and the more sophisticated and more conventional annual statement from George Spencer Limited.

George Spencer Group

Vedonis knitwear and underwear

The forty-first annual general meeting was held on 30th January in Nottingham.

	Year Ended 19th September	
	1969	1968
	£	£
Group Turnover	5,234,332	4,596,460
Profit before Tax	531,705	410,374
Taxation	237,584	168,268
Profit after Tax	294,121	242,106
Dividends for year 25% (22½%)	117,429	108,237
Profit retained	176,692	133,869

Mr. George H. Spencer reports a record achievement.

PROFIT: Net profit before tax has increased from £410,000 in 1968 to £531,000, the highest ever achieved by the Group. Taxation takes £237,000 and dividends £117,000.

SALES: Generally, throughout the year, activity remained at a high level. Sales to outside customers reached a record figure of £5,234,000 and, in addition, a great deal of internal activity among the various Companies within the Group has taken place.

EXPORTS: Goods exported totalled £165,000, an increase of £95,000 over 1968. Exporting entails a great deal of hard, unremitting work, not only in the securement of the orders but in their execution which is not helped by the frustration of dock strikes, pilfering and the like. However, we have made—and are making—special efforts to increase our export sales and we are confident that these will become an increasing feature of our business.

TRADING: The improved activity and profits were not easily obtained. Competition was, if anything, keener than ever, whilst there was an insufficiency of labour to cope with the demand for our merchandise and services. Few, if any, of our costs remained static during the year and most items showed a persistent increase. However, as the Group operates on a wide basis in the textile field, it is able, with its useful spread, to deploy and efficiently use its resources to the best advantage and to develop and promote the most profitable sectors.

OUTLOOK: The Group's plant, machinery and buildings are not only being kept up to date but expanded to meet the demand for our products and services. The present economic climate does show a temporary downturn in many consumer goods but our Group is rich in both human and material resources and, with our forward programme, I have every confidence in our long term prospects.

Copies of the Report available on request from the Secretary
GEORGE SPENCER LIMITED, BASFORD, NOTTINGHAM.

Financial news is never dull—although some financial news is more exciting than others. Some examples of some recent more lively financial reports.

Don't say down —say Bovis

THIS year it has not been nearly as easy to pick winners on the stock market as it was in 1968. From a starting level of 506.4 the Financial Times index has now dropped 103 points—around 20%—taking many of the favourites with it.

A section that has been out of favour is the one dealing with the building and construction industry. This is mainly because of the adverse effect the credit squeeze has had on companies under this heading.

The index referring to this area of the market has fallen nearly 14% this year and only a handful of firms managed to stay within striking distance of their " peaks."

Bovis Holdings is one of the few. Its present price is only fractionally below a high for the year of 47s. and at this level the gain on the year is a handsome 27%.

Throughout the year there has been a flow of gloomy reports from building concerns about a fall off in orders and cutbacks brought about by the harsh credit squeeze.

But Bovis has moved against the national trend. Forward order books and work programmes have increased substantially so much so that the chairman has forecast profits of more than £1,700,000 for 1969, a minimum increase of 50% on last year

This follows a 72% rise in profits in 1967 and a gain of 50% in 1968.

One aspect of the company—best known as the group which looks after the building needs of the Marks and Spencer stores group—that appears to hold a great deal of potential is management contracts.

These are operated on the basis of one company, for a fee, supervising the whole of a particular project including the handling of sub-contracts.

At the moment Bovis has a management contract for the new £6,000,000 Players cigarette factory at Nottingham.

More City Page 6

THE MONEY IN BUNNIES

by City Editor David Malbert

WHEN THEY BUILT the Playboy Club in Park Lane for about £1,500,000 3½ years ago, plenty of people said it was going to be a white elephant—or perhaps rabbit was the word.

The British, they muttered, were not interested in such titillations, preferring the more earthy fare available in Soho.

But enough money is, in fact, being made at the Playboy to set all fluffy tails wagging.

Mr Victor Lownes, European boss of the Hugh Hefner club and magazine empire based in Chicago, has been telling me the financial facts of Playboy life.

Members and their guests sent the pre-tax profits soaring from £374,885 to a record £831,313 in the year to last August.

The money flowed in even faster in the first four months of the current year with the figures leaping from £251,554 to £522,274.

Lownes, who was one of the founding fathers of the group, proudly says that the London operation is the best money spinner of the 20 clubs.

He gave me this break-down of where the money came from in the year to last August.

In the bag

Top of the list was gaming which pulled a golden stream of £857,000, just over half of the total gross income of £1,671,000.

Some £330,000 of drink was sold and £190,000-worth of food. Members paid £145,000 in fees and £102,000 on entertainment.

Lownes has just won the Gaming Board's approval to apply for a new gaming licence. He believes this means it is in the bag.

In fact, he is now running his eyes over several sites in Manchester and if he can again please the Gaming Board will open his second British operation there.

If that fails he is toying with the idea of setting up a chain of restaurants and nightclubs.

A new Bunny Club is planned for Rome and an hotel and

> The British bunny warren is 100 per cent. owned by the American company but its shares are held by four trustees—Lord Hirshfield, founder and chairman of the Trades Union Unit Trust, Clement Freud, Arnold Finer and Lownes.

holiday resort is to be built in Spain.

The Playboy empire was started in 1953 by Hefner, then a young cartoonist with 600 dollars he borrowed.

The magazine was still struggling when Victor Lownes left his family firm of industrial time lock manufacturers and joined him.

Today Hefner and Lownes are both millionaires. Lownes tells me he paid about six cents for each of his shares in the privately-owned empire. The last time the shares changed hands about a year ago the price was 60 dollars.

Safe

Lownes, a handsome 41, has a job many Playboy readers dream of. Apart from being surrounded by all those beautiful bunnies, he drives an Aston Martin DB5, has a company Rolls, owns a house in Connaught Square and a villa in Spain.

Any ideas that he had about floating the British operation on the Stock Exchange have been cast aside now the gaming licence is safe.

And Hefner has no intention of letting the public into his U.S. master company. "If he did I would be a much richer man," said Lownes with a grin.

Goldsmith's plan

Emperor Jones...

In week when a million was added to shares

Tom Jones relaxes, Napoleonic-cum-Hollywood-style...the man everybody loves

LIFE has never been better for Welsh singer Tom Jones. America loves him . . . his fans love him . . . even the Stock Exchange loves him.

Dealings in the shares of the company which looks after him added a million pounds to the value of the stock on Monday.

Tom is now in America, making the world's most expensive TV series, "This Is . . . Tom Jones."

Suitable

He has rented a house in Beverly Hills suitable to his eminent position in showbiz.

It belongs to actor Paul Newman, and has all the usual luxurious appointments without which Hollywood living, it seems, is impossible.

Including a remarkably large and ornate bed, which gives the 29-year-old singer from Pontypridd a rather Napoleonic air.

Loose tiles restored

Back in 1965 **Pilkington's Tiles** was paying a dividend of 22½ per cent. It was cut by 10 points the following year and remained at 12½ per cent for the next three years. But in response to some outstandingly good results for the year to September 30, 1969, the board is doubling the distribution to 25 per cent and adding a one-for-one scrip issue. The 10s shares are also to be sub-divided into 5s units.

Profits for 1968-69 were 57 per cent higher at £512,000 and the increase improves to 64 per cent if devaluation benefits in the previous year are ignored. As profits were 43 per cent higher in the first six months, there has been a 68 per cent improvement in the summer months.

Pilkington's has a useful trade in the do-it-yourself market, which lends welcome support when the building industry is in the dumps, but the big surge in profits owes less to a growth in trade than to more efficient working. Sales were only 10 per cent up at £6.2m, but margins have strengthened from 5.8 per cent to 8.2 per cent.

Undoubtedly the results have been assisted by steps taken in the previous year to deal with uneconomic working at Carter Panels and Art Pavements and Decorations. The former has been wound up and the latter has been absorbed into Carter London to tighten efficiency.

Earnings come out at 63.2 per cent, which puts the shares on a PE ratio of 11.9 at 75s 6d, after a rise of 3s 6d on the news. A year ago, when the shares stood at 39s 6d, we said that there should be something to go for this year. Despite the big rise that has taken place since then, we see no reason to take a profit. Pilkington's performance in a difficult year promises much when building takes off again.

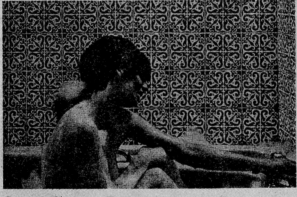

Sena Sugar Estates

Is a 9½ per cent yield for the shares of **Sena Sugar Estates** fully commensurate with the risks attached to such an operation? If an optimistic assessment of the stability of this Portuguese territory is made then the current price of 9s for the 10s shares, where the PE ratio is exactly 7½, could have sunk too low from the 1969-70 high of 14s 6d. On the

ever the verdict, the shares remain an interesting speculation.

The present setback to the share price, down by 1s 6d last week, follows the announcement that estimated profits for the year to end-December will be 64 per cent lower at £1.1m. Calculated on the same ‥‥tio as the p‥‥s period ‥‥re

One of the main problem the last year has been the fal from the previous record of to 139 tons. This reduction to the fact that the ratio of sugar was 9.3 tons of sugar ton of sugar compared with age of 8.6 in the previous t Meanwhile the amount of s fined in Portugal at the sul refinery was much the same tons. There are at this stage mates given for the curre prospects but one point in th favour is that its crop is so protected markets of Portug colonies and is thus largely the fluctuations of world su

Electro-Hydrau suffering from Jetstream upse

After announcing halfway £178,000, the directors of **Hydraulics**, maker of fork-l and hydraulic components, 60 per cent owned by Rube predicted at least the same second half, making a total profit of £356,000, compar the previous year's figure of (excluding a credit of £128 balance of overheads and p settlement of a cancellatior In fact the pre-tax profit of which includes a previous ye of £30,000, is 32 per cent the estimate.

The difficulties of the se are attributable to a greater of margins than anticipat setback in the production carriage and hydraulic equ the *Jetstream*, following th ment of a Receiver to Han

Electro-Hydraulics has p full for the trade debt of £1(from Handley Page, leaving profit of only £81,000 and e only £12,000. However, this i apparent tax charge of 80 which, presumably, is o because of the provision for ba If a straight 45 per cent ded made earnings come to 2.6 However, if the exceptional is added back and tax de 45 per cent, earnings are 8.9 and the PE ratio 15.8 with at 6s 9d. This looks high en the cr‥ m‥ ‥an give a full‥

You too can get a piece of this action

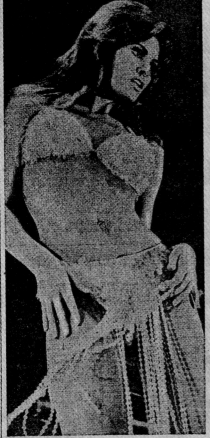

RAQUEL WELCH—an investment attraction

HOW would you like to own a piece— unquantified of course—of sex symbol Raquel Welch or if that, looking at the picture on the left, is too much what about Natalie Wood, Joanna Woodward, Mia Farrow, Gina Lollobrigida, or Barbra Streisand?

Not surprisingly there is no lack of takers for this amazing opportunity, even if it is restricted more mundanely to a slice of the high-powered earnings of these and a myriad other super-stars.

And the rush has already started professional investors in London and Wall Street hot-foot after shares in an until now little known American company called Creative Management Associates.

For C.M.A. is *THE* " Mr. Ten Percent " of show business, acting as agent for close to three-quarters of the biggest Hollywood, Broadway and Tin Pan Alley names.

Last week the company's brokers were in London drumming up interest in the stock and have created a large amount of buying power.

Already two major "go-go" unit trusts have gone in, while some leading merchant banks are showing keen interest on behalf of their investment clients, despite having to pay the 25% dollar premium.

As a result of this, and a mirrored amount of activity on Wall Street, shares in C.M.A. have shot up in the last few days from 75s. to 125s., pricing the group at £6 million plus.

C.M.A. has been in business for many years but has only started to catch the eye following a change in management some 18 months ago.

This brought in a group of top managers and agents led by

Paul Newman

Freddie Fields, manager to Peter Sellers and Rock Hudson, and ex-Columbia Pictures man Sid Cohn.

The directors own a big slice of the C.M.A. shares while another large block is held by a group of Canadian institutional investors.

And they have embarked on a major expansion plan based on signing up big stars on one year sole agency contracts covering films, TV, records, theatre and cabaret performances.

At the ——— ——— ast year C.M.A. has no ——— that the stars will ——— ontract, but a ———

IP C MERGER: **Scotch sales**

——TH SIDES ——— slipping

——FE

You too can get a piece of this action

Special sales

meeting and rambling over the events of the year. Almost a cross between a headmaster's speech at Open Day and the Queen's Christmas message. During the war, companies began to circulate it with the report and accounts. The practice caught on. It became formalised. And now practically every company under the sun has its chairman's statement.

It is either included in the annual report itself like Reckitt and Colman, IPC, Baker Perkins, Vickers or United Biscuits or it is left and given as a speech at the annual meeting like ICI, Courtaulds and Rolls-Royce. A few companies do both. Selection Trust, for example. Chairman, Mr A. Chester Beatty, wrote a 1,500-word message for the annual report and then gave a 3,000-word speech at the annual meeting on 17 July 1969 as well. But this is unusual. Each method has its advantages By including it with the annual report itself, the chairman's statement can provide, as the Society of Investment Analysts says, 'an interesting verbal alternative to the accounts for the benefit of those who cannot cope with figures'. An important point to bear in mind if there is a wide range of shareholders in a company. Says Jones, 'The value of the chairman's statement is a medium to amplify the accounts and notes on the accounts cannot be stressed too strongly'.

From the publicity point of view, however, it might be better to omit the statement from the annual report and let the chairman have his say at the annual meeting. Bearing in mind the length of time it takes to prepare an annual report, its unlikely that any statement by the chairman will still be newsworthy by the time the report is distributed to shareholders. The chances of getting any publicity out of the statement, as opposed to the report itself, are therefore slight. If, however, the chairman is kept in reserve and allowed to fire his salvo at the annual meeting, the company stands a good chance of not only capturing publicity with the report but with the chairman's statement as well. It also means a double opportunity for impressing shareholders. By including the statement with the report, the company has only one mailing. By splitting them in two, the company has two mailings: first, the report itself and then after the meeting, a copy of the chairman's speech. A company with an enormous shareholding, however, would probably find the cost prohibitive.

In many respects, therefore, preparing the chairman's statement is like walking through a minefield. Even the most flamboyant chairmen baulk at making a 'bullish' statement about profits and prospects. If they can under-play the figures they do. First, because they are unwilling to give hostages to fortune. Second, because they fear the consequences. Reporting a dramatic increase in profits, they fear, will attract competition. Other companies will spot the money to be made and begin moving in. It would also increase the chances of wage claims and perhaps, force a reduction in prices. It would certainly mean more taxes and, most dangerous of all, accustom shareholders to increased dividends, which might prove impossible to match in following years.

L

Ace journalist Hugh Cudlipp, now Chairman of the giant International
Publishing Corporation, for example, began his 1969 statement:

'Your board, during my first year as Chairman, has carried out an
intensive review of the Corporation's operations and resources and has
agreed upon its short-term and long-term intentions, some of which for
good commercial reasons cannot yet be announced. . . . The immediate
future presents major challenges and opportunities, particularly in the
area of loss-making and low-yield operations and the level of return on
our substantial resources.'

Turgid, clichéd and, in some places, quite meaningless. Not surprisingly
Cudlipp was called to order over the report at the annual meeting on 17 July
1969. 'It is not exactly hogwash, but it is tautological and verbose', said a young
man in black spectacles near the front of the meeting. 'Knowing your journalistic style, I am surprised to find you using post-Einsteinian Marxist-Leninist
phraseology.' But Cudlipp is certainly not the worst offender. The prize goes
to Sir Basil Goulding, Chairman of the fertiliser-to-jewellery Goulding
Group. Witness the start of his 1969 report:

'The balance sheet exemplifies in almost Disney fashion how you can
apparently get wealthier as you expend; despite our drab net earnings
and our overspending of them on dividend you may observe that the
net current assets have risen. . . . This kind of contradiction, which so
baffles bunnies, is airborne by the magic carpet of cash flow. . . . The
company finds itself well able to motorise a good diversification project,
even of scale should it be confidently evaluated as bosker.'

The more he continued, the worse it got. Jewellery, for example, became
'our own native stones, the literally downtrodden runestones, found to hold
glories hitherto unfolded'. Pre-tax profits of £340,000 did not simply become
£10,000 after tax and minority interests. 'But lo! this tolerable sum was
almost wholly devoured by taxation provisions and by minority interests so
that only £10,000 survives', said the chairman. Generally one would 'expect
to find that the scum of overheads has been much diluted, allowing the
profit to bubble through merrily', he continued. But, unfortunately, high
costs and too low prices had 'entered burglariously upon our premises'.

Suffice it to say that Goulding Group is an Irish company.

The ideal style, therefore, should be short, sharp and to the point. People
will read a chairman's statement for facts and relevant comment. If they are
missing, the readers can be counted on one hand.

'I am pleased to report record sales and profits. Group sales totalled
£161,142,000, a rise of 14 per cent on the year. Group profit before tax
increased from £7,901,000 to £9,261,000—a rise of 17 per cent and the
profit attributable to Tilling shareholders was £7,861,000 or 19 per cent
up on 1967.'

(Sir Geoffrey Eley, Chairman of Thomas Tilling Limited in the 1968 Report and Accounts)

'1968 was a year of substantial progress in every section of the business. Sales increased by 24 per cent to £76,700,000, trading profits by 43 per cent to £5,977,000 and profits before tax, after substantially increased interest charges, by 28 per cent to £5,331,000.'

(Lord Craigton, Chairman of United Biscuits (Holdings) Limited, 1968 Annual Report and Accounts)

'With trading profits up by over 50 per cent Vickers had a much better year in 1968, and there was also a significant improvement in the return on capital. Pre-tax profit stood at its highest level since 1963 and return on capital at its highest since 1962.'

(Sir Leslie Rowan, Chairman of Vickers Limited, 1968 Report and Accounts)

The temptation to retreat into platitudes and figures of speech, therefore, should be resisted. A vigorous chairman's statement has immense shareholder appeal.

It gives shareholders a view from the boardroom

The views of the chairman and the directors are important. If they are play-safe merchants, the shareholders have a right to know. Similarly if the board are research- or marketing-orientated. This can come across in the statement.

'You can often judge a man's character and competence by his communications to shareholders', says financial journalist, Margot Naylor. 'Does he spend his time wailing about profit margins being squeezed, rising costs, different export markets and labour problems? Or is he finding new markets and new products which will make better profits for shareholders? Does he regard the company simply as a comfortable source of executive salaries—and labour, customers and shareholders as crosses he has to bear? Or is the company research-minded, skilled in labour relations and respected by credit providers such as banks and trade suppliers? You should ask yourself all these questions when contemplating buying shares in any company.'

It gives shareholders an insight into the industry

Too many chairmen seem to live in ivory offices, judging by their reports. They have plenty to say about their own backyard. But little or nothing about their industry. Which seems odd. For industrial developments and trends are as interesting and as useful in measuring the success of a company as the figures in the individual reports and accounts. Engineering companies, however, are the exception. Chairman of Alenco Limited, a member of the Charterhouse Group, Mr W. R. L. Warnock, for example, found the going hard in the industry generally and said so in his 1967 report.

'The past two years have not been easy ones for the engineering industry and Alenco is no exception. Pressures on management and staff at all levels have been and continue to be considerable to achieve changes, mechanical and organisational, necessary to meet intensifying competition now experienced from overseas as well as from within this country.'

Chairman of Alfred Herbert Limited, Mr R. D. Young, made a similar point in his 1968 report.

'We worked hard in the past year to mitigate the effects on workers and shareholders alike, of the unusually long depression in machine-tool demand.'

Mr D. B. LeMare, Chairman of Norwest Construction, made a similar point about the construction industry in his 1969 report. The private housing development companies had a successful year although some reduction in demand was experienced in the second half. Local authority housing contracts were also going to more than offset any decline in private home sales.

It gives shareholders a clue to the relationship between the company and the economy

Again, this is just as important as the relationship between the company and its industry. It's also likely to appeal to chairmen, eager to take a swipe at Government controls and influence, whenever they can. Chairman of GKN, Mr Raymond P. Brookes, for example, described the persisting low percentage of surplus to turnover as disturbing in his 1968 report, reflecting as it did failure to balance ever-increasing wage costs with higher productivity and to contain other endemic widespread inflationary factors. He went on:

'It is imprudent for Government or others to persist in the fallacious belief that these adversities can be indefinitely offset by management ingenuity and sinew, technological innovation and capital expenditure. These resources are not inexhaustible.'

Sir Geoffrey Eley, Chairman of Thomas Tilling, went a stage further and gave the general national economic background to the whole year's operation in his 1968 report.

'The year began in the sharp shadow of devaluation and under the threat of further measures to restrain the economy. At first the trading pattern of the Group was mixed. Some companies serving the capital goods industries found themselves in an unhelpful climate with orders difficult to obtain, whilst others linked to consumer demand enjoyed a minor boom as customers rushed to buy before prices went up. During this time we continued to make every effort to increase, wherever possible, exports and to tighten efficiency throughout the Group to meet the challenges in the home market. The budget brought additional taxes, and trading in Great Britain inevitably became harder. At the half year whilst we were able to report good figures, it seemed that some slowing down in the growth of profits during the second half might have to be anticipated, especially in the light of the temporary effect of exceptional revenue expenditure designed to increase the long term profits of our Volkswagen distribution network. In November fresh difficulties arose in the international monetary field and the Government felt itself forced still further to raise indirect taxes; to intensify the credit squeeze; and to introduce the Import Deposits Scheme.'

This kind of economic panorama is useful for investors. It enables them to jud ge how much the company is affected by national policy.

It gives shareholders the opportunity of hearing additional information about the company which could not be slotted into any other place in the report
John Davis, Chairman of the Rank Organisation, used his annual report, out September 1969, to release additional information about Rank's proposed bid for De La Rue, the reference to the Monopolies Commission and the subsequent banning of the takeover by President of the Board of Trade, Anthony Crosland. Crosland's announcement on 2 June that he intended to stop Rank's offer was made without giving the Rank board an opportunity of reading the commission's report or discussing its contents, he said. The principal reason for the decision was that a number of De La Rue executives would have resigned if the merger had gone through. 'It is well known and accepted as reasonable that in the heat of a contested bid the executives of a company for which a bid is being made support their own board', said Davis. 'But we can hardly believe that if the merger had gone through the executives would not have continued to support their company. The report suggests that a Government-appointed body can make wiser decisions on highly complex financial matters than the owners of the business.'

Sir Leslie Rowan used his 1968 statement to Vickers shareholders to give his side of the Barrow strike, which hit the headlines and led to a Court of Inquiry headed by Sir Jack Scamp.

'In view of the national interest aroused by the Barrow strike, I should perhaps make it clear that a close examination of industrial relations in the Vickers Group shows an outstandingly good record. Until the 1968 strike Barrow had experienced no major stoppage for many years. In the rest of the Group the annual average of working days lost per 1,000 workers during the five-years 1964–68 was 15—less than one-seventh of the average for the United Kingdom.'

Chairman of Selection Trust, Mr A. Chester Beatty, used his 1969 annual statement to stress how much the company relied on the men in the field and to explain their 'field participation scheme'.

'Exploration has always been a major point of policy in this company's history, and so has the principle that those who contribute to success in that field should share in the benefits produced. . . . Firstly, I do not think one can adequately reward a man, by orthodox means, for working for months on end in temperatures of 30 or 40 degrees below zero or above 100 degrees fahrenheit, separated from his family and, in many cases, from any civilised community. Secondly, there are obvious economic limitations on the amount of salary payable to such field men, because their work is not productive in the ordinary commercial sense of the word for possibly very long periods of time. Thirdly, since it is not practical, from an economic point of view, to pay salaries which take account of hardship, it is essential to provide an incentive which enables a man to identify himself very personally with the team effort which is necessary to bring results in the unusually demanding, and often disappointing, work of field exploration.'

Selection Trust, therefore, were planning to put their present scheme, which sets aside 5 per cent participation in any potential mining development resulting from the work of the exploration team, on a global basis. So that field staff operating anywhere in the world would have the chance of participating in the success of their colleagues working elsewhere.

8.4.7 DIFFERENT ASPECTS OF COMPANY AFFAIRS IN CHAIRMAN'S REPORT
There are seven different aspects of a company's affairs which should also be included in every chairman's report, although they will probably be of more interest to the investment public, generally, than to individual shareholders.

Progress
Has the company's progress during the year been good, bad or indifferent? The chairman should say so. Gross revenue, profit, earnings per share, dividend should be spelt out together with comparisons with previous years. Its no good saying sales were at their highest level. If 'the highest level' means a mere one per cent jump over the previous year. Similarly the statement should assess the various market shares held by the company's products and give some indication whether they are increasing or not.

Lord Craigton gave a copybook report on progress in the 1968 United Biscuits statement. After referring to the 'substantial progress' achieved during the year, he spelt out the percentage increases in sales, trading profits and profits before tax. He then went a stage further and reported that earnings per ordinary share had increased also from 2s 1d to 2s 6d and covered the dividend 1·9 times. Precisely the kind of information that interests both the professional investor and the potential investor.

Internal reasons for progress
If the company launched a new product and captured 90 per cent of the market

in one fell swoop, it should say so. The chairman should also give the promotional expenditure which helped to catapult the product into the position as well. Similarly if new production machinery has been installed; a new factory opened or just an efficiency drive, the shareholder is entitled to know. The chairman also should report on any over-all rationalisation moves made during the year as well as outlining their benefits.

Chairman of the Reed Group, Mr S. T. Ryder, for example, outlined the steps they were taking to boost their production capacity for packaging boards in the United Kingdom in his 1968 report. The major conversion of one of their large machines had been completed in the second half in 1967.

'The test jute liner made on this machine is based on the re-use of specially sorted wastepapers and a product of high quality is now being produced at rates in excess of our expectations. This machine gives us a greater potential for import savings through the availability of a first-class product competitive with imported materials.'

But then, Ryder was a journalist. So, of course, was Mr R. P. T. Gibson, Chairman of S. Pearson Publishers, who really went into detail discussing Westminster Press in his 1968 report.

'The encouraging feature of the increase in advertisement revenues is that it was mainly due to a higher volume of advertising. Indeed, the effect of rate increases during the year accounted for only about 3 per cent of the 19 per cent rise in total advertisement revenues achieved in 1968 in comparison with the previous year. Although higher selling prices have brought increased sales revenues from most daily papers, it was noticeable that these price increases affected circulations more than on previous occasions and daily paper sales were about 3 per cent down on the previous year. However, improved methods of marketing are now being applied to the circulation of our newspapers, and sales generally are responding well.'

External reasons for progress

This is takeover territory. Many companies have grown at a fantastic rate because they have grown by acquisition. The chairman should spell out the details. He should also mention—in outline—whether the company would continue to hit the takeover trail. Sir Geoffrey Eley said in the 1968 Thomas Tilling report, 'Naturally we would hope that our bids for public companies will normally be made in agreement with their Boards; but we do not exclude the possibility of contested takeovers in certain circumstances.' Sir Geoffrey and Tillings, of course, are very open-minded. Few company chairmen would go so far as that. But they should. It pays tremendous dividends in the long-term.

The industrial environment

If the whole industry is on a winning streak, the chairman should explain the reasons and warn readers how long it is likely to last. If, however, things are on the down-turn generally, he should try and explain why. Mr R. D. Young, Chairman of Alfred Herbert, had a different story to tell in his 1968 report. He had to report an 'unusually long depression in machine-tool demand'. But he gave the reasons, as well.

> 'Important sectors of industry needed time to assess the consequence of wholesale re-organisation following mergers. Others have delayed normal spending while studying technological developments and their implications for production methods. The upshot was that the machine-tool industry had to contend not only with the deferment by its customers of their investment in new capacity but also with a continuing reluctance by many even to maintain normal replacement.'

The national environment

This is where many chairmen go to town. They lash out at everything from the Prices and Incomes Board to the Monopolies Commission. They attack Governments and praise the Opposition. Colonel W. H. Whitbread, Chairman of Whitbread, the United Kingdom's third-largest brewery, for example, accused the Government of 'interference' in his 1968 report. He went on to reveal that his company had contributed £20,765 to various Conservative Party associations because 'we believe that this is the least we should do for our shareholders'.

But that's exceptional.

Staff

Everyone from managing directors down to the men on the shop floor. They have all invested their lives with the company. The chairman, therefore, should thank them for their efforts. Admittedly, it can appear patronising. That is no reason for not doing it. Some chairmen manage to express their appreciation in a reasonable, adult fashion. Take Dorland Advertising, for example:

> 'The wider range of services demanded by the advertiser provide, of course, a constant challenge to the staff. We are fortunate in being in a business where the real basis of any organisation's success—the ability and motivation of its employees—is so readily recognisable. And so we would like on behalf of Members, as well as the Board, to thank directors and staff of our subsidiary companies for their excellent efforts over the past year.'

The Hargreaves Group went a stage further. Chairman, Mr Kenneth Hargreaves even congratulated Mr F. A. Robinson on becoming Chairman of the National Council of Coal Traders. 'A post he should fill with distinction', he added.

The future

This is cliché corner. Chairmen are frightened of having their hands tied—let alone tying their own hands. Hence the platitudes. Yet the future is important. The chairman should at least give some indication about the current trend and whether it is on target or not. If he can mention the order-book, so much the better. If not, he should give one or two indications about sales, profit even dividends. Admittedly, he must not be over-cautious. But he should be realistic.

Lord Thomson managed to combine the two in his summing up on the 1968 report of the Thomson Organisation. After stressing that profits for 1969 and the reduced level of development expenditure were both ahead of budget, he added:

> 'This, I am sure you will agree, is a highly satisfactory situation. If our expectations are fulfilled, we shall have more than trebled our profits during the ten years in which I have had the privilege of being your Chairman. This by itself says all that needs to be said about the skill and dedication of the Directors, executives and staff of your Company which have made this possible.'

8.4.8 THE DIRECTORS' REPORT

Before the Companies Act, 1967, the directors' report was barely a note on trading profit and dividend with, perhaps, a comment about the odd board-room re-shuffle. Now, virtually designed for the investment community while the chairman's statement is for the non-specialist, it is the guts of the annual report. The Act lays down a set of twelve requirements for the directors' report. This (see above) covers everything from the principal activities of the company to the average number of employees. Then there are the Stock Exchange's own requirements as well as the obligations accepted by the company in the General Undertaking. A veritable tangle of facts and figures. Yet with ingenuity and a good designer, the information can still be well presented and meaningful.

Albright and Wilson manage to cover everything in just two pages—or 13 paragraphs, some as short as 20 words. Admittedly, it generally refers to another part of the report:

> 'The proposed transfers to and from reserves are set out in the Notes on the balance sheets on page 18.'

Rolls-Royce were a little more expansive. Their 1968 Directors' Report numbered 12 paragraphs and stretched to three pages in a 24-page Report and Accounts. Rio Tinto-Zinc, by comparison, packed their report with a mass of information and covered seven pages while our old friend, Thomas Tilling, went one further and covered eight pages.

Long or short, the essentials that must be covered are as follows.

The principal activities of the company and its subsidiaries during the year as well as any significant changes of activities that occurred during the period
ICI once covered this point in just four paragraphs. So it is possible. Rentokil in their 1968 report, however, followed the Albright and Wilson school and commented tartly: 'The activities of the Group are set out on page 1'.

The British Printing Corporation were more helpful. 'The principal activities of the company and its subsidiary companies are in the general printing field with substantial interests in the allied businesses of publishing, packaging and paper', commented their 1968 report. But that's not all. They broke down the proportion of sales and the contribution to profit on trading for all three activities together with the comparable figures for the previous year. On top of that they gave the inter-Corporation sales as well. Courtaulds were expansive. In 1968 for the first time man-made fibres accounted for more than half the total consumption of fibres by the British textile industry, said their 1968–69 report before launching into details about their own activities during the year. The 1969 report from IPC seemed to demand a definition of the word 'significant'. After saying there were no significant changes in the Corporation's activities during the year, it went on to explain that a new subsidiary had been bought; a 40 per cent stake in the leading Dutch trade and technical publisher had been acquired; similarly a minority interest was taken in a German publishing house; a mail order and gramophone record company had been launched in Australia together with a 50 per cent share taken in an Australian publisher.

The names of directors
This is promotion. Previously this was listed after the notice of meeting. Now they should be in the directors report. Auditors, registrars, bankers and solicitors were all passed over by the Act. But some companies still list them. Albright and Wilson, for example, even include the staff solicitor, Mr P. R. White, as well, although they fail to mention the positions and responsibilities of the board members. Rolls-Royce forget the staff solicitor but list the responsibilities of the board. Many companies also detail directors interests in this section as well. Thus killing two birds with one stone.

Few companies give any real information about their directors. Probably, because they are shy, self-effacing men. Yet there is no reason why brief biographical details as well as job responsibility should not be included. This gives the Investors and Shareholders Association their favourite ploy at annual meetings. One of their representatives gets up and asks what the principal duties of a particular director are. 'It is a disarmingly simple question which almost invariably produces on the face of the Chairman a look of blank amazement and confusion, just as if he does not know', said their October 1969 Newsletter. 'Members might like to try it sometime.' But, of course, there is no reason why companies should not give their directors responsibilities. ICI, in fact goes about as far as it can go. Their 1968 report gave the lot: the executive directors control group membership; the division liaison directorships; the functional and field directorships; the overseas policy group membership and his territorial directorships. IOS Limited (SA), however, beat them in one respect. They included full-page, full-colour photographs of each of their directors.

Any significant changes in the fixed assets of the company or any of its subsidiaries
Again, different companies have different ways of presenting the information. The Hargreaves Group list their fixed assets—land, buildings, mineral leases, etc.; transport vehicles, craft, etc.; plant and equipment—and give two yearly sets of figures. They add a word of caution: 'In the opinion of the Directors, any differences between the market values and the net bank values of the Group's freehold and leasehold properties at 31st March 1969 are not significant for the purposes of these accounts'. Rolls-Royce are crisper. Three sentences cover property and plant; depreciation and negotiations about the sale of assets of minor Canadian businesses.

Details of any share issue as well as the reasons for making it
Alfred Herbert, for example, referred to two additional 'B' Ordinary Shares of £1 each being issued to the Birmingham Small Arms Company in accordance with an agreement between the two companies dated 13 December 1966 at a premium of £59,385, in their 1968 report. Rolls-Royce in the same year mentioned a rights issue of Ordinary shares involving an increase of £9,568,718 in the issued share capital of the company; a further £495,583 Ordinary Stock issued as a result of the conversion of £1,126,325 7¾ per cent Convertible Unsecured Loan Stock 1987/92; an issue of £10 million 8¼ per cent Debenture Stock 1990/95; and issues of Workers (1955) Stock, at par to employees amounting to £180,077. Rio Tinto-Zinc detailed the arrangements they had made in 1968 for a Eurodollar bond issue.

Information about any contract with the company in which a director had, either directly or indirectly, an interest
This is unusual. Few directors' reports will have to face this question. If they do, they should give as much relevant information as possible. Any suggestion that the company was trying to conceal any details would be practically guaranteed to make shareholders see red. It is better to be generous.

Any arrangements that had been made to enable directors to acquire shares or debentures
This was the question raised by Chairman, Mr A. Chester Beatty, in the 1969 report of Selection Trust. Shareholders were being asked to approve two share incentive schemes, The Selection Trust Employees Share Trust Scheme and The Selection Trust Share Option Scheme which would enable senior employees of the company, including salaried directors and alternate directors to have a personal interest in the equity of the company. The Directors' Report gave all the information, stressing that the scheme would be restricted to 200,000 shares of 5s each, roughly 1 per cent of the issued capital, subject of course to appropriate adjustments in the event of capitalisation issues or other capital re-organisations.

The number of shares and debentures in the company and its subsidiaries held by directors
Some companies include this information with the list of directors mentioned above. Either way, its quite straightforward. The beneficial interest of each director should be listed together with any holding he controls as a trustee. Corresponding figures for the previous year should then be given as well. But beware. This can be a sensitive spot for shareholders particularly if directors begin selling substantial numbers of their shares. If they do so, therefore, directors should be prepared to give their reasons.

The turnover and profitability or otherwise of different businesses where there are different businesses involved
Thomas Tilling faced this problem in their 1968 report by giving three annual sets of figures covering building materials; engineering; glassware; insurance; textiles; vehicle distribution; wholesaling and merchandising and their other interests, such as aerosols, printing, publishing and road haulage, all lumped together.

The average number of employees and their wages total for the year
This is the nitty-gritty. In 1968 Reed Group reported 43,000 employees in the United Kingdom with a total annual wages bill of £39·95 million. GKN gave the totals in the entire Group:

United Kingdom			74,969
Overseas	Asia	10,771	
	Australasia	9,156	
	Europe	2,496	
	North America	266	
	Southern Africa	3,158	
			25,847
World total			100,816

But they only gave the aggregate remuneration in the United Kingdom: £82 million. Rentokil, by comparison, was minute. In 1968 the average number of employees working in the United Kingdom was just 2,032. Their total remuneration: £2,407,930.

Political or charitable contributions
More than £250,000 was given to the Conservative Party in 1968 alone, according to the returns disclosed under the Companies Act. The City banking firm, Hill Samuel gave £25,000. Beechams, Dunlop and Hambros Bank gave £20,000 each. Baring Brothers handed over £15,188—an odd amount. Ranks stuck to the £15,000 mark. Joseph Lucas Industries gave £12,000; Brown Shipley Holdings £10,000; Tate and Lyle £7,758 and Taylor Woodrow, the round £7,000. Schweppes and Page Johnson gave £5,000 each. Reyrolle Parsons and Eagle Star Insurance, both £4,000 and Wilmot Breedon Holdings, £3,000. Guest Keen and Nettlefolds seem to hit the jackpot with their £33,431 contribution. A further £2,500 went to Aims of Industry; £1,250 to the Aldnor Trust; and £3,780 to the Economic League. When companies donate any money for political purposes as defined by the Companies Act, 1967, it seems as though they should at least give a reason. GKN, for example, said nothing. It seemed a pity.

Exports—for certain companies
This, of course, is a much more expansive subject. Lord Thomson, for example, in his 1968 report made the point right at the very beginning:

> 'As I have said in previous years, we are not normally regarded as being a major exporting industry; even so, our total revenue in 1968 from the export of newspapers, books and periodicals, and from services provided for overseas customers, amounted to £4,424,623, an increase of 8 per cent over 1967.'

Some companies, however, still play it cool. Reed Group, for example, said flatly in their 1968 report: 'Goods to the value of £9·5 million have been exported by United Kingdom companies during the year'. The Hargreaves Group take the same attitude. 'The value of goods, exported from the United Kingdom during the year was £1,490,835', said their 1969 report. Courtaulds, however, seemed quite pleased with their successes. And made a 'bull' point about exports at the same time in their report the same year:

> 'Record sales of fibres and a contribution of £7·6 million from new subsidiaries were the principal factors in the considerable rise in exports from £50·9 million to £81·6 million. The figures reflect credit on all concerned in the United Kingdom and overseas. For the second

year running Bull Royd Mill, specialists in lightweight men's wear fabrics, received The Queen's Award to Industry for outstanding export achievement. Exports were 96 per cent of Bull Royd Mill's sales.'

The right note. Sufficient information. Shareholders would feel pleased with the success of their company reading that report.

Any other details essential for the understanding of the company—unless it would harm the business
Impossible to be specific. But, obviously, any radical plans or achievements of the company should also be mentioned. It might be rationalisation plans; perhaps, a more active takeover policy or a startling breakthrough on the horizon. Its a difficult position. On the one hand, the company is under an obligation to reveal any such information. But on the other, it must be careful not to harm its reputation or, in the case of a breakthrough, alert its competitors before the time is ripe.

8.4.9 AUDITORS REPORT
'The auditors of a company shall make a report to the members on the accounts examined by them, and on every balance sheet, every profit and loss account and all group accounts laid before the company in general meeting during their tenure of office', says the Companies Act, 1967. Which means auditors should do just that: report that the books have been kept properly. There is no need for all their involved rambling statements. They should simply report that the books have been kept properly:

'In our opinion the accounts comply with the Companies Acts, 1948 and 1967, and give a true and fair view of the state of affairs of the company and, so far as concerns the members, of the state of affairs and profits of the group.'

Auditor's reports, however, can have another important effect. They can help an investor assess the value of the company shares, according to President of the Association of Certified and Corporate Accountants, Mr E. A. Lediard Smith. On 24 November 1969 he told his annual meeting about the clergyman who liked to dabble on the Stock Exchange. Whenever he got an annual report, he would turn to the auditor's certificate. If he could then sing the report to the tune, Crimond—'The Lord's my shepherd, I'll not want . . .'—he would immediately invest in the company's shares. If not, he would pass them by. And it worked. The singing clergyman was able to keep ahead of the Financial Times index.

8.4.10 ACCOUNTS
'The aim is to produce a set of accounts firmly based on the best accounting

practice, fully informative but not too fussy, attractively designed and printed and capable of telling the investment analyst and the institutional investor what they are fairly entitled to know or, at least, of providing them with the data for finding out for themselves. The same accounts must also be intelligible to the old lady in Leamington who owns a handful of shares in the company', said a chartered accountant in the September 1965 issue of the *Stock Exchange Journal.*

Right at the start, two points should be stressed. First, the Period of the Accounts. Even though the accounts cover a year, it might not be the same year for every subsidiary company. Courtaulds, for example, in their 1969 accounts stressed that the period of account covered the year ended 31 March 1969 with two exceptions:

1 Companies whose accounts covered a period of one year ended between 30 September 1968 and 31 January 1969.
2 Companies which had been recently formed or acquired and whose accounts covered periods of more or less than one year ended on or before 31 March 1969.

ICI turned this question of balance sheet dates into a 'bull' point in their 1968 report:

'Owing to seasonal trade or local conditions and to avoid undue delay in the presentation of the Group accounts, it is impracticable for 207 subsidiaries to make up accounts to 31st December. The accounts of such subsidiaries are made up to dates varying from 30th June to 31st October 1968: 195 of them are made up to 30th September or later.'

Second, comparative figures. The Companies Act, 1967, even threatened 'summary conviction to imprisonment for a term not exceeding six months or to a fine not exceeding £200' to drive home the point. Many companies, however, have recognised the value of comparative figures to serious investors and included periods covering as much as ten years in their annual reports. Financial records covering anything up to ten years are becoming more and more common, particularly among investment trusts.

Balance sheet

There are two kinds: the horizontal double-sided balance sheet and the more modern, vertical balance sheet. The horizontal style is the conventional lay out. It is used by companies like Selection Trust, John Harvey and Sons and the British Printing Corporation. Admittedly, it is convenient. Corresponding items can be printed opposite each other. And there is plenty of space for notes and explanations. But it does have one drawback, its difficult to understand. The layman can be baffled.

A typical horizontal balance sheet

Ordinary Share Capital	Current Assets
Reserves	Current liabilities
Ordinary Shareholders' Funds	Net Current liabilities
Preference Share Capital	Fixed Assets
Debenture Stocks	Investments
Loans	Subsidiary Companies

The vertical lay-out, by comparison, is crystal clear. It starts with the capital at the top of the list. Then, by taking everything into account—assets and liabilities—step by step, one can show how the money is employed.

Albright and Wilson, for example, began their 1968 balance sheet by detailing the Sources of Funds. These were Ordinary stockholders; preference stockholders; minority shareholders in subsidiaries; tax equalisation; deferred liabilities to pension funds and borrowed money. Clear and concise. It then detailed the 'Employment of Funds' and gave the fixed assets; unquoted investments; net current assets less, of course, creditors, current taxation and dividends payable. Fisons do a similar thing—with one aid: figures representing deductions are printed in italics.

There are slight variations. Some companies start with current assets then current liabilities plus fixed assets. Others begin with capital employed and then move on to employment of capital. Either way the figures for the preceding year must also be given.

A typical vertical balance sheet

Assets employed	Fixed Assets
	Goodwill
	Interests in associated companies
	Net current Assets
Financed by	Capital and reserves
	Investment Grants
	Deferred taxation
	Loans

Notes to the Balance Sheet
This is the small print. A comprehensive set of notes can turn a jungle of figures into an easy-to-follow exercise. A company should, therefore, devote two pages at least to explaining the accounts to the reader in plain English. Fisons go a stage further. Instead of just giving a note they gave further sets

of accounts in their 1968 report to explain how the balance sheet was composed. The note on Land, Buildings, Plant and Equipment, for example, gave comparable figures for both Fisons Limited and the Group for the freehold; leasehold over 50 years; leasehold for 50 years and under as well as plant and equipment for both the year to June 1967 and June 1968. This was further broken down into:

> Net bank amount as at 1 July
> Expenditure
> Sales and disposals
> Added on revaluation
> Depreciation—charge for the year
>   —adjustment for disposals, etc.
> Net bank amount
> Accumulated depreciation and amounts written off
> Valuation 30 June 1968
> Valuation 30 June 1959
> Cost at 30 June 1948

Clearly, this is preferable to a meaningless sentence or, worse still, nothing at all.

Share capital
This is straightforward:

Issued
3,524,917 Cumulative 5% Preference stock units of £1 each
65,517,897 Ordinary stock units of 5s each

Unissued
382,435 Ordinary shares of 5s each

AUTHORISED SHARE CAPITAL

In some cases details of share options should also be given.

Reserves
This can range from a simple two-line statement of the revaluation of a subsidiary, for example, as well as the figure for retained profit. ICI, however, give eight different sets of figures: reserves at the beginning of the year; profit of the year retained in the business; share premiums received; losses less profits on disposal of investments and fixed assets; miscellaneous capital receipts (less tax); deferred overseas taxation adjustments; changes in percentage holdings and other adjustments; and, of course, reserves at the end of the year. Albright and Wilson go further still, including information on overseas government grants, provision of terminal losses on the closure of a particular works and so on.

Taxation

GKN give three sets of figures: United Kingdom Corporation Tax on current year's profits; other United Kingdom taxation; and overseas taxation. ICI, however, split the taxation figures in two. The first details United Kingdom Corporation Tax less double taxation relief and less the amount deferred due to accelerated capital allowances. The second merely gives the overseas tax together with the corresponding amount deferred due to accelerated capital allowances.

Fixed assets

The most detailed information on fixed assets is given by ICI. First, they divide them in two: land and buidings; and plant etc. Each group is then further divided into cost or as revalued; depreciation and, of course, the net bank value. But in doing this they also give: the figures for the beginning of the year; new subsidiaries; capital expenditure; sales; demolitions, etc.; and depreciation. On top of that come the dates of different revaluations and the value of freeholds as well as both the long and short term leases.

Investments

Some companies have massive investments in other groups. Rio Tinto-Zinc, for example, have major investments in Rhokana Corporation, British Petroleum, Cia Esp de Minas de Rio Tinto and Le Nickel SA among others. The Reed Group have a share in the Canadian Prince George Pulp and Paper company as well as International Pulp, the New Zealand Tasman Pulp and Paper company and the British Kimberly-Clark. When it comes to presenting the information in the annual report some companies merely detail the bank value and the market value of the investments. Others give the gross income receivable for the year; the share of profit and loss for both the past year and the previous one as well as—in a few cases—the cumulative retained profit. Then, of course, come the unquoted investments. Again, in some cases the straight figure is given. Alternatively, it can be broken down into cost less amounts written off and script issues giving the bank value.

ICI go a step further. They give the income before taxation of investments in unquoted equity shares as included in the previous year's accounts; their share of aggregate profits less the losses before taxation and after taxation in the latest accounts received; their share of the aggregate undistributed profits less the losses since acquisition and, finally, the aggregate amounts provided by ICI in respect of such losses. This meets the demands of the Companies Act, 1967, on shareholdings and subsidiaries.

Stocks and work in progress

Any reference to stocks should include the basis of valuation. This is generally cost or net sales value—whichever is lower. GKN commented in their 1968 report: 'Stocks have been consistently valued at the beginning and end of the year at the lower of Group cost and net realisable value'. Courtaulds, the same year, added the helpful statement: 'Cost includes factory overheads'.

Interests in subsidiaries
Once again the Companies Act, 1967, has drawn back the curtain. 'Where, at the end of its financial year, a company has subsidiaries, there shall, in the case of each subsidiary, be stated in, or in a note on, or statement annexed to, the company's accounts laid before it in general meeting: (*a*) the subsidiary's name; (*b*) if it be incorporated in Great Britain and if it be registered in England and the company be registered in Scotland (or vice versa), the country in which it is registered, and if it be incorporated outside Great Britain, the country in which it is incorporated; and (*c*) in relation to shares of each class of subsidiary held by the company, the identity of the class and the proportion of the nominal value of the issued shares of that class represented by the shares held', it says.

If a group consists of a large number of companies, this can be a headache. In some cases, they might be allowed just to list the companies which contributed to the bulk of profit, loss or assets. If not, they should all be listed across a number of pages in the report. Courtaulds, for example, not only give the names of their major subsidiaries, their main trading activities but their share of both the ordinary and preference capital as well. Then they give similar information about their principal associated companies. Some companies make a virtue out of the necessity and refer to the chief executives, the locations, products and so on.

Contingent liabilities
Again, one can give the uncalled share capital of certain associated companies; the undertakings to subscribe for or purchase shares and bank and other guarantees and liabilities on negotiated bills or one can give even more information. ICI's 1968 report went into detail about contracts, expenditure sanctioned but not yet contracted, the eight annual instalments they were committed to pay to the Workers Pension Fund and the seven instalments to the Staff Pension Fund.

Profit and loss account
Here the vertical form is king. It starts with turnover—an essential, thanks to the 1967 Act—then trading profit and other forms of income such as investment income. Taxation and depreciation allowance are then subtracted giving the final dividend and reserves allocation. Beware. There are problems. It's not only necessary to give the turnover nowadays. The company must also explain how they arrived at the figure, whether the figure includes any internal sales, purchase tax or excise duty. It's even more detailed if a company operates outside the United Kingdom. In that case, the Stock Exchange also insists on a geographical breakdown in either figures or percentages as well.

Similarly taxation. Both United Kingdom tax and overseas taxation must also be included.

A typical profit and loss account

TURNOVER
TRADING PROFIT
        after charging: Depreciation of fixed assets
                        Bank finance charges
                        Auditors' remuneration
                        Pensions and contributions to Pension Fund
                        Hire of plant and equipment
      Investment income (gross)
                        Associated companies
                        Other investments
      Debenture and Loan interest
GROUP PROFIT BEFORE TAXATION
    Taxation on profits for the year
    Net profit attributable to outside interests in subsidiaries
NET PROFIT ATTRIBUTABLE TO PARENT COMPANY
    Preference dividend (gross)
PROFIT ACCRUING TO THE ORDINARY CAPITAL
    Ordinary dividends
PROFIT RETAINED IN THE BUSINESS

Some companies go even further and include an operating account in the profit and loss account as well. This covers sales expenses, advertising, research, everything that makes a business tick.

Notes to the profit and loss account
Again the 'child's guide' to the figures.

Turnover
This represents the sales by group companies to external companies. Ideally it should be divided into home trade and exports—less sales to overseas subsidiaries—overseas subsidiaries sales. This should then be divided on a geographical basis as well as in product groups. A few companies which do this hammer home their message by printing the profit alongside the turnover in each case.

Trading profit
First, the deduction. The note on depreciation of fixed assets can either take the form of a short comment or, as in the case of Fisons, a complete breakdown

of their land, buildings, plant and equipment account. Bank finance charges are almost self-explanatory. So is audirors' remuneration. Some companies, however, take this opportunity of also including details of their directors' and senior employees' £10,000-plus remuneration as well. In most cases they merely list the number of directors which fell into a particular salary scale, with corresponding figures for the previous year. ICI go a stage further and list the take-home pay as well. The point is made that if a man is earning around, say £10,000, his take-home pay is £6,400. But if he is earning between £52,000 and £55,000 his take-home pay is still only £10,500 while his tax is £44,500. If a director has waived his rights to any salary or commission, this is the place to mention it. Similarly, any interests held by directors' families in the company. Some companies also list their chief executives here as well.

Group profit before taxation
This is divided in two: United Kingdom and Overseas. United Kingdom taxation covers Corporation Tax less, of course, relief for overseas taxation. Overseas covers the relevant overseas taxes on profits as well as the sum transferred to tax equalisation account in respect of taxation deferred by capital allowances.

Ordinary dividends
For the average reader of annual reports probably the most important paragraph. The interim figures and dates should be given together with the proposed final—and the corresponding figures for the previous year.

8.4.11 EXTRAS
The Companies Act, 1948. The Companies Act, 1967. The General Undertaking. Stock Exchange requirements. They are all forcing companies to reveal more and more. Yet in spite of their enthusiasm for revelation, there are still plenty of other opportunities for taking the investing public into a company's confidence.

Policy
Its a good idea for the company to outline its policy. Thomas Tilling, for example, call themselves a 'family of companies'. This gives readers an insight into management objectives. The International Publishing Corporation, however, went the whole hog in their 1969 report. They devoted a whole page to 'The Purpose and Objectives of IPC', a kind of commercial state of the nation. Their purpose was stiaightforward:

> 'To be a prosperous and expanding international corporation maintaining leadership in our field of business and meeting the reasonable requirements of the public, our shareholders and our employees within the constraints set by the social obligations of our times.'

They then explained what this meant for the three most important groups:

'For the community, a service of news, information, opinion and entertainment of the finest quality and reliability, and the maintenance and defence of the freedom of the press and of communications generally;

'For shareholders, an increasing return on corporate earnings per share;

'For employees, not only increasing earnings but also an opportunity to develop their individual capabilities and to enjoy personal fulfilment in serving the interests of the corporation.'

They had five objectives in the field of business ranging from marketing to the community 'information for instruction, commercial and professional use and the better fulfilment of leisure' to developing all their activities on an international front and two objectives in terms of growth:

'To achieve a rate of growth of earnings per share and a level of management efficiency which will bear comparison with the best-managed companies operating in similar spheres.

'To maintain, through initiation and acquisition, our place as a leader in our field of business by increasing the profitable exploitation of current activities, and discovering and profitably exploiting new activities within that field.'

Its development
If the company started in a single room above a shop in the East End of London and is now spread all over the world, it's worth making the point. List all the company's sites, the areas they cover and include one or two illustrations as well. Courtaulds, in fact, have been including a leaflet about their two-volume 828-page, 370,000-word economic and social history written by Dr D. C. Coleman, Reader in Economic History at London University, with their annual reports. It is also worth inviting shareholders to visit the various business centres.

Its products
It's amazing. But it's possible to read annual reports put out by many companies which do not even mention the products manufactured by the company let alone the industry. Of course, it is possible to go to the other extreme. Seager Evans and Company, for example, not only include descriptions and pictures of their wines and spirits, they even include order forms as well. ICI seem to strike the happy medium. In 1960 they produced a 30-page booklet listing all the company's products that stockholders and employees could identify and buy in the shops. A new edition was sent to stockholders in 1965 and, again, five years later in 1970.

Sales
It is possible to discover the amount of money a company has spent on

advertising. So it's not too difficult to discover the effect on sales. Yet wild horses wouldn't draw the information from the average company chairman. Companies should cover this ground in detail. Sales, after all, are the key area of any company's organisation. If a company is gaining an improving share of a major market it should say so. Similarly they should report on new or improved marketing and distribution facilities as well as the hiring of any new advertising agency.

Cash flow
Print a cash flow chart in the annual report and you're a pacemaker. Few companies have got round to this. Yet it is an important addition to the company's accounts.

A typical cash flow account

CASH RECEIVED FROM:
    Sources within the company
        Profit retained in business
        Depreciation retained
        Increased tax retention
        Sale of investments
    Sources outside the company
        Issue of new ordinary stock (if any)
        Loans (less repayments)

CASH DEVOTED TO
    Buildings and plant
    Increased working capital
    Interests in associated companies
    Intangible assets

Increase or decrease in liquidity

Rationalisation
If a company is closing down a centre, it should mention it in the report. It might mean an increase in profits or it might not. The company should say. They should also mention the arrangements being made to look after any employees that are being declared redundant in the process.

Productivity
Productivity is everywhere. And it's news worthy. A company should report on its plans for boosting productivity. They should spell out the effect in terms of output as well as in sales per employee. Again, it could have an important effect on the company as a whole.

New directors

Research has shown that investors study the management when following a company. If a company appoints a new director with a proven track record in terms of profits and efficiency, it should be mentioned in the report. Shareholders and investors have a right to know the qualifications and abilities of people being appointed to the board.

Shareholder breakdown

The Companies Act, 1967, insists on holders owning more than 10 per cent of the nominal capital revealing their identity. Similarly the General Undertaking insists on 'substantial' holdings being revealed in the annual report. Companies, however, can go a stage further and detail the shareholder profile of the company. Interesting reading it is too, from the financial public relations point of view. Thomas Tillings share ownership analysis at 31 December 1968, for example, revealed that the majority of their shareholders held between 500 and 2,500 shares, an average of just £235 a head. Eight-thousand odd shareholders held around £450,000 of stock, an average of £54 a head. For GKN, the figures were lower still. Approximately 60 per cent of their stockholders held between £101 and £500 worth of stock. A further 10,000 held £100 or less. IPC's shareholder statistics revealed the entire composition of the stock: the categories of ownership, the number held, the percentage, the number of shares and the percentage of total shares.

Company calendar

The key date is 5 April 1965, the base date for capital gains tax. It is a great help if companies print their share price on that day. Similarly with the dividend and interest payment dates as well as the scheduled publication date of the interim and annual reports. These, of course, vary from company to company.

8.5 Distribution of the annual report

Companies should not wait until the annual report is ready before releasing their annual figures. The New York Stock Exchange, for example, urges its member companies to publish their annual earnings to the press as soon as the audited figures are available, without waiting for the actual printing and distribution of the annual report. Similarly in the United Kingdom. Companies should release their preliminary figures—and advertise them as soon as they are ready. Plus, of course, a brief comment from the chairman. When the report is available, however, it must still be sent to every shareholder and debenture holder 21 days before the annual meeting. This also acts as notice of the meeting. For companies like ICI, with its 650,000 stockholders, this is a major problem. After all kinds of experiments they finally decided to instruct their printer to send Mount Pleasant each day's print as soon as it came off the presses—about 80,000 copies per day for eight days. Doing it any other way, would mean blocking the post office for weeks. Four copies must be sent to the Quotations Department of the Stock Exchanges on which the shares are quoted. The annual report and accounts, themselves, must be laid before the annual meeting.

Now the financial public relations media. The press should receive copies the day the report is mailed to shareholders—or earlier. An embargo should be placed on publication, however, so that nothing appears until shareholders have—or should have—received their copies. Some City Editors receive as many as 500 reports a week. Others, on the more popular and less business-minded papers, receive around 100–150. Either way, it is clearly an impossible task to study and analyse each one.

In that case, it is wise—and helpful—to attach a digest press release to the copies sent to the press. First, give the company name, state when the annual meeting takes place, and say whether the information is for immediate release or not. Then give the relevant information. This, generally, need only cover three points:

1 FINAL DIVIDENDS Give details for the different kinds of stock, the totals for the year and the corresponding figures for the previous year. And state the end of the financial year and, the date dividends will be payable.

2 RESULTS A statement setting out the profit for the financial year should be given. In some cases, where there is a great deal of information, this is given on accompanying sheets.

3 ANNUAL REPORT Give the salient points—the chairman's comments on the results and especially on the future for the chairman commented on the figures when the preliminaries were released—and the date the annual report will be circulated.

One Liverpool company had some harsh truths to tell when they released their annual results on 27 August 1969.

'The Directors regret the delay in submitting to you the preliminary announcement of the results of the Group for the year ended 31st December, 1968 largely due to the untimely death of our Chairman on 30th June, 1969. The Directors announce that the results of the Group, subject to audit, for the year ended 31st December, 1968 were as follows: Year ended 31st December, 1968—Loss £32,275 (1967 Loss £70,755). 1968 was not a good year for the Group. Trading conditions continued to be difficult and whilst we began to feel the benefits of rationalisation we still ended with a loss and your Directors do not recommend the payment of a dividend.'

It was harsh. But honest. And that's what counts more than anything in financial public relations.

At the other end of the scale, companies like Slater Walker, produce masses of additional financial and statistical analysis for the press. This helps them to arrive at a realistic assessment ot the company's trading position. Remember, journalists by definition are always working against the clock. Anything a company can do to help them, the better. Press conferences, however, are generally out. There is rarely a case for calling a press conference to mark the publication of the annual report. It is a waste of time for both the company—and the press. If the annual report requires additional explanation, the answer is to produce a better annual report. Not to call a press conference. It is also dangerous. A chance remark at a press conference by a chairman inexperienced in dealing with the press could have a serious effect on the stock market. It's not worth the risk. If, however, it is absolutely vital, any press conference should take place after the markets have closed.

Then there are the remaining financial public relations media.

'The annual report should be sent to new shareholders when their shares are registered; to selected investment managers (for example, of pension and insurance funds) and investment analysts; to selected libraries, universities, business colleges; to dealers and major customers', says Nightingirl. Derriman goes further. He suggests reference libraries of places where the company has factories or major offices; trade associations; principal suppliers, dealers and customers; MP's for constituencies in which the company is based; leaders of the local communities; as well as friends and associates such as managers, the intelligence department of the company clearing bank and chambers of commerce with which it has links. And, of course, to employees. Apart from being, at the lowest, good manners, it can also have other benefits for management.

It will help correct misconceptions

The annual report is probably the only occasion in the year when the company is in absolute agreement about what it can say and what it can't say. The printed facts and figures are undeniable. If employees have been under the impression the company has been making excessive profits, the annual report will tell.

It will help strengthen morale

There is little point in the chairman thanking the staff for all their working during the year, if they never hear about it. It won't double productivity overnight. But it will enable employees to see everything in perspective.

It might boost sales

This depends on the company. Some companies run superb sales organisations. But, inevitably, they forget their own backyard. Employees are a pretty captive market.

It might persuade some employees to become shareholders

It's a fair bet that a number of a company's employees are buying shares through the Stock Exchange. It's only fair that their own company should give them a chance—and, perhaps, some encouragement—in buying shares in their company as well. Watney Mann, for example, devoted six pages to extracts from the 1968 annual report in their February 1969 issue of *Red Barrel*.

'The difficulties of the past year and the external constraints within which we have been forced to operate have placed great burdens on all members of the Group at all levels and not least upon the tenants and managers of our houses. I would like on your behalf to thank them all for their continued loyalty and determination in most difficult circumstances', wrote chairman, Mr D. P. Crossman.

The breakdown of holdings of ordinary shares was given—92 per cent held by individual shareholders—as well as the Group balance sheet. Here Watneys produced a superb, easy-to-follow, vertical balance sheet written not in accountants mumbo-jumbo but in everyday English:

THE GROUP BALANCE SHEET

How we stood at 30th September 1968

We owned

Breweries, public houses, off-licence shops, plant, fixtures and motor vehicles, at cost or valuation, less amounts provided to replace them

Investments in other concerns and Government securities and loans to customers

Stocks of raw materials, beers, wines, spirits and miscellaneous stores

....

Less bank overdrafts

....

We were owed

By our customers and by way of loans

....

But we owed

To people who have lent us money on the security of our assets

To our suppliers for goods and services

Money deposited with us, including club funds

For current taxation

For dividends due but not paid

....

A share of the Group's assets attributable to outside shareholders

....

The Group's working assets which comprise the investment of the shareholders of Watney Mann Ltd therefore amount to

Watneys then went on to treat their profit and loss account the same way.

THE GROUP PROFIT AND LOSS ACCOUNT
The profits earned in the year to 30th September 1968
and how we dealt with them

The Group's trading profits and income from rents,
investments and other sources were
The interest paid on our permanent Loan Capital was

....

Out of this we provided depreciation for replacing worn-
out plant, machinery, vehicles and other fixed assets

....

The remaining profit before taxation was
Taxation amounted to

....

Leaving a Group net profit, after taxation, of
Undistributed portion of income from a trade investment
The profit attributable to shares in certain of our subsidiaries held by shareholders outside the Group
The net profit available to our ordinary and preference
shareholders was therefore
Of this they received dividends which, grossed up for
income tax, totalled

....

The balance, which was placed to reserve for further
development was

Em, the house magazine of one of IPC's six divisions, went a stage further
following the publication of the group annual report. They produced their
own divisional annual report with a commentary by division Chairman,
Arnold Quick, in July 1969. First, they analysed the source of each £1 of
income—8s 8d from advertising, 9s from cover sales, 1s 6d from offers and so
on—then they examined where each £1 of turnover went—2s 8d on salaries,
10s 6d on materials, 4s 7d on overheads and 2s 3d profit for the group—and
finally they explained where all the profit went. Because of its enormous size,
Unilever publish a special four-page newspaper containing extracts from the
annual report for their employees.

Some companies have even produced their annual report on records. Some
have straightforward reproductions of the chairman's statement. Others have
been documentary guides to the company and its employees. American

Telephone and Telegraph, for example, produce their annual report in Braille and on records. A few companies even go as far as publishing different sections of the report in different languages. As investment becomes more international, this is bound to grow more and more.

8.6 Survey

A sophisticated financial public relations operation would now launch a research programme to discover whether the annual report had the desired results. If the message had failed to hit the target, the company should know. It can then try and correct the shortcomings in following years. If it doesn't undertake even the most rudimentary research programme, it will continue firing off ammunition in the dark. Which is both expensive and dangerous. A straightforward postal survey would do. The questions could be mailed to a representative sample at a reasonable cost. It wouldn't cost much to analyse the results for, basically, there are only four questions a company would want answered.

1 Which sections of the annual report did you read?
2 Were you able to understand them?
3 Did you give the report to anyone else to read?
4 Have you any suggestions for next year's report?

A full-scale research operation, however, would be more effective. This ICI did in 1968. They took every 560th name on their register of ordinary stockholders giving them a total universe of 1,000. Then, in the most comprehensive research programme ever undertaken into the effectiveness of annual reports, they asked for their opinions.

8.6.1 READERSHIP OF THE ANNUAL REPORT

More than three-quarters (77 per cent) said they had read the report although it appealed to men (84 per cent) more than women (69 per cent). There was little difference, however, between different groups of people. Seventy-six per cent of under-45's claimed to have read it compared to 78 per cent of the over-45's. Seventy-four per cent of manual workers said they had read it compared to 78 per cent of non-manual workers. And 75 per cent of those with ICI connections compared with 78 per cent without.

8.6.2 REASONS FOR NOT READING THE REPORT

Only 1 per cent said they had not read it because they had seen a summary in the press. Two per cent said it was too long. Another two per cent said it was too dull. Three per cent said they were not interested in it. Four per cent said it was too technical. Five per cent said they did not feel there was any need for them to study it. While 10 per cent said they didn't have the time.

8.6.3 THE EXTENT TO WHICH THE REPORT IS READ

Trading results were top of the financial pops. They were read by 41 per cent of shareholders. Finance came second with 35 per cent. Then came research and development with 30 per cent; Exports with 28 per cent and the Year's Activities in the United Kingdom with 24 per cent. At the other end of the scale came Personnel (11 per cent); Investment in Associated Companies (15 per cent); Details of Directors (18 per cent) and the Accounts themselves with a mere 18 per cent. The research also discovered that although three out of four shareholders might read the report, on average they only read four items.

8.6.4 ATTITUDES TO THE REPORT

Only one per cent wanted it improved. Nearly 40 per cent said the next report should be exactly the same although 38 per cent asked for a shorter summarised form. As for the contents, only 15 per cent wanted more detailed information: eight per cent about aspects already covered and the remainder on topics not covered at all. Surprisingly, perhaps, five out of seven in this group wanted more information on ICI products.

8.7 Public relations annual report

All financial public relations consultancies are private companies so they don't have to practise what they preach. One consultancy, Financial Public Relations, however, does publish its own annual report. Wrote Chairman, Lord Alport, in the 1969 issue:

> 'The accounts show a decisive swing from £2,147 loss in our first account-ing period to a profit of £4,827 before tax and £3,244 after tax. This has enabled the board to recommend a maiden dividend of 12 per cent costing £600, and, after taking the adverse balance into account, still to show a carry forward of £497. The results reflect a 79 per cent increase in turnover to £34,831, which by the year-end had reached an annual rate of £45,000.'

And he added:

> 'We expect continuing growth in fee income as awareness spreads through British boardrooms of the importance of financial public relations.'

Chapter 9

Annual general meetings

9.1 Classic farce with elements of slapstick

Not an old-time Whitehall comedy. But the annual shareholders meeting of the Communications Satellite Corporation, according to 'New York writer, John Brooks (*Business Adventures*, Victor Gollancz, 1969).

> 'Mrs Davis decked out in stage make-up, an orange pith helmet, a short red skirt, white boots and a black sweater bearing in white letters the legend: "I was born to raise hell" had placed herself squarely in front of a battery of television cameras . . . as the cameras ground, she launched into an ear-splitting tirade against the company and its directors because there had been a special door to the meeting room reserved for the entrance of "distinguished guests". Mrs Davis in a good many words, said she considered this procedure undemocratic.'

Chairman, James McCormack, was sorry. 'We apologise and when you go out, please go by any door you want', he said. Not content, Mrs Davis continued.

> 'Eventually Mrs Davis's speech built up to a peak of volume and content at which she began making specific allegations against individual Comsat directors, and at this point three security guards, two beefy men and a determined-looking woman, all dressed in gaudy bottle green uniforms that might have been costumes for "The Pirates of Penzance" appeared at the rear, marched with brisk yet stately tread up the centre aisle and assumed the position of parade rest in the aisle within handy reach of Mrs Davis whereupon she abruptly concluded her speech and sat down. "All right", Mr McCormack said, still grinning. "Everything's cool now!" '

It's virtually impossible to organise an annual meeting which would satisfy everyone. But a company must try. Because its the one time in the year they go on parade before their investors.

Here the United States is much more shareholder conscious than the United Kingdom. Marvin Chandler, President of the Northern Illinois Gas Company, writes to every shareholder inviting them to attend:

'You are cordially invited to attend the meeting, which will be held at the East High School of Aurora on June 9. Stockholders will note that this location is different from the meeting place of the past several years. East High has superior facilities for the meeting, including ample parking space. Following the formal meeting we will have a short programme of interest to stockholders and a buffet luncheon. The latest appliances and other outstanding displays will be exhibited.'

He also gives them detailed directions for finding the School:

'A map showing automobile routes to Aurora and the location of East High School appears below. If you do not drive, Aurora may be reached from Chicago on the Chicago, Burlington and Quincy Railroad and the Bluebird Coach Lines. Please let the Secretary know if you wish to have a copy of the train and bus schedules. Transportation will be provided to and from the station or bus terminal and the School. In addition, a transportation booth will be available for your convenience at the meeting.'

Most companies, however, tend to dismiss the value of annual meetings. 'It has been easier to get a quorum since lunch has been added to the agenda', said the chairman of a drinks company. 'It's when shareholders turn up for meetings that I begin to worry', says another. 'You may think a stockholder is a nuisance', says Richard E. Cheney, senior Vice-President of Hill and Knowlton Incorporated, the giant American public relations consultancy. 'But its surprising how charming, attractive and interesting he becomes if he is contemplating a tender offer for your company's stock or reading an inimical proxy statement that may cost you your job. When and how did you last talk to him in frank and understandable terms about what you are doing on his behalf? Are there other additional ways you can reach him effectively?'

9.2 Benefits of a good shareholder relations programme

The benefits of a good shareholder relations programme are enormous.

9.2.1 IT IMPROVES COMMUNICATIONS BETWEEN MANAGEMENT AND INVESTORS
Instead of running long, dull and boring meetings more and more companies are trying to make them more interesting to shareholders. Some drink companies, for example, are beginning to distribute samples of their various products before and after the meeting as an ice-breaker. One company has even taken to showing films of different beauty contests they have organised during the year. Then there are the extras. Folland Aircraft Limited, for example,

lay on cars to meet shareholders travelling by train. Tesco provide lunch. 'Tesco a la carte', said *The Guardian* (26 July 1969). 'After a company meeting on a warm day a spot of refreshment is welcome, and shareholders were glad to accept the invitation of Sir John Cohen after the London annual meeting.' Says Jones:

> 'A few other companies have earned a reputation for hospitality once a year and it is difficult to believe that publicity of value does not result from this policy.'

One company whose annual meetings virtually spell hospitality is Fitch Lovell. First, because of the vast quantities of 'goodies' given away to shareholders every year. Then there is the champagne and refreshments. At their 1969 annual meeting in October, for example, more than 1,000 shareholders packed into the Connaught Rooms, some crowded round the walls, others on the balcony. As each shareholder filed in, he was given a ticket entitling him to a bag of foodstuffs to be collected at the end of the meeting. That's not all. It was also the last annual meeting for Sir Ambrose Keevil after more than 50 years with the group. What did they do? They all stood up and sang 'For he's a jolly good fellow'. It was enough to bring tears to the eyes of Mrs Davis.

Mr Maxwell Joseph is another chairman who knows how to pack in the shareholders. When one of his companies, Giltspur Investments, was meeting on 15 October 1969 he decided to write to shareholders urging them to attend. He also promised to throw in a visit to the Motor Show if they did. For the company had a car body conversion subsidiary, E. D. Abbott, which was responsible for a special Ford Capri being featured in the show. It worked. More than 200 turned up for the meeting—and 90 per cent of them went on to the Motor Show afterwards. It was the biggest turn-out ever of Giltspur investors.

9.2.2 IT CONSOLIDATES INTEREST IN THE COMPANY

Chairman, Mr William D. Barnetson took the opportunity of describing the early days of United Newspapers at the fiftieth annual meeting in July 1969.

> 'The occasion is significant not because we can claim for our original assets any pattern of continuity or even survival. It is significant for the very opposite reason—the remarkable extent to which the group has changed in its ingredients, in its image, in its objectives, and in its ramifications. Indeed, practically all that is left of the original mixture is the label on the bottle. When our predecessors met at Salisbury Square half a century ago to study their accounts, they were concerned primarily with two national newspapers—the *Daily Chronicle* and the *Sunday News*. Between them, about ten years later, these two journals were operating at a loss of around £9,000 a week, and soon disappeared as

N

independent entities, the one merged with the *Daily News* to form the *News Chronicle*, and the other absorbed by Lord Camrose's *Sunday Graphic*. Happily enough, however, the company's fairly modest provincial interests were salvaged from the chaos and the wreckage. . . . These provincial interests formed the foundation upon which the group has since been built. . . .'

The *UK Press Gazette* picked up the story and not only ran it on 7 July 1969, but set the story in Jubilee type 'as a mark of respect' as well.

9.2.3 IT BOOSTS THE COMPANY IN THE EYES OF THE FINANCIAL PUBLIC RELATIONS MEDIA

Facing a determined shareholder like Mrs Davis is bad enough. But many companies have to put up with strong criticism as well. When this happens, all eyes are turned to the annual meeting to see whether the management will capitulate or fight back.

Robert Butlin, head of the Butlin's holiday camp group, put up a valiant battle at his annual meeting on 23 July 1969. One shareholder accused the board of 'gross mismanagement'. Another said, 'Something is radically wrong —you have done nothing to diversify your interest. Get someone dynamic on the board'. In his reply, Butlin played the trump card. Since the unsuccessful bid for the company the previous October, he said, Butlin's shares had declined 21 per cent. This compared with a 24 per cent fall in the *Financial Times* Share Index, a 21 per cent slide in the value of fellow-entertainment group, Mecca and a 52 per cent drop in the shares of Phonographic, the company which made the bid.

'Armed with a good few statistics, Bobby Butlin managed to take most of the sting out of his shareholder critics', commented the *Sun* the following day. And, bang on time, out came a four-page photo-feature with words by Clement Freud on Butlin's Bognor Regis camp a few days later in the August issue of the monthly 88,450-circulation *Fashion*.

9.2.4 IT INCREASES CONFIDENCE

There is a long delay between the annual report and the annual meeting. Hence the opportunity for another look at the profits forecast. At IPC's annual meeting on 17 July 1969, Chairman, Mr Hugh Cudlipp, stressed the difficulty of forecasting with any certainty the level of profits for the year but maintained that the board had every confidence that, in the absence of unforeseen circumstances, profits for 1970–71 would show a further significant increase.

'Mini-skirts are not popular with Mr John Bedford, the man who runs Marshall and Snelgrove, Harvey Nichols, Debenham and Freebody, Swan

and Edgar and a host of other departmental stores around the country in the Debenham group. Commenting on 'the girls who are wearing next to nothing these days', he told the company's annual meeting today, 'Their passion for mini-skirts hasn't helped our fashion business at all'.
(*Evening Standard*, 7 August 1969)

A badly handled annual meeting could have disastrous results—like the case of a major shareholder who decided to attend an annual meeting for the first time. He was so put off he stormed out, called his broker and sold his shares on the spot. The price dropped. And rumours began.

9.3 Date

After the strictures of the various Company Accounts, the General Undertaking and the different Stock Exchange rules, the regulations governing annual meetings are remarkably lax. Once a company has been incorporated, it must hold its first annual meeting within the next 18 months. Once that has been held, annual meetings must follow every year—with a maximum of 15 months between each one. This gives companies plenty of room for manoeuvre. The depths of the winter can be forgotten. So can the height of the summer. Neither are likely to produce a packed attendance. Then there is the question of clashing. It would be unwise, for example, to hold the annual meeting the same day as ICI or GEC–EE, the giant electrical engineering group. But the ideal date depends on two points: First: will it clash from the shareholders point-of-view? This obviously, depends on the size of the company and the importance of the industry. Second: will it clash from the financial press point of view?

With around 150 annual meetings taking place every week, obviously, some must suffer. But there is no point in inviting a brush-off. Its best to check with the financial diaries of previous years to ensure, as far as possible, the meeting will not be passed over.

It's also wise to look out for Bank Holidays, Derby Days, Budgets—and Fridays. It's wrong. But nobody will be interested if the annual meeting takes place, say, Budget Day. Fridays, however, are wrong for a different reason. There is precious little space in Saturday's papers to cover annual meetings. Hence the risk. It's best to play safe and hold the meeting earlier in the week.

9.4 Time

This is a problem. The earlier the meeting is held, the more convenient it is for the press. The later it is held, the more convenient it is for the shareholders. The usual time for the quick ten-minute in-and-out instant annual meeting is around 11.00 am. It suits the board. It's ideal for the press. And it doesn't interfere with lunch. But it's inconvenient for shareholders. Admittedly, some of the major shareholders may be able to attend. But the small investor is likely to find it impossible. Hold the meeting later in the day and the situation is reversed. The board will still come. The press won't—unless it is a major news event which is unlikely. But shareholders will.

'One has yet to hear of a company asking its members what time of day they would prefer', says Derriman, '*by order of the board* wins hands down over *by wish of the members*'.

9.5 Location

Too often companies faced with their annual meeting, choose either their own offices—one major company packs its entire board, shareholders and press representatives into a 40-seater cinema, with plenty of room to spare—or a hired room outside. This is safe—if unexciting. Annual meetings at the company's premises can usually be combined with a see-for-yourself tour of the works. Outside meetings, usually in hotels, can mean painless entertainment facilities. But there is an alternative: regional meetings. Most companies have shareholders spread all over the country. Unless they live on the doorstep of the company, they are unlikely to even consider attending an annual meeting. Take the meeting to their part of the country, however, and things are likely to change.

Says Cheney, 'Regional stockbroker meetings should be re-examined with the possibility in mind that they not only will strengthen stockholder loyalty, but can also be used to build sales under certain circumstances'.

There is, of course, one problem: persuading shareholders that it is in the company's interests to do so. Mrs Davis, the American AGM rebel, took Frederick R. Kappel, Chairman of the world's largest company, American Telephone and Telegraph, to task for switching the venue from New York to Detroit. She complained that it meant she had to come all the way from New York by bus. This made the mid-western stockholders furious. They were only able to attend the meeting because it was held in Detroit and not in New York, they claimed.

Once again General Mills has been in the vanguard of running effective annual meetings. As far back as 1939 they were holding a series of meetings in different parts of the country for shareholders. 'We believe they not only broaden communication with our owners but also serve as a springboard for reaching important members of the financial community', says vice-president, Nate L. Crabtree. In 1959 they went a stage further and linked all the regional meetings with the main centre in New York through a giant closed-circuit coast-to-coast television link-up. Three-years later they were again experimenting. Stockholders in New York, Boston, Chicago, Detroit and San Francisco were all linked by amplified telephone to the Minneapolis meeting.

'With regional meetings, we obviously invite more queries or comments than we would receive at one location alone and it is well to be prepared for them', says Crabtree. 'We therefore attempt to anticipate a wide variety of questions and assist management in preparing answers ahead of time. Every regional meeting we have had since 1939 has been followed by warm thanks from those attending. Shareowners seem to appreciate our efforts to keep them posted on company affairs and appear to enjoy the opportunity to meet company officials.'

Republic Steel, America's third largest steel corporation with 96,000 shareholders, however, still insists on meeting in Flemington, NJ, a two-and-a-half-hour journey from Manhatten. Only 65 people bother to turn up.

9.6 Layout

The annual meeting is still a selling operation. The company is selling itself to its shareholders. Display panels covering the development and progress of the company should be on show. If, like the Northern Illinois Gas Company, it's possible to exhibit some 'latest appliances' as well, so much the better.

Apart from that, the layout of the room is much the same as any business meeting. As people come in, their names should be checked against the register and recorded. There should be plenty of chairs, and at the top of the room, the main table, complete with name plates, for the chairman and his fellow directors. On left, could be a set of tables and chairs for the various company advisers—auditors, solicitors, perhaps even public relations advisers and so on—as well as a secretary taking a shorthand note on the proceedings. On the right should be the press table, stocked with copies of the annual report, transcripts of any additional speeches being made and background information on the company and its products.

9.7 The two sides

The Companies Act, 1948, believe it or not, only insists on three as a quorum for an annual meeting. Which is absurd. The company, because it is their one open day of the year, should go all out for more than three and invite:

1 DIRECTORS It's not essential but every company director—especially those coming up for re-election—should be present at the annual meeting together with the company secretary.

2 SENIOR MANAGEMENT The annual meeting is the only opportunity in the year for shareholders to meet the men who run the company they are investing in. Directors are the top of the iceberg. Senior management should also be present to meet shareholders as well as to answer any detailed question raised during the meeting.

3 JUNIOR MANAGEMENT A number of companies have started inviting a

group of younger executives to the annual meeting as well. It's valuable experience. It also helps them to see the company's operation in perspective.

4 EMPLOYEES If the company runs an employee shareholding scheme, this is a must. Ideally, all employees with shares in the company should be invited not only as shareholders but employees as well. If, however, the vast majority of employees hold shares, this is obviously out of the question. It's no good shutting the company down for the sake of the annual meeting. Either a representative selection of employee-shareholders should be invited to attend. Or a special meeting especially for them should take place before the annual meeting itself. This, Cadburys have been doing since the early 1960's. At the annual meeting in June 1969, for example, attended by about 250 people, questions ranged from diversification into ice-cream to developing containerisation.

John Laing and Son, which was running an employee shareholding scheme as far back as 1920, take over Brent Town Hall for their annual meetings. Staff often come from Canada, Saudi Arabia and Spain as well as from sites and offices all over the United Kingdom to be present. After the formal meeting long-service awards are presented to employees who have been with the company for 25 years. On 27 June 1969 a film was also shown on the 65-mile Bilbao-Behobia Motorway, the company were helping to construct for the Spanish Government. All in all a copy-book annual meeting for employees. Or as the house newspaper, *Team Spirit*, said afterwards, 'Strong sense of family at annual meeting'.

5 ADVISERS The auditors, of course, should be present. But so should the company's solicitors, bankers, brokers—and public relations advisers.

6 BUSINESS NEWS MEDIA In the US, this includes television as well. But the chance of a television company wanting to film an annual meeting in the United Kingdom is slight. Which is, perhaps, a measure of the gulf which still separates the importance of annual meetings in the United States and the United Kingdom. The financial press should, of course, be invited. That's a priority. But there is no reason why the other press groups which are interested in the company should not be invited as well.

7 OUTSIDE EXPERTS. If the company's own brokers are invited, there is no reason why the various jobbing firms who deal in the company's shares shouldn't be invited as well. Then there are other brokers with a special interest in the company. Not to mention selected investment analysts as well.

9.8 Agenda

This is really the Notice of Meeting, which appeared in the annual report.

The same seven points generally apply to every company. They are usually taken in the same order as well.

'To receive the Report of the Directors together with the Accounts for the year ended . . . and the Report of the Auditors thereon.'
Or words to that effect. Some, for example, say 'consider'. The Companies Act, 1948, however, merely says they should be 'laid before' the annual meeting. There is nothing in the Act about 'receiving', 'considering' or even 'approving' them. It does, however, give shareholders a chance to have their say.

'To declare a final dividend on the ordinary shares of the company for the year ended . . .'
This is crucial. Directors can only 'recommend' a dividend. It takes a general meeting of the company to actually 'declare' them. Only when that has been done are shareholders entitled to their dividend. Interim dividends are slightly different. There, directors are entitled to both 'recommend' and 'declare' dividends at the same time.

'To elect Directors: . . . who retire by rotation, being eligible, offer themselves for re-election.'
Once again, a formality. But it shouldn't be. Details about directors coming up for re-election, should be included in the annual report. They should also be at the meeting. If shareholders have any questions about their ability, the directors should be prepared to stand up and reply. One American AGM rebel, Mrs Wilma Soss, with the backing of an organisation of women stockholders, caused a riot among 4,000 stockholders who attended the 1966 annual meeting of the American Telephone and Telegraph Company when she nominated a psychoanalyst, Dr Frances Arkin, to the board. Not only should the company have a woman on the board, she maintained. But some of the company's executives would benefit by the occasional psychiatric examination as well. There was uproar. Chairman, Frederick Kappel, said he would not stand for any more abuse. The floor microphone Mrs Soss was using was switched off.

> 'Followed at a distance of 10 to 15 feet by a uniformed security guard, and to the accompaniment of deafening booing and stamping, Mrs Soss marched up the aisle and took a stand in front of the platform, facing Mr Kappel who informed her that he knew she wanted him to have her thrown out and that he declined to comply', said Brooks.

Four hours later, with only a few hundred exhausted stockholders left, Mrs Soss's nomination went to the vote. She won 19,106 votes. The board, however, crushed her with a massive 400 million votes.

'To re-appoint the auditors in accordance with Section 195 (2) of the Companies Act, 1948, and to fix their remuneration.'
This is an annual meeting decision by tradition. Nothing else. The 1948 Act merely says the remuneration should be arranged 'in general meeting'. In other words there is nothing to stop the board deciding the fee among themselves.

'To consider and if thought fit, pass the following Ordinary Resolution: . . .'
There are not many annual meetings involving resolutions. If there are, they generally involve boosting the authorised capital of the company by launching further ordinary shares. Again, largely a formality.

'To transact any other ordinary business of the company.'
This is the rag-bag of the meeting. If the chairman wants to up-date his annual statement, he does so now. Or he can give an additional speech altogether. Mr Eric Quinton Hazell, for example, usually regales the shareholders of his car spares empire, Quinton Hazell, with a few well-chosen words about the British tax system. 'The thing that got me going was the wealth tax idea', he said. 'It made me see red.'

   Unilever, however, have the best idea. Each year the Chairman, Lord Cole, speaks about different aspects of the company. In 1963, for example, he spoke about Unilever in a Changing Europe. The following year it was Investment in Food. The 1965 talk was devoted to Packaging; 1966 to Raw Materials and Pricing; 1967 to Government, Private Enterprise and Profits; 1968 to Our Changing Customer—the Consumer; and 1969 to Consumer Satisfaction and Protection. Each talk, around 3,000 words, was also given at the same time by Mr H. S. A. Hartog, Chairman of Unilever NV, at their twin annual meeting in Rotterdam. The impact on investor and consumer alike has always been invaluable because, year after year, the chairmen have given an improved insight into the company, its operations and, of course, its potential. As, for example, in their 1969 outline of the scope of Unilever's research programme:

   'Every new ingredient of a food product, every new formulation of a cleaning product or a toilet preparation, has to be cleared as safe. We have an elaborate system of testing, some tests lasting many years. Whatever be the ingredient or the formulation, if we have not used it previously, the final clearance for safety has to be endorsed by the Head of Research. It is not necessary for us to test everything ourselves, as quite often the tests we need have been done by some outside authority on whom we feel we can rely like the American Food and Drug Administration. Nevertheless we spend £885,000 a year in our own laboratories, on testing the biological effects of experimental new products and also in investigating the nutritional values of our foods. . . . We try to take every precaution we can, but if by any chance we miss some reaction that has no precedent, some rare allergy, for instance, and it comes to our notice after the product comes on the market, we withdraw it straight-away, however much time and effort we might already have spent on testing the product and on bringing it to market.'

After a comment like that, Unilever shareholders can feel pleased. Of course, there are plenty of companies with equally rigorous standards. The trouble is that they don't talk about it. Unilever does—and, of course, benefits. They also reprint the talk as a booklet.

9.9 Entertainment

This really depends on the location. If the annual meeting is held in a hotel, the least a company can do, is to provide light refreshments. It could go as far as Tescos and provide a buffet lunch. If, however, the meeting is held at the company's offices, it should be possible to arrange a tour of the centre. Watneys, for example, which regularly attract 150–200 shareholders to their annual meetings, lay on a tour of their Mortlake Brewery afterwards. 'They are very good at informal shareholder meetings', says their public relations adviser, Russell Cobb. But then that's a natural. Everyone enjoys touring a brewery.

There is, of course, the opposing view. 'Such a fatuous disposition of mind indicates that a paternal smile from a director and a glass of dry Spanish sherry are more important than the yield on the capital employed', says Alex Rubner, author of *The Ensnared Shareholder* (Macmillan, 1965) which is absolute nonsense. Nobody suggests a glass of sherry makes up for a poor return. Tours are an ideal way of letting shareholders see how a company operates.

9.10 Annual meeting reports

This takes us back to fundamentals. The annual meeting is held for share-holders. Few shareholders are able to attend. But all shareholders as well as the financial public relations media, having heard the preliminary figures, are entitled to hear what takes place at the meeting. A company, therefore, is under an obligation to ensure that as many people as possible get a report on the meeting. Says the Society of Investment Analysts in their *Company Reports and their Presentation*:

'A major defect, in both law and practice, is that no provision is made for informing shareholders who were not present in person of what actually took place at the meeting. An interesting innovation in the United States and Canada has been the circulation of minutes of the annual general meeting with the text of questions and answers to them and a list of the shareholders present. In printing and general presentation the minutes are arranged as an addendum for easy filing with the annual report. It should be a statutory requirement that minutes of an annual general meeting be circulated in a sufficiently complete form to contain any statements by the Chairman supplementing his printed review, the comments (if any) of the auditors and the substance of questions (whether they are put by shareholders or their authorised reps) and the answers to them.'

The South African Companies Amendment Act goes even further. Whenever a company advertises or circulates a report of a meeting, it insists that it should be a full report complete with a fair summary of all the material questions and answers raised as well. This should be adopted also in the United Kingdom.

9.10.1 PRESS RELEASE

This is basically the straightforward press release operation—except that it is more important than ever not only that all the facts are given but that they are all absolutely accurate as well. A medium-sized engineering company, for example, was negotiating a takeover for a company in a larger group. All the details had been finalised. It was agreed that the chairman would make the announcement at his annual meeting. To ensure that nobody jumped the gun and started a hare, he released the information to the press the previous day. But he embargoed it until 1.00 pm the following day when the annual meeting was taking place.

'*Press announcement for release at 1.00 pm Thursday, September 4th, 1969* Agreement has been reached in principle between A company and the B Corporation whereby B Corporation will purchase for cash the whole of the share capital of C company. It is expected that a formal Agreement will be signed within the next two weeks.

The total purchase consideration will be based on the net asset value of C company at August 8th, 1969 plus an agreed figure for goodwill and is expected to total £x.

The main business of C company is the design and supply of continuous casting and further processing equipment in the non-ferrous field and this proposed acquisition by B corporation reflects their intention, as reported by its chairman, Lord X, in his statement to shareholders, to develop into the non-ferrous industries based on aluminium and copper.

The combination of C company and B corporation furnace equipment will enable the B corporation to offer completely integrated foundry installations in this wider field.'

Not the best press release in the world. Not the most informative. But it gives the facts in a straightforward way. Handled properly, therefore, there are a number of different opportunities to capture the attention of the financial press.

Pre-publication publicity
Every newspaper likes to be first with the news. If the chairman is going to make a special announcement at the annual meeting, it might be worth giving some of the details to selected journalists. This would certainly help to draw attention to the importance of the annual meeting. But it depends on the nature of the company and, of course, the nature of the information.

Feature publicity
Occasionally a company has that additional information which ensures that they are not only recognised by the news columns but by the feature columns as well. This is a great help.

> 'The word *amari* means happiness in the African Hausa language. But the shareholders of the company bearing the name, derived from its Nigerian mining venture, have had little reason for joy. This year, they saw the profits dip and the share price fall from a high of 18s in 1968 to 8s now. But the chairman, Mr Ray Whiteway, is optimistic: he told me he had just bought 25,000 shares.'
> (*Investors Chronicle*, 25 July 1969)

News publicity
Lord Stokes hit the front-page headlines in a big way with his hard-hitting speech about strikes and the motor industry at British Leyland's annual meeting on 25 February 1970. It was the lead story of the *Daily Express*, *Daily Mail* and the *Financial Times* the following day. *The Times*, the *Daily Telegraph* and the *Guardian* all gave it front-page prominence as well.

> 'Lord Stokes, head of a giant British Leyland car firm, yesterday launched a massive counter-attack against the wildcat strikes which are throwing the motor industry into chaos.
>
> He talked of "planned and deliberate disruption". Later he said: "The attitude of the country has gone quite berserk over pay".
>
> His attack came on a normal day for the car industry—ten unofficial strikes running, causing nearly 10,000 men to be laid off.
>
> Lord Stokes first attacked the wildcats in a speech at the annual company meeting of British Leyland.'
> (*Daily Mail* 26 February 1970)

9.10.2 A SPECIAL INDIVIDUAL SHAREHOLDERS REPORT
University Computing Company produced a glossy 12-page booklet, tailor-made for a foolscap envelope, following their annual meeting in Dallas on 29 May 1969.

The cover simply said: UCC, Annual Shareholders Meeting, May 29th, 1969.

Page two showed a photograph of Chairman, Sam Wyly, addressing stockholders.

Page three carried a message to shareholders:

> Our 1969 Annual Meeting was held in Dallas on May 29th and it was a pleasure to welcome approximately 500 shareholders and guests who were able to attend. At the meeting, UCC officers reported on the Company's progress and invited shareholders to ask questions about out-operations and plans. In an adjoining room we conducted demonstrations of what we believe to be the world's fastest plotter, a new graphic display device made by our subsidiary Computer Industries Inc and FASBAC, the newest UCC remote computer terminal system. This summary of the meeting is being sent to all shareholders, and we hope it will be informative for those who were unable to attend.
> Sincerely, Sam Wyly, Chairman of the Board.

Pages four and five began the Report to shareholders where Wyly gave the revenues, earnings after taxes, net worth and earnings per share for each of the five years of the young company's existence.

Pages six and seven featured seven different photos of the meeting itself.

Pages eight and nine saw the end of the report including the following comment,

> 'I would like to introduce Mr Walter Haefner, the fine and able gentleman who founded and built ACI, and Dr Tobias Schuler, the general manager of ACI's multi-national operations. (applause).'

The end of the page began a summary rather than a verbatim transcription of the questions raised by shareholders.

Pages ten and eleven continued the questions and answers.

Page twelve, the back cover, merely gave the full name of the company, together with the address of their executive offices.

Few companies in the United Kingdom are as ambitious. Courtaulds, for example, merely reprint the statement made by their Chairman, Lord Kearton, at the annual meeting as a straightforward booklet. The Weir Group publish a flimsy four-page leaflet covering sales, exports, earnings, assets and employment. There is a three-year summary; an easy-to-follow breakdown on where the money goes and points from the chairman's statement. Yet such booklets would provide an invaluable service to shareholders unable to attend annual meetings.

9.10.3 ADVERTISING

This is the familiar Chairman Statement advertising. Or 'Chairmanitis' as it is known in the advertising business because of its extreme conservative handling and presentation compared with general advertising campaigns. It remains, however, the only way a company report can gain extensive publicity, largely without abbreviation or editing, in the financial public relations media. There are two points. First, where should the advertisements appear? 'Annual report advertising', says Smith, 'should depend, year by year, on who your shareholders are—and where they are'.

The old-school annual statement—Mark I
This is 'Chairmanitis' at its worst. Many companies still insist on advertising their annual statements in the style of news stories at the turn of the century. Pick up any national newspaper and you'll see them:

XYZ Company Limited
ENCOURAGING OUTCOME OF A DIFFICULT YEAR
Policy of diversification actively pursued
CHAIRMAN ON BENEFITS ACCRUING FROM MERGER

The 47th annual general meeting of the XYZ Company Limited was held on September 12th at UVW Town Hall, Worcestershire. Alderman A. N. Other JP (the chairman) presiding. The Secretary read the Notice convening the meeting and the Chartered Accountants read the report of his firm. The following is the report of the chairman which had been circulated with the Report and Accounts for the year ended April 3rd, 1969.

And so on. Column after column of dull type with equally dull cross-heads: The End of an Era; First Object of Merger; Second Object of Merger; Associated Companies; Accounts; Expression of Thanks. Yet buried away at the bottom of the report there is probably a story about a unique break-through in nuclear engineering that will bring untold benefits to the company, the shareholders and the underdeveloped world. What happens? Nothing. Nobody, except perhaps the chairman and directors of the company, have got time to read the report. So the company languishes unrecognised and neglected.

The old-school annual statement—Mark II
This is almost as bad. It is just that it doesn't take up so much room. Many companies, obviously, recognise the need for publishing their annual statements. Yet, probably through a mixture of fear and lack of finance, they seem frightened to take the plunge and produce an eye-catching display. Instead they dip their toe in with a three-inch, double column box, that is usually tucked away at the back of the paper.

XYZ and Sons Ltd
BICYCLE MANUFACTURERS
Extracts from the statement by the Chairman, Sir ABC:

The Accounts for the year ended 31st March 1969 show a consolidated net profit of . . . Total dividend . . . Conditions have improved somewhat but they are not yet back to normal. We have, however, taken the opportunity to effect many further improvements.

How have conditions improved? How long will it be before things are back to normal? And what on earth are the improvements the chairman is talking about? These are probably all 'bull' points for the chairman to make to shareholders. It's little use running extracts from a chairman's statement unless one is going to give many more facts. It doesn't convince anyone.

The no-nonsense modern

This is straightforward and to the point. One company takes a four-inch double column box in the major financial news media to announce just four lines:

Sales up 60 per cent
Exports up 71 per cent
Profits up 67 per cent
Dividend up to 20·7 per cent

You can't argue with that. It presents the progress of the company in a dramatic, telling way. There is no mass of figures to wade through. And yet, superb though it is as a record of the past, shareholders and the financial public relations media deserve a little more information about the future of the company. Warner Holidays used this approach to advertise their 1969 results—and to create a brand new style of their own at the same time. The only figures mentioned in the advertisement were profits: 'The Chairman reports profits for the year ended 31 March 1969: 1968—£270,000; 1969—£430,000', said the headline. Nothing more. Then came a plug for their new Mediterranean hotel: 'We are opening our new overseas hotel in Majorca for June 1970', it said. 'We hope to see you there.' Alongside—sex rears its head in financial advertising—was a photograph of a rather awkward looking girl in a swimming costume. And underneath, a coupon requesting their Majorca brochure. The advertisement—a six-inch double in *The Times* on 16 October 1969—didn't even say the profit was a record. But Managing Director, Alan Warner, seemed pleased. 'We believe the interests of our shareholders are best served at the present time by insuring that all our advertising is selling and direct response advertising', he said. The George Spencer Group were more sophisticated. Their 1969 report, published in the *Investors Chronicle* on 6 February 1970, featured a far more elegant model displaying their Vedonis knitwear. In fact, not only the figures of the annual report were eye-catching.

Another company, Staffordshire Potteries (Holdings), perfected this approach two months later. They published a four-inch treble giving highlights from the Chairman's Statement as well as both 1968 and 1969 figures for issued share capital; net profit before taxation; net profit after taxation; dividend for year; rate of dividend and carry forward. Alongside—instead of a girl—they featured a 'Stop Press' box covering exports and prospects for the current year. It was eye-catching and effective. An idea worth adopting where there is a limit on the amount of space available for annual statement advertising.

Modern

The standard chairman statement advertising found in most financial media. The company's name runs across the top of the display. Underneath comes a photo of the chairman together with an accompanying quote, such as, 'Active and successful year'. The body of the advertisement is then taken up with a blow-by-blow account of the annual meeting.

> 'The eighty-first annual meeting of the XYZ Company was held on May 17th in Nottingham. The Right Honourable Lord WXY (the chairman) who presided said, "As the reports and accounts have been in your hands for the required time, I hope you will agree that they may be taken as read (Agreed). It was with very much regret that I have to report the death in March last of. . . .'

It starts so well. A bold display. A photograph. Yet in the end its still an old-school annual statement. With great respect, is the death of a director really the most important thing that happened to the company during the year?

Modern with line drawings

More and more companies have struck out and made an impact with this technique. And very effective it is. A single line drawing can bring an annual statement to life. It catches the eye and—if the copy is good—holds the readers attention until he has absorbed the message. If a chairman's statement advertisement can do that, it is a successful advertisement. Higgs and Hill, the building and civil engineering contractors, made a tremendous impact with their 1968 annual statement. At the top was a compelling quote from chairman, Sir Rex Cohen: £44,000,000 order book for Higgs and Hill. Then came the statement, crisply written and packed with facts. At the bottom was the company's name again, together with a line drawing of a builder complete with his HH helmet.

The Distillers Company Limited adopted the same style in a whole-page advertisement featuring their annual statement in August, 1969. 'Mr Alex McDonald reports Distillers' exports over £86 million', ran the headline. The copy, broken down into product groups with their separate headings, then ran around an attractive line drawing of one of the company's pot-stills at Talisker, the only distillery on the Isle of Skye where they have produced a distinctive blend of malt whisky since 1830. William Cory and Son Limited, however, have developed this technique to the ultimate. In an advertisement featuring Chairman, Lord Leathers' statement, they included four neat line-drawings illustrating the successes achieved by their oil division; their fleets of tugs, colliers and bulk carriers; their modern dredgers and their warehouses and cold stores. The copy also takes a different line. Instead of being straight extracts from the chairman's statement, they mixed the report with the chairman's actual comments.

> 'The Group's trading profit for the year ended March 31st, 1969, before tax, is £3,132,183 compared with £2,865,783 for the preceding year, and after tax and retentions in associated companies £1,616,823, as against £1,416,724. The chairman said: "Not only are the results satisfactory, but I am confident that we are now in a position to make fuller use of our resources". Paying tribute to employees, he said: "It is a truism that bears repetition. There can be no success without an enthusiastic and efficient staff and your company continues to enjoy the services of people with these qualities. We are grateful for their constant support!"'

Nationale-Nederlanden NV, Holland's leading insurance group, made a nice point with a line-drawing they included with their 1968 annual statement. It showed the statuette in the entrance hall of their head office at The Hague. 'It is by the Dutch artist Louk van Meurs', said the caption 'and embodies The Family—symbol of Peace and Joy of Family Life, which can be doubled by the sense of security given by good insurance cover'.

Modern with photographs

There are three kinds of photographs being featured in annual statements: the presentation photograph, the attraction photograph and the action photograph.

British Leyland Motor Corporation used presentation photographs of various cars and trucks manufactured by the group in their 1968 annual statement. A quote from Chairman, Lord Stokes, came at the top of the display: 'The future potential of the Corporation is enormous'. Underneath came the photographs of the cars, fanning out in all directions. International Distillers and Vintners went a stage further with their 1969 report. They took a whole page advertisement in the *Financial Times* on 19 December 1969, annual meeting day. Photographs of all their drinks were there. So was a quote from Chairman, Mr Cecil Berens as well as charts showing both the geographical distribution of sales and the divisional structure of the company. But instead of being in traditional black-and-white, the advertisement was in full colour. Action, of course, spells Purle. A photograph of chairman, Tony Morgan, racing head down, bulging brief case in hand, from a helicopter, graced his annual statement advertising in June 1969.

Modern with charts

This is the Jim Slater approach. And very effective it is too. The 1968 chairman's statement, which appeared as a full-page advertisement in the *Financial Times* and a half-page in *The Times*, began with the heading: '115% Growth in earnings per share in 1968. Last year the Group achieved very substantial organic and internal growth and we see no reason why this should not continue for many years to come.' Next came 13 starred paragraphs, the bull points from the chairman's statement. Then, at the foot of the page, came three charts illustrating the dramatic growth per share from 1964–1969. The first covered net earnings after tax. The second, gross dividends. And the third, net equity assets. In each case the 1969 column showed the estimated or forecast totals.

The Rank Organisation were equally bullish. 'Rank sets profit record for eighth year running: an increase of 30 per cent on 1968,' said their annual statement advertisement on 17 October 1969. Two charts were there: the consolidated profit and loss account and a five-year financial review. Then came chairman, Mr John Davis's statement to shareholders. Plessey, however, went overboard. Their annual statement advertisement two-days later on 19 October 1969 had the bold heading: 'for Plessey the best year ever' followed by a quote from Chairman, Lord Harding, 'Our order books are fuller than ever before . . .' Four charts gave the background: ordinary share price growth; earnings and assets per ordinary share; a ten-year summary of results and—a very good idea—the first quarter results for the year 1969–1970. Finally there were seven different photographs showing various Plessey developments in microelectronics, air traffic control systems and communications.

In a category of its own comes the extravagant two-page black-and-white and full-colour advertisement on the 1969 annual meeting of the giant Matsushita Electric, which makes more profit size for size than any other Japanese company, that appeared in *Time* magazine on 21 November 1969. First, there was a photograph of the annual meeting showing hundreds of shareholders packed row-after-row into a giant conference hall. The caption: 'Big Daddy is watching you'. Then came the copy which explained how Big Daddy Matsushita, facing a record $1·7 billion sales record, had launched a revolutionary plan to replace seniority by productivity and efficiency as the guide-lines for promotion and pay rises. As a result TV production had trebled while the number of workers had only doubled. The case of foreman, Kuniaki Ando, 31, was explained in detail as evidence of the success of the scheme—and, opposite, were photographs of Mr Ando and his family having dinner.

Also in a category of its own is the annual report published by The Golden Egg Group in January 1970. 'Our Chairman tells a tasty story', said the headline. And a tasty story it was too:

'Phillip Kaye, Chairman of the Golden Egg Group serves up his tasty Report and Accounts at today's AGM. A delicious £517,000 profit

o

including a beefy contribution from the Angus Steak Houses Limited. The taste of things to come from an expanding hotels division. A profitable froth from the Shorts public developments and a spicy tale from the speciality restaurants.'

One wonders what would happen if companies adopted this approach and then had a disaster to report. Would it be a case of 'minced profits, rancid dividends and—unbelievably—cooked books'?

Chairman Statement advertising is, of course, only one half of the question. Companies should also advertise the proceedings of the annual meeting itself. Clearly, if the chairman has startling progress to report to the annual meeting, which often takes place well into the first quarter of the following year, i should be communicated to the investing public generally. And that means advertising, more often than not.

Altogether, therefore, chairman statement advertising should cover:

1 Preliminary figures
2 Report and Accounts
3 Annual meeting

Chapter 10

Extraordinary general meetings

Extraordinary general meetings can be called for all kinds of extraordinary reasons. The bitter four-hour meeting on 10 October 1969 when Mr Saul Steinberg's Leasco Data Processing Corporation ousted Mr Robert Maxwell and gained control of Pergamon Press was an extraordinary meeting. So was the brief meeting called by Guardian Properties (Holdings) to approve a resolution increasing the share capital.

> 'Twenty-four-year-old joint Managing Director Mr Harvey Soning is interested in seeing his company, Guardian Properties (Holdings) in the Guinness Book of Records. He, his fellow directors and shareholders held an extraordinary general meeting the other day which took only 58 seconds. The meeting was called to approve a resolution increasing the share capital so as to facilitate the recently announced takeover of W. B. Properties. Thankfully no questions were asked and a spokesman was able to race to the nearest telephone and ask the Guinness people whether a record had been established.'
> (*Investors Chronicle*, 15 August 1969)

Extraordinary meetings can be called by either the directors or the shareholders. Meetings called by directors generally involve changes in the company's memorandum or articles of association. The shareholders can insist that the directors call a meeting for virtually any reason under the sun provided the shareholders concerned control both one-tenth or more of the paid-up capital together with the voting rights. If the directors refuse, the shareholders can go right ahead and call the meeting themselves. After that, the mechanics of an extraordinary meeting are much the same as for the annual meeting. Although the amount of attention it will attract, obviously, depends on the reasons for calling the meeting.

Notices of the meeting must be formal. They must also contain all the relevant information:

'Notice is hereby given that an Extraordinary General Meeting of the

XYZ Company will be held at the Waldorf Hotel, Aldwych, London, WC 2 on Friday, 9 October 1969 for the purpose of considering the following resolutions.'

It is also wise to add a note on proxies:

'Any member entitled to attend and vote at the meeting may appoint one or more persons to attend and upon a poll to vote in his or her stead. A proxy need not be a member of the company. To be effective the proxy together with any power of attorney or other authority under which it is signed or office copy of such power or authority shall be deposited at the offices of the company's registrars . . . not less than 48 hours before the time appointed for the meeting.'

The date and time are just as important. So is the location. If the various resolutions are formal as in the case of Guardian Properties (Holdings), there is little point in holding the meeting in a large room. If, however, the meeting is likely to attract a great deal of attention as well as a big attendance by shareholders, then much larger premises are necessary. This, in turn, will decide the facilities for the business news media. In the case of Pergamon, for example, it meant catering for radio and television as well.

The opportunities for news and feature publicity are also relative. In any case a press release should be issued after the meeting and circulated to the relevant business news madia. Shareholders who were unable to be present should also be notified of the result of the meeting. If the meeting was of major importance, advertisements should also be taken in order to make as many people as possible aware of the result.

'The board of directors of Pergamon Press Limited elected at the Extraordinary General Meeting held on Friday, 10th October 1969 to meet the same evening. At this meeting:
  (a) Sir Henry d'Avigdor-Goldsmid, Bart., D.S.O., M.C., M.P. and Mr D. A. Hunter Johnston were elected members of the board.
  (b) Sir Henry d'Avigdor-Goldsmid was appointed Chairman of the board with overriding executive powers.
  (c) Mr M. Abbott, Mr Robert Hodes, Mr R Oliver, Mr Bernard Schwartz and Mr Saul Steinberg resigned from the board.'
(*Financial Times* advertisement, 13 October 1969)

In most cases, therefore, it is simply a matter of repeating the public relations programme for an annual meeting.

Takeovers and mergers

*Knife and fork millionaire Mr Charles Forte made an £8,000,000 takeover
bid yesterday for Skyway, who owns hotels at London Airport, Southampton
and Miami in America.*
(*Daily Mirror* 5 August 1969)
*Allied Ironfounders, the bath makers, and Painton, the electronics firm,
are the latest to go under the hammer. Allied are fighting and Painton
talking—both shares went soaring shillings over their market prices. And
signs are that better things are coming.*
(*Sun*, 6 August 1969)

Gone are the lazy, hazy days of management. The top of the corporate
pyramid is just as precarious nowadays as the shop floor. For any day, a
merger merchant or takeover tyrant can strike. At the least, it means a bitter
struggle. At the worst, it could mean a clean sweep through the boardroom.
It is this aspect, the threat of management dismissal especially, which has
made takeovers a number-one story for the press. Even the word 'takeover',
according to financial journalist Paul Bareau, was coined by a hard-pressed
sub-editor who was desperately searching for a synonym for 'amalgamation'.

11.1 Mergers and takeovers are big business

Sir Isaac Wolfson, Charles Clore, Lord Fraser, Lord Thomson, Jim Slater—
they have all built enormous organisations in a few years through takeovers.
When Wolfson and Clore started in the 1950's, takeovers were rare. Ten years
later they were an accepted fact of business life. Even the giant ICI was raiding
a sleepy Courtaulds although it was soon beaten off. Whole areas of industry
were completely re-shaped. Tired, exhausted companies were snapped up,
shaken and turned into profitable money-makers by the takeover tyrants.
Although the actual number of companies acquired annually since 1964 has
fallen from 939 to 598, the amount of money involved has soared more than
three times from £502m to £1,653m in the same period. And the average
consideration has shot up from a measly £500,000 to £2·8m. (See Table 11.1.)

Table 11.1 Mergers and acquisitions 1954–68*

	Number of company mergers			Number of Public company mergers, % of total	Value of company mergers			Number of Public company mergers, % of total
	Public	Private	All		Public	Private	All	
1954	42	233	275	15·2	59·6	45·6	105·2	56·6
1955	49	245	294	16·6	45·8	42·8	88·6	51·7
1956	44	202	246	17·9	54·4	76·9	131·3	41·4
1957	70	231	301	23·2	98·4	37·2	135·6	72·5
1958	60	273	333	18·0	79·6	40·6	120·2	66·2
1959	98	461	559	17·5	216·0	91·3	307·3	70·2
1960	81	655	736	11·0	160·6	177·8	338·4	47·4
1961	64	568	632	10·1	225·4	142·2	367·6	61·3
1962	62	574	636	9·7	191·3	166·7	358·0	53·4
1963	77	808	885	8·7	157·4	174·5	332·0	47·4
1964	71	868	939	7·5	262·0	240·0	502·0	52·2
1965	75	920	995	7·5	347·0	160·0	507·0	68·4
1966	78	727	805	9·7	330·0	117·0	447·0	73·8
1967	84	557	641	13·1	630·0	151·0	781·0	80·7
1968	140	458	598	23·4	1,516·0	137·0	1,653·0	91·7
Totals	1,095	7,780	8,875		4,373·5	1,800·6	6,174·2	

* *Financial Times*, 30 December 1969

It's the same in the United States. Before 1960 the tender offer was practically unknown. Five years later the New York Stock Exchange reported 56 companies involved in tender offers. The American Stock Exchange reported another 30 the same year. By 1969 there were around 230.

Stagnant profit margins. A share price worth about half the assets. Low sales. Low earnings. Low market rating. And low dividends. These are the ingredients for most takeovers. But in other cases, companies are snatched up because their assets are worth more than the price the shares are selling at. In other words, they are worth more dead than alive. Or because a company wants to move into a new industry and finds it cheaper to take over an existing organisation with the necessary skills and expertise rather than start up from scratch. They are worth more to an outsider than they are to themselves.

There are six points that bring tears of joy to any takeover merchant:

1 Low management stock ownership. The less stock controlled by management the better.
2 Small institutional holdings. The less chance of the big boys ganging up against a bid.
3 Disenchanted stockholders. The more the merrier. The better the chances of success.

4 Speculators. Again, the more the merrier. Their loyalties will be minimal. They will only be interested in the price.
5 Wide distribution of stockholders. Less chance of stockholders getting together and having a decisive influence.
6 A rising market.

Essentially there are three different kinds of merger and takeover. First, the merger by equals—when two companies in the same industry and about the same size decide to join forces. It is merger by amalgamation. Second, the merger by unequals. This happens when one company gains control of another by actually buying control of the larger or smaller partner. This is merger by acquisition. Third, the contested merger. For not all marriages are made in heaven. Quite often the groom has to be coaxed towards the altar with a shotgun. Says Vincent H. Gannon, a Vice-President of Hill and Knowlton (*Current Thoughts*, M. W. Lads Publishing Company, New York, 1968), 'The shotgun in this case is called a tender offer—a company advertises that it wants to buy a specified number of shares of another company's stock, usually enough to assure control, at a price temptingly higher than the going market price. The 'groom' may be a company in a turn-around position; higher earnings are in sight but are not yet reflected in the price of its shares. Or it may be a company with a tax loss that would bring a tax saving and higher earnings to the acquiring company. Or perhaps the acquiring company wants to diversify or enter a new market; the tender offer may be cheaper than starting from scratch or negotiating an acquisition. Or still another possibility, the earnings of a company undervalued in the stock market may add to the market appeal of the acquiring company and justify the premium paid.' This is merger by takeover.

Mergers and financial public relations—or lack of—always go together. Says Cocking, 'Takeover bids invariably hit the financial headlines. City Editors will publish their own advice to shareholders. It is, therefore, important that any board of directors should be poised to communicate its case to the press forcibly and at the right psychological moment. Merchant banks are the skilled duellists in any takeover struggle but it is the financial public relations consultant who can best advise on the form and timing of statements to the financial press in order to achieve maximum impact and to rally the widest support.'

Derriman quotes a merchant banker who goes even further.

'In contested bids, financial public relations are of supreme importance. Quite apart from the enormous disadvantage of the man who has ignored all this in the past, there is no doubt that in an evenly balanced situation public relations can very well win or lose the battle. The effective arguments in the end may not lie in the technical financial field, because the shareholders may decide by what is the right thing for the employees, and by their local loyalties.'

11.2 Fighting off a raider

But it's no good sitting back and trusting to the skills of a financial public relations consultant when the bidder strikes. The kind of financial public relations that is invaluable in fighting off a corporate raider, is the kind of public relations that is developed throughout the years. This means following the advice outlined so far and developing a two-way relationship with the financial public relations media.

11.2.1 MAINTAIN AN EFFECTIVE SHAREHOLDER RELATIONS PROGRAMME

The company that lives together, stays together. Those glossy annual reports could be the cement that keeps a company intact in the face of a raid. Not because shareholders are hoodwinked. But because attractive, readable and informative statements engender confidence. And like it or not, turnout at annual meetings is a good barometer of shareholder confidence. 'Probably, the most effective precaution', says Jones, 'is for management to take shareholders into their confidence to the maximum practicable extent. The company that presents its accounts in a simple, informative manner, reinforces the statutory accounts with effective explanatory statements, gives a welcome to members at general meetings and perhaps circulates interim reports at not less than half-yearly intervals, is far less likely to find itself at the wrong end of a takeover bid.'

11.2.2 MAINTAIN AN EFFECTIVE EMPLOYEE RELATIONS PROGRAMME

This doesn't just mean building a valuable employee shareholder scheme, inviting representatives to annual meetings and so on. Although it is desperately important. It also means ensuring that employees—as shareholders—are wholly satisfied with the development of the company. A large slice of employee-owned shares does not automatically guarantee they will follow the company line. The employee retirement fund at Kropp Forge Company in Chicago, for example, turned down a plan to merge with Gulf and Western and voted for a management-opposed takeover by Anadite Incorporated, a Californian metal-producing company instead. An effective employee relations programme, however, helps. Put yourself in the position of a raider. How would you reckon your chances if a large slice of the company belong to the employees?

11.2.3 MAINTAIN AN EFFECTIVE FINANCIAL PUBLIC RELATIONS PROGRAMME

Shareholders are important when it comes to repelling a raider. But so are the financial public relations media, which influences them. This was the point made by the Chairman of the London Stock Exchange, Mr R. F. M. Wilkinson on 8 May 1968. 'Communications with the shareholder and the investing public generally must be a continuous and continuing process designed with a clear understanding of the needs of those for whom it is intended and supported by the company making the communication', he said. 'It means creating good and favourable relations with the wider investing public, the City and the Press.'

11.2.4 CHECK THE MESSAGE IS GETTING HOME

Good financial public relations is expensive. Bad financial public relations is damned expensive. It could cost a company its life. For a bad communications programme could leave a company defenceless in the face of a raider. A company should, therefore, regularly check that it is hitting the target. An example of the kind of research a company can undertake is the ICI research into the effectiveness of their annual report. See page 173. If in doubt—take a survey. This need not be an elaborate affair. Just a random check to find out how the financial public relations media rate a particular company. Says Cheney (Ohio State Bar Association's 12th Annual Institute on Corporate Legal Problems, 8 November 1968):

> 'If you take a survey, you would be in a lot better position to judge your vulnerability to a tender. You might be like one new client who was shocked to learn that, for all his talking to analyst societies, the financial community believed he had, as one analyst put it, "delusions of adequacy". This does not mean asking around the investment community to find out if anyone has heard rumours about a possible tender for your stock. This is one of the best ways ever discovered to start the rumour mill churning. I am advocating only that you try to find out what the financial community thinks of your company and its management.'

11.2.5 MAINTAIN AN EARLY WARNING SYSTEM

'It usually happens when you're not ready', says Leo Cavendish, 29-year-old head of Financial Press Information Services. 'If companies are susceptible to takeover offers they should have the documents ready to rebuff the approaches.' Watch the volume of trading. If it suddenly increases for no apparent reason, find out why. Keep an eye on the price. If it suddenly shoots up leaving the rest of the industry behind, something is happening. It could be the first signs. Check the names of new stockholders. It could be significant. 'You must determine who the opposition is', says Beveridge. 'And this is sometimes difficult. You'll want to know what kind of people they are, because if they're racketeers, you'll want to crucify them. And, before you do, you had better be sure that you can prove what you are going to say.'

Better safe than sorry. Companies should keep a close watch on developments in their industry. If a particular company suddenly turns ambitious, they should have all the necessary background information at hand. The company secretary together with the financial public relations adviser ought to maintain a draft defence in case the company is suddenly raided out of the blue. The best possible arguments for use against attack together with the necessary figures should always be in draft form. Similarly the financial public relations department ought to know how quickly they could mount a defence operation: calling press conferences, preparing statements and figures for the press and, of course, mailing details and advice to shareholders.

11.2.6 MAINTAIN AN ACTION PROGRAMME OF ATTACK

Once a raid is on, there is little time for planning. Often the most vigorous response pays dividends. Financial public relations advisers have a skeleton advertising programme on file together with a media list and cost schedule. If a company wants to repel boarders, speed is the essence. Similarly with editorial men. Lists should be on hand detailing them in order of importance. Top financial journalists welcome private briefings for top executives. This should be arranged within minutes, if necessary. Lists of major shareholders should also be available. Again, companies should be in a position to mount a personal lobby of all major shareholders to explain their side of the story—first. Says Cheney:

> 'If a tender comes, establish a position of calm, careful attention to the interests of the owners, the employees and public. Nothing is so apt to damage your cause as panic and attacking the management of the company making the tender is almost as bad. If Ho Chi Minh makes an offer, stockholder opinion might be so outraged that the tender would fail, but assuming the tender is made by a mine-run American raider using cash, it is to the raider's advantage if the stockholders think he is a horse thief. The possibility that the tender might succeed and the horse thief take over will cause the stockholders to get rid of their shares all the quicker.'

11.3 The six stages of a takeover

Any takeover bid broadly falls in six separate stages.

11.3.1 DECIDING ON A TAKEOVER BID

Checking the research. Deciding the tactics. Assessing the chances of success. These are all essential in the vital pre-bid planning stage. So is telling the financial public relations advisers. Even though they are always in contact with the press, it does not mean they will immediately bleat out every scrap of information to the press. They can respect a confidence just the same as any other businessmen, if not more so. In the long run, it benefits the company. For the financial public relations people can draw up their plan of action; prepare the necessary research and decide the strategy to be adopted in releasing and projecting the information. Says Cheney:

> 'The public relations man for one tendering company, for example, who

had been brought into the planning in advance of the tender, was adequately prepared once the tender was sprung to come into the headquarters town of the victim company and appear on television and radio. He explained what good things were in store for the community and employees if the tender offer succeeded. He visited with the local editors and got editorials favouring the tender. The management, who had neglected its press relations over the years, was flabbergasted. They wanted to oppose the tender, but they had lost an important opportunity to use fear of changes to enlist local support and encourage local stock purchase.'

That's only one aspect. Once the financial public relations advisers are taken into the company's confidence they can also begin planning their assault on the financial public relations media proper: the City, City institutions, brokers, bankers and so on.

11.3.2 RUMOURS

There are two kinds: unsubstantiated and substantiated. Any possible bid has a number of signs. First, a sudden up-surge in the volume of trading. This is not too difficult to detect. Second, a corresponding increase in the price. Most newspapers list the major price changes every day. It doesn't take a financial wizard to spot a company whose price has been moving up over a period. It doesn't necessarily mean a bid is in the offing, of course. But it could be a straw in the wind. The real insider would now start checking further. It might be possible to discover the buyer. If its a single company, it could mean a bidder. Or it could mean they were only interested in a limited stake. It depends how far they go. The real insider would probably go further still. He would try and discover how fast the transfers were being made. If they were being made regularly, everything is probably alright. If, however, they were being delayed, it could mean a bidder was building up a stake in the company before revealing his hand. Or it could mean nothing. Again, nobody knows what it means until somebody says something. As a result, the rumours begin simmering whether there is any foundation for them or not. If there is no foundation for them, the sooner the companies concerned say so the better.

Now the substantiated rumours.

'Almost on the first anniversary of the initial whisper, last night saw the most rumoured bid of this year, and maybe any other year, become a fact. Surprise, surprise, it is the long-looked-for offer from "Players" and "Wills" cigarette combine, Imperial Tobacco, for frozen foodsters, Ross Group.
(*Daily Express*, 7 August 1969)

'After a month of rumours about a possible bid for Lombard Banking it

was revealed last night that Britain's biggest clearing bank, National Westminster, was having "preliminary discussions" with Lombard "with a view to the possible combination of their instalment credit interests!" '
(*Financial Times*, 10 September 1969)

When is a bid a bid? When it has been made. If companies are merely talking about the possibility of a merger or takeover, they are under no obligation to say anything.

The City Code on Mergers and Takeovers merely says:

'Where there have been approaches which may or may not lead to an offer, the duty of a Board in relation to shareholders is less clearly defined. There are obvious dangers in announcing prematurely an approach which may not lead to an offer. By way of guidance it can be said that an announcement of the facts should be made forthwith as soon as two companies are agreed on the basic terms of an offer and are reasonably confident of a successful outcome of the negotiations.'

Lombard Banking zoomed 4s to 44s in late deals on 9 September 1969. Rumours were suggesting a bid from National Westminster. They were right. The following day came the confirmation, as the City Code suggested:

'The National Westminster Bank and Lombard Banking have confirmed that they are having bid talks. This could lead to an offer worth upwards of £40 million being made for Lombard, the deposit banking and hire purchase group. Informal talks have been going on for some time.'
(*Daily Express*, 10 September 1969)

As the Code says, 'The vital importance of absolute secrecy before an announcement must be emphasised'. David Koonce, an account executive with the giant American Carl Byoir and Associates PR consultancy, for example, went to almost absurd lengths to maintain strict security while his client, Omark Industries Incorporated, Portland, Oregon, maker of welding equipment were negotiating to buy Briles Manufacturing, a privately held firm based in El Segundo, California. First, he installed a special hot-line telephone in the offices of the president and the chairman of Omark. All calls to El Segundo were made on the line and not through the switchboard. Only secretaries who had to know were told anything. The rest were kept in the dark. And then—the final touch—Koonce typed two press releases, one saying the two companies were negotiating, the other that agreement in principle had been reached, so that he was ready for a possible leak. 'I put these in two sealed envelopes, put them in my briefcase and even took them home with me at night', he told the *Wall Street Journal* on 9 October 1968. 'I even took them when I went out to lunch. If there should be a hint of a leak, I wanted to be prepared to make immediate disclosure, using the appropriate release.' Executives involved in the deal had trouble on the home front as well.

They had to tell their wives they were going out of town for a few days without being able to say where they were going. Koonce even found that right in the middle of things, his wife decided she'd like to buy a few more Omark shares. 'I had to talk her out of it without being able to tell her why', he told the Journal. A preliminary agreement was reached over a weekend. On the Monday the market was lively. Without being sure there hadn't been a leak, they decided they couldn't maintain the strict security right up until the final agreement had been signed. They decided to release the 'agreement in principle' statement. 'It sounds sort of cloak and dagger. But its not enough to be clean. You must be aseptic', said Koonce.

11.3.3 MAKING THE BID
The nearer the time comes to make the actual bid, the more the rumours start to fly. This is a dangerous time for the bidder and the victim. For rumours can rock a company from top to bottom. They can also attract press censure. The City Code tackles this dangerous period in rule 5.

> 'When any firm intention to make an offer is notified to a Board from a serious source (irrespective of whether the Board views the offer favourably or otherwise) shareholders must be informed without delay by Press notice. The Press notice should be followed as soon as possible by a circular.'

But (see previous section) the Panel is less certain when it comes to the pre-bid stage.

> 'Where there have been approaches which may or may not lead to an offer, the duty of a Board in relation to shareholders is less clearly defined. There are obvious dangers in announcing prematurely an approach which may not lead to an offer. By way of guidance it can be said that an announcement of the facts should be made forthwith as soon as two companies are agreed on the basic terms of an offer and are reasonably confident of a successful outcome of the negotiations.'

It goes on to make two further points about publicity and speed which should be borne in mind.

> 'In any situation which might lead to an offer being made, whether welcome or not, a close watch should be kept on the share market; in the event of any untoward movement in share prices an immediate announcement accompanied by such comment as may be appropriate should be made. . . . Joint statements are desirable whenever possible, provided that agreement thereon does not lead to undue delay. The obligation to make announcements lies no less with the potential offeror company than with the offeree company.'

But what is a 'firm intention'? *The Times* took the Chairman of Ross Group,

Mr Alex Alexander, to task on 7 August 1969 following the bid for the Ross Group from Imperial Tobacco.

'One major complaint to be made about the whole affair is Mr Alexander's denial of an offer yesterday afternoon. Mr Alexander lunched yesterday with Kleinwort, his merchant bank advisers, discussing the terms of the possible bid. The denial may have been technically correct, since agreement was not reached until late afternoon. But it was undeniably misleading in the circumstances. A considerable number of Ross shares were sold after the statement by holders who took it at its face value. It would have been much better if Mr Alexander had admitted that negotiations were in progress—or even refused to comment at all.'

David Malbert, City editor of the *Evening News*, made the same point. 'It looks as if the takeover scene is again being muddied by leaks', he said. And yet—what is a 'firm intention'? *The Times* returned to the problem the following day.

'What is needed is a much clearer indication to directors of quoted companies and their advisers as to what they should say when negotiations towards a takeover bid are in progress. Clearly an offer is not an offer until it is an offer. There are a great many graduations before that stage is reached. Much the most satisfactory statement for shareholders and the health and reputation of the market is for as many facts as possible about approaches or negotiations to be made public at the earliest stage. But equally no company wishes to be named as a potential victim, or something less than a victim, when nothing comes of the negotiation at the end of the day. It is generally bad for the company's reputation and its credit. Yet far less satisfactory are denials even in the best faith of events which materialise within hours. Directors need to be helped by the Panel on this. And at the same time the Stock Exchange would enhance its reputation for efficiency and good sense by announcing in a clear and firm voice that it is instituting an investigation into dealings because of suspected leaks. It is ridiculous to neither confirm nor deny that enquiries are in progress when anyone in the least close to the scene knows perfectly well what is going on.'

So much for the 'firm intention'. But how can it be 'notified'? What is the best way of informing the Press 'without delay'? Imagine the position. A company has just slapped in a bid. A press release is prepared within seconds. Messengers are despatched hot-foot with the news to all City editors. That probably comes within the City Code. But don't forget there is bound to be a long delay between the City editor at the top of the list receiving his copy and the City editor at the bottom of the list. Should the releases be telexed straight to newspaper offices instead? That certainly seems to come nearer the spirit of the City Code. Then there are other problems. If you are going to notify the press, for heaven's sake make certain that both companies are in agreement. Blaw Knox–Babcock and Wilcox came in for some criticism from *The Times*—again—on this point (9 August 1969):

'As it was, the initial statement was satisfactory in all respects except that it did not state the objects of the talks, and when the press inevitably inquired, the spokesmen for the two parties gave conflicting explanations. For a while after, the market for Blaw shares had some of the characteristics of roulette and no semblance of equality of risk, the hallmark of an orderly stock market.'

Once the bid has actually been made, however, there are communications problems for both the raider and the victim. Says Cheney:

'The tender price does make a difference in a tender offer but a company's relations with the public and the press, whether it is a raider or a target company, are also important in a tender situation. Ignoring stockholders and public sentiment and emotion can slow a raider down, raise his costs and even cause him to fail.'

This means keeping the financial public relations media informed. Above all, the financial public relations adviser will have his time cut out ensuring management fight the real enemy not an imagined adversary with real weapons. Brainerd Chapman, partner of Pritchard, Chapman, Pennington, Montgomery and Sloan and a veteran of US takeover battles says:

'You'll want to see yourself as others see you. You may want to anticipate some of the charges which the opposition is planning to say you should have done, because this will take the wind out of their sails.'

The business news media

Attackers hold all the trumps. They are go-ahead, dynamic, usually trying against all the odds to carve an empire out of nothing. All the ingredients that go to make a good news story. Bill de Vigier, Chairman and Managing Director of Acrow, was described as 'something of a legend' in a *Times* business diary profile when he was making his £18 million offer for Allied Ironfounders. A Swiss emigré, he arrived in Britain at the age of 24 in 1936. He started Acrow, named after his lawyer, Arthur Crow, with £50 of savings from his apprenticeship days in a Swiss iron foundry. The cornerstone of the company was a revolutionary steel prop for use in the construction industry, which he manufactured initially underneath Bow Arches in the East End.

The Oriental Carpet Manufacturers Ltd.

The Directors of the Oriental Carpet Manufacturers Limited ('OCM') announce that they are having discussions with the directors of Ralli

Brothers (Trading) Limited ('RBT') with a view to obtaining the whole of the issued share capital of that company. In view of the size of the proposed acquisition the directors of OCM have requested the Council of The Stock Exchange, London, to suspend temporarily the quotation of the shares in the company pending an announcement of the outcome of the discussions. If terms for the acquisition are agreed, full details will be sent to the shareholders of OCM as soon as possible (28 August 1969)

'Sitting in front of a large-scale wallchart tracing the growth of Acrow and clutching a foot-long Jamaican cigar, Bill de Vigier explained to us yesterday his motives for the Allied Ironfounders bid. It was right in line with his product philosophy of "make it, sell it and forget it". He has no time for products which require after-sales service: so Allied's baths, drainage goods, kitchen appliances fit well with this school of thought.' (6 August 1969)

Charles Forte did even better when he slapped in his £8 million plus bid for Skyway Hotels. He was the subject of one from-rags-to-riches profile after another.

'Bermuda, Paris, the Mediterranean . . . now Florida? At the last count, the Fortes hotel empire, founded on ice-cream and milk bars in postwar London, comprised 38 establishments with a total of more than 8,000 beds. They are dotted at airports and holiday resorts around the world from Birmingham to Bermuda, but the acquisition of Skyway opens up the US market for the first time and plugs a vital and significant gap in the planned network.'
(*The Times*, 5 August 1969)

Yet defenders are not out in the cold altogether. Dickenson, probably the first PRO to utilise the press in a takeover battle, made a tremendous impact during the Glaxo struggle for British Drug Houses. Hambros were called in by BDH to fight off the bid. Public relations was part of the service. 'We made the point that it was terribly relevant to shareholders—not pie in the sky. This was the first news of the British pill. It was also the first time the *Daily Mirror* gave a takeover a big spread', he says. Hambros went on to win the fight on behalf of BDH.

When it comes to the details of the offer documents and so on, its in a company's interests to prepare special summaries for the press featuring the main points of the argument. If a bid is complicated, it is worth arranging special press briefings. This, for example, was arranged by Rothschilds during the Showerings bid for Harveys in 1965. It is also invaluable to have one man responsible for liaison with the press. Takeovers and mergers are difficult times. They always come out of the blue which generally means confusion. In the midst of confusion, however, the press should be able to rely on at least one source of reliable up-to-the-minute information. If they cannot, they tend to rely on speculation and rumour. Which, in turn, can cause even more confusion. It is worth the effort.

Enots, the Birmingham-based manufacturers of pneumatic control and centralised lubrication systems equipment, introduced a novel angle into the takeover scene with a full page advertisement in the *Financial Times* on 24 November 1969.

'This page was to be a prospectus for Enots. Then someone thought of making a bid for us. Our 6,000 customers know why. You might like to know too.'

The copy went on to tell the story of the company—'Enots is Stone spelt backwards. That's the only backward thing about us'—which was founded the year before Waterloo; how they now market 2,000 different products throughout Western Europe, South Africa, Australia, New Zealand, Israel and Brazil; and how their profits have risen 50 per cent each year since 1967. In fact, they had grown so much that in 1965 they began moving from Birmingham to brand new premises at Lichfield. With a 250,000 sq ft factory, with room for further expansion, phased for completion in 1972, they already had 140,000 sq ft fully operational. Then came a note from the directors. While they had been finalising the arrangements for obtaining a quotation for the company's ordinary shares, they had received preliminary notification of a proposed share exchange offer for all the ordinary shares of the company. As a result, they decided to postpone the offer for sale while they considered the approach. (They also, of course, had time to consider the investing public as well—in a highly individual and effective way.)

Employees

To employees, there is much more at stake than cash. Their jobs, their very livelihood could be in jeopardy. Companies fighting a takeover battle owe it to them to keep them informed—right from the start. Yet in only two instances out of eight takeover case histories studied by Dennis Brooks and Randall Smith in *The Human Factors of Mergers* (Acton Society, 1966) were any efforts made to keep the work force informed. In the other cases, the work staff were left to ferret out their information from rumours or the news media. Obviously, this is wrong. Employees should be put into the picture as soon as the official announcement has been made. Delay is dangerous. The longer employees have had to absorb the rumours, the more difficult it is for a company to put its case. Don't forget, employees can have a decisive influence in a takeover.

Courtaulds was, of course, the classic example of this form of defence. The battle with ICI was a long and bitter struggle. The two giants stepped down into the market place and fought tooth and claw. As a result, many wild

P

accusations were slung backwards and forwards. But if the bid was to succeed, it meant that many top executives in particular would have to swallow the insults and knuckle down under new masters, who had made their attitude perfectly plain. Said the *Financial Times*:

'To take over and digest an organisation the size of Courtauld's is not an easy matter at the best of times. To do so in the face of hostility on the part of Courtauld's personnel would be an immense undertaking in human and managerial terms. One has only to think of the disruption which was caused by the departure of top management when the coal industry, for example, was nationalised, to see the problems ICI might have to face. It seems clear that if ICI does succeed in its bid there will be considerable resentment among Courtauld's executive and research staff—after what ICI has said about the company's record—and this is not going to make it easy to establish the sort of relationships which will enable the marriage to be a happy and fruitful one.'

The Rank Organisation found its bid for De La Rue rebuffed for the same reason. Therefore, it is in the interests of both companies concerned—attacker and defender—to try to gain their support. The attacker should stress right from the start their plans for staff reorganisation if their bid is successful. If they foresee redundancies, they should give an indication of the extent and timing of the cut-back. They should also release full information on any redundancy payment schemes they envisage. Defenders, however, are in a stronger position providing, of course, the employees are on their side.

Speculators
This is rife in the United States. Although it is probably kept within reasonable bounds in the United Kingdom. Cheney suggests one way to keep arbitrageurs, brokers who buy and sell at the same time to take advantage of the price discrepancies, at bay.

'One of the best ways to give them pause about coming in on a tender is to throw a lawsuit at a raider that looks as if it might stick—particularly a good antitrust action. Arbitrageurs don't want a big inventory on a target company's stock on hand with the possibility of their not being able to complete the tender and take their profit. A lawsuit will often drive them away. On the other hand, with the arbitrageur's attitude toward risk in mind, if you are hit with a tender, think twice before announcing that you are getting cozy with another suitor. Of course, you may be forced to make such an announcement ultimately under the timely disclosure rules. But prior to that, remember, arbitrageurs are more apt to move in if management reacts to a raid with an announcement that it is discussing a merger with a shelter company. It is true that such an announcement may tend to dissuade your Aunt Jane stockholders from tendering to the raider or selling. If you have a lot of stock in the hands of conservative stockholders, the promise of a friendly merger may keep stock on the market so the arbitrageur cannot accumulate enough to make any difference. But if your stock has attracted a lot of traders, beware. The prospects of a bidding contest will bring arbitrageurs on the double. If you decide to go ahead anyway and talk about a shelter merger, you'd better be sure you deliver a deal better than the one your enemy has to offer. Otherwise, the arbitrageur is going to be encouraged to buy a big block of stock that will wind up on your enemy's doorstep.'

Shareholders

'It is essential that after an offer has been announced the offer document and a letter setting out the views of the Board of the offeree company should be circulated as soon as possible', says the takeover code. If a company which has made an offer, however, and does not go ahead with the formal offer within a reasonable time, they must be prepared to justify the position to the Panel. The raider must despatch the terms of his offer, approved by the Stock Exchange, to his victim at least three business days before he circulates it to shareholders. At the same time copies should go to the Panel Secretariat. Offer time is a difficult time for a raider. More than 20 of the Takeover Panel's 35 rules cover the ground. Then there is the Prevention of Frauds (Investment) Act, 1958; the Licensed Dealers (Conduct of Business) Rules, 1960; and the various Stock Exchange requirements laid down in The Admission of Securities to Quotation. Where an offer is made for more than one class of share, the Companies Act, 1948, must also be taken into account. Separate offers must be made for each class with the attacking company announcing that it will resort to compulsory acquisition powers only in respect of each class separately. Offers, in fact, must be treated virtually the same as prospectuses. First the obvious essentials. The bidder must be clearly identified. The value of the securities must be given.

The reason for the bid. If the proposed move represents a significant move in rationalisation of the industry, the document should say so. It should also spell out the advantages to the industry, the company and, of course, the shareholders. If there are conditions attached to the offer, they must be given.

The result of the bid. Any takeover or merger means economies. Economies, however, could mean redundancies. The offeror should spell out its policy towards rationalisation, its effects—if any—on the directors and employees of the company concerned.

Forecasts. Two can live together almost as cheaply as one. At least, that's the theory. A combined company should stand a chance of making bigger and better profits and, of course, providing higher dividends to shareholders. Forecasts are difficult. Hence phrases like, '. . . it is anticipated that, if trading conditions are maintained, the improvements established in recent years should continue . . .'. But they are essential.

Recommendations. There is little point sending out an offer unless the company makes it absolutely clear that it is urging shareholders to accept. In some cases, the wording is so tortuous that it is difficult to understand what it is all about, let alone get the message. That is absurd. But the offeror should ensure that the message goes home loud and clear.

Shareholders must be given all the facts. Says the Takeover Code:

> 'Shareholders must be put into possession of all the facts necessary for the formation of an informed judgement as to the merits or demerits of an offer. Such facts must be accurately and fairly presented and be available to the shareholder early enough to enable him to make a decision in good time. The obligation of the offeror company in these respects towards the shareholders of the offeree company is no less than its obligation towards its own shareholders.'

It goes on to show how much information it means.

Assets. It is no good the Board saying that assets had been revalued. The basis of the revaluation must be given together with the opinion of independent professional experts as well.

Mechanics of the formal offer. Rules 20–24 of the Takeover Code lay down what a company can bid for, the amount of the equity share capital involved, what should happen if a company fails in its attempt, the timing of the various moves involved in takeover battles and so on. Rule 25 lays down that 'the obligations of the offeror company and the rights of the offeree company shareholders under Rules 20–24 must be specifically incorporated in the offer document.'

Profits. Forecasts must not only be compiled with the greatest possible care but the assumptions, including the commercial assumptions upon which they are based, must also be included. If they cover a period in which trading has already started, then the latest unaudited figures for the expired period together with the corresponding figures for the same period the previous year must also be given. That's not all. Auditors or consultant accountants must examine and report on both the accounting bases and the calculations of the forecasts as well. So must the merchant bank or any other adviser mentioned in the document.

Resources. If the offer is for cash—or includes an element of cash—an adviser or any other independent party must confirm that the resources are available to satisfy the full acceptance of the offer.

Service contracts. The offeror company must say in its offer documents whether its directors' emoluments will be affected by the takeover or not.

Similarly the offeree company must detail all the service contracts in force for its directors as well as for directors of any of its subsidiaries who have more than 12 months to operate. They must also say whether any of the contracts were entered into within six months of the date of the document. If so, details of the contracts and particulars of any immediately preceding contracts must be given.

Shareholdings. If the offeror company has any shareholding in the offeree company, the offer document must say so. It must also give the total of the shareholdings in the offeree company in which directors of the offeror company are interested. Similarly when the offeree company advises its shareholders whether to accept or reject the offer it must give the following information about its shareholding:

1 The extent of the shareholding of directors of the offeree company in both the offeree company and the offeror company.
2 The extent of the shareholding of the offeree company in the offeror company.
3 Whether the directors of the offeree company intend, in respect of their own shareholdings, to accept or reject the offer.

There is one other point. If any of these shareholdings have been taken up within six months of the date on the offer document, all the details—date, cost and so on—must be given. If, however, no shareholdings had been purchased, that fact must also be made.

Mergers are more involved but less complicated. The offer document goes out just the same. But this time, although there is no legal obligation, it is generally accompanied by a letter from the chairman giving the board's reasons for wanting the go-ahead with the merger. If not, it should. For obvious reasons.

'The merger will represent a significant move in rationalisation within the industry. Furthermore it will result in a Group which will provide additional and more flexible capacities to meet the increasing demands in industry at home and overseas and through the facilities afforded by an enlarged marketing and sales organisation should lead to a greater share of the potential world markets. XYZ Ltd is expanding under energetic and enterprising management and in recent times has made marked progress. It is clear that the experience and acumen, gained over the last few years, has been consolidated into an effective force, with the knowledge, drive and leadership capable of profitable achievement. All this along with net assets, largely in the United Kingdom, valued at more than twice those attributable to UVW shareholders, gives your Board a sense of fairness in the values of the proposed financial arrangements as well as confidence in the fundamental strength of the new group.

In view of the foregoing your directors strongly recommend these proposals as being in the best interests of the shareholders.'

Any changes in the company's prospects since the last annual or interim report should be added. It would also be wise to mention the effects the merger would have on employees, especially if there is a large employee shareholding in the company.

11.3.4 AWAITING THE RESULT
This is three weeks of limbo. The timing is strictly laid down by the Takeover Panel:

> 'An offer must initially be open for at least 21 days after the posting of the offer and, if revised, it must be kept open for at least eight days from the date of posting written notification of the revision to shareholders: an acceptor shall be entitled to withdraw his acceptance in any case after the expiry of 21 days from the first closing date of the initial offer, if the offer has not by such expiry become or been declared unconditional; such entitlement to withdraw shall be exercisable until such time as the offer becomes or is declared unconditional.'

No offer, revised or otherwise, can be declared unconditional 60 days after the date of posting the initial offer. Nor can it be kept open—unless it has previously become or been declared unconditional. If, however, a competing offer is made or becomes unconditional, a formal offer may be withdrawn, but the Panel must give the go-ahead first.

There are other rules on timing as well. After an offer has become or is declared unconditional, it must remain open for acceptance for not less than 14 days—unless the offeror company has given ten days notice in writing to shareholders of the offeree company that the offer will not be open for acceptance beyond a set expiry date when the offer becomes or is declared unconditional. But if the unconditional declaration becomes void and is subsequently reinstated, the 14-day period can run from the date of the second declaration.

All this provides headaches for the company and its advisers and opportunities for the financial public relations experts. Every deadline is an opportunity for hammering home the message and rallying support. There should be a regular series of briefings for the various financial press media. Contact should be established with employees, customers, suppliers and all the other financial public relations media.

In the meantime anything can happen.

The victim could surrender
If the offer makes sense, it would be foolish to turn it down. The directors of the offeree company could go ahead and recommend acceptance. If, however,

the shareholding of the directors effectively control the company they must ensure that the remaining shareholders get the same offer. When it comes to mergers all shareholders are equal. Or should be. As the Takeover Code says:

> 'Directors whose shareholdings, together with those of their families and trusts, effectively control a company, or shareholders in that position who are represented on the Board of a company, and who contemplate transferring control, should not, other than in special circumstances, do so unless the buyer undertakes to extend within a reasonable period of time a comparable offer to the holders of the remaining equity share capital, whether such capital carries voting rights or not. In such special circumstances the Panel must be consulted in advance and its consent obtained.'

The victim could fight back

The victim could fight back for a number of reasons. Perhaps the price was wrong. Perhaps they were not right for each other. Perhaps there was a better match with another company. Either way there is plenty of scope for the offeree's financial public relations advisers. The victim could go a stage further and begin attacking as well. Says Cheney:

> 'An action programme to get the company growing should be started immediately. One fairly common method today is to make acquisitions. Obviously this has some side advantages. Through stock consideration used in acquisitions, it is possible to put stock in what presumably are friendly hands. If in the process earnings per share are increased, the price of your stock may improve, making a tender more expensive. All this may be obvious, but usually the company that says it is obvious also says that it is too long a process for the emergency they face. One well-managed company, for example, who faced a tender, went on such a successful acquisition programme under the direction of a new chief executive that the company has tripled its sales and doubled its earnings per share in two years.'

It might get even worse with the victim company producing facts and figures proving that life would be impossible with the attacking company, that they would run down the business, close factories, throw men out on the streets in the name of rationalisation. Or they could take the Courtauld's, De La Rue line and warn the bidder that key executives would quit if the bid went through. Either way financial public relations is vital. Derriman quotes a merchant banker:

> 'In contested bids, financial public relations are of supreme importance. Quite apart from the enormous disadvantage of the man who has ignored

all this in the past, there is no doubt that in an evenly balanced situation public relations can very well win or lose the battle. The effective arguments in the end may not lie in the technical financial field, because the shareholders may decide by what is the right thing for the employees, and by their local loyalties.'

Probably the finest financial public relations drive mounted by a company under attack was the Saint-Gobain campaign against their long-time rival French glass group, Boussois-Souchon-Neuvesel. The 300-year-old sleeping giant was against publicity and PR—until the blow struck late December 1968. A double-page BSN advertisement aimed at Saint-Gobain shareholders appeared in 66 daily papers on 7 January. A poll by *France-Soir* revealed the extent of its impact. Saint-Gobain's image was decidedly flabby. They decided to fight back. Saint-Gobain boss, Arnaud de Voguè, despatched his first 'No' letter to shareholders. The typical reaction. But then he called in Publicis, the giant French advertising agency. They decided to change the company's image, a mammoth operation at any time. In the heat of a takeover battle, it was virtually an impossible task. But they set to work. Polls were already showing that 40 per cent of the company's 200,000 shareholders were thinking of accepting the bid. Then the campaign started with *France-Soir* the main medium. By 6 January the flabby image was disappearing. And support for BSN was now down to 17 per cent. Another shareholders letter followed. A radio interview was arranged on Europe 1. A telephone inquiry bureau was set up. And—the biggest coup of all—the Saint-Gobain open-house programme got under way. Twenty-one factories, two research centres and 11 offices were thrown open to visitors. More than 120,000 took advantage of the offer and went to see for themselves. By now less than 12 per cent were likely to accept the BSN bid. On 13 January BSN fought back. A huge information meeting increased their catch to 45 per cent. Saint-Gobain, however, came up with a free share offer. They also exploited a chance remark by BSN's Antoine Riboud. 'I am an enthusiast of glass', he said. De Voguè turned up at a rival meeting with a bottle—in plastic, illustrating the group's diversification for the future. A bomb was thrown through a window of Riboud's house. De Voguè announced dividends would be 'trebled'. Acceptances were now back down to the 12 per cent mark. By 27 January, decision day, only 8 per cent were in favour of BSN. Saint-Gobain had won.

There could be a counter-bid
This is real hand-to-hand fighting. In each corner, a rival bidder. Waiting anxiously at the side to see who is going to win her hand is the victim. In the place of swords and pistols, there are circulars and press releases. The offer documents are the opening blast. These are followed up by circular after circular each taking the battle a stage further. At the same time the press need keeping informed.

'Having sent out full reasons for their rejection of an offer for Armstrong Equipment, the directors of Toledo Woodhead Springs last night received an unexpected rival offer, worth £2·6 million, from fellow spring-makers, Jonas Woodhead and Sons. Terms are three Jonas Ordinary and 30s of 9½ per cent Convertible unsecured loan stock 1989–94, for every four Toledo Ordinary.'
(*Financial Times*, 18 October 1969)

Releases and special briefings must be given regularly to the business press. In the heat of battle, this is certainly the quickest line of communication with shareholders and the financial media. But there might be drawbacks. The press might not be reporting the battle in sufficient detail to attract vital shareholders. This means advertising. It is the fastest way of contacting shareholders—and answering an opponent.

The November 1966 battle by AVP Industries Limited to gain control of Barry Stains Limited involved press advertising. So, of course, did the GEC–AEI battle the following year. International Distillers and Vintners Limited advertised a circular which had just been posted to shareholders during their battle with Showerings Limited the same year—'for the benefit of shareholders who may not as yet be on the share register or may be away from home'. A shrewd move. And good public relations as well. Jessel Securities also advertised in *The Sunday Times* urging Falks shareholders to accept their bid, which they claimed would increase their income by 42½ per cent or 90 per cent on the dividend before the bid. And so on.

The Monopolies Commission could intervene

If a takeover involves acquiring assets exceeding £5 million, watch out. That's one of the opportunities for the Board of Trade to step in and refer a merger to the Monopolies Commission. Another is the threat that a merger would mean a monopoly, one-third or more of the market of a particular product or service in the United Kingdom. If, however, the Board of Trade looks at a proposed merger and decides against referring it to the Commission, it must issue a statement giving the facts. This allows battle to recommence. But if the Board goes ahead and refers the merger to the Commission, it can mean the end of negotiations until the Commission reports, which could be anything between six and nine months. Subsequently, if the Commission turns down the merger, the Board of Trade can forbid it to take place. Or, if it has already taken place, it is promptly broken up again.

During the moratorium, the bid negotiations might be frozen. But there's no reason why the financial public relations programme shouldn't go ahead at top speed. If Saint-Gobain could reduce the likely number of acceptances from 40 per cent to 17 per cent and then from 45 per cent down to a winning 8 per cent in just 27 days, the opportunities for effective financial public relations work in six to nine months must be enormous.

11.3.5 THE RESULT

Decision day.

The Panel insists that by 9.30 am at the latest on the first working day following the expiry of the first offer, or of any extended or revised offer, the offeror company must both announce and inform the Stock Exchange either

1 That the offer has become or is declared unconditional. If so he must give the total number of shares for which acceptances of the offer have been received; the total number of shares held before the offer period; and the total number of shares acquired or agreed to be acquired during the offer period.

or

2 That the offer has been allowed to lapse.

If the offeror company is unable to keep to the time-table, the Stock Exchange can consider not only the suspension of dealings in the offeree company's shares but the offeror company's shares as well until the necessary information is given. Things are even more stringent against the offeror company, which declares an offer unconditional, yet still fails to provide the necessary information by 3.30 pm the relevant day. Its unconditional declaration can be declared void. As a result any acceptor is immediately entitled to withdraw his acceptance until the offer is again declared unconditional.

If the battle is still not decided, the victim company can go ahead and rally its supporters. The Express Dairy Company Limited took space to warn holders of its 'A' ordinary stock during its fight with Grand Metropolitan:

> 'Although Grand Metropolitan Hotels Limited has declared its offer unconditional you should be aware that it has only received acceptances for 2 per cent of the 'A' Ordinary Stock and now holds less than $3\frac{1}{2}$ per cent of the total equity capital of Express Dairy. Your Board will be writing to the Stockholders as soon as possible. Please do not take any action on the GMH offer until you have received your Board's letter.'
> (*Financial Times*, 4 September 1969)

Grand Metropolitan fought back with a novel ploy. In a last minute attempt to woo reluctant shareholders, Mr Maxwell Joseph sent out more than 14,000 telegrams to all shareholders in Express Dairy—other than the big institutions—to remind them that the final day for acceptances of Grand Metropolitan's offer for the group was fast approaching. Warburgs, Grand Metropolitan's bankers, estimated that the cost of the operation was in the region of £4,000. But shortly after midday on T (for telegram)-Day, it was reported that Grand Metropolitan Hotels had more than 50 per cent of the non-voting 'A' shares of Express Dairy.

11.3.6 WHEN THE BATTLE IS FINALLY WON

The amount of information to be released and the form it should take depends on which of the four different Stock Exchange categories the bid falls into.

1 Where the value of the assets acquired comes to more than 15 per cent of the assets of the successful company, Stock Exchange, the Press and shareholders must be informed directly.
2 Where the value is less than 15 per cent, Stock Exchange and the Press must be informed directly. In this case there is no need to mail a circular to shareholders.
3 Where any transactions involve substantial interest on the part of a major shareholder or group of shareholders, Stock Exchange must be informed. The Stock Exchange may insist that a circular be mailed to shareholders as well. But it is not always necessary.
4 If the consideration is completely in cash and the proportionate value of assets and profits is less than 5 per cent, no announcement at all is necessary.

The PR-conscious companies, however, will go ahead and release all the necessary information to the financial media.

'Rexmore has acquired John Singleton, a Manchester-based textile converting concern for £250,000, satisfied by the issue of 175,000 Ordinary shares and £625 cash. The shares will not rank for the interim dividend in respect of the year ending March 31 next. Singleton's activities tie in well with Rexmore. The company had net assets at June 30 1969 of £198,832 of which £70,000 was cash or readily realisable. Pre-tax profits for the year to the same date were £77,700.'
(*Financial Times*, 17 October 1969)

Cough + wheeze + splutter = £400,000
The foreign threat to the British way of life went one stage further last week when Owbridge's, probably the biggest-selling cough mixture in the country passed into Dutch hands. The privately owned Hull firm of W. T. Owbridge was taken over, for just under £500,000, by KZO, the Dutch drugs, paint and chemicals group. Within 24 hours the Chairman, Tom Norfolk (whose father, a chartered accountant, has been brought in as an independent chairman) and all the board, except the managing director, had resigned; and it was clear that KZO intended to use the Owbridge name, previously a largely one-product United Kingdom-only affair, for a wider range of medicines and a wider export spread for the well-known soothing syrup.
(*Sunday Times*, 20 July 1969)

Two facts are important in any takeover announcement: the consideration as well as any details about deferred payments and the value of the assets involved. It is also worth including:

1 Details of the company being taken over or merged, its name, its business as well as any other relevant information.
2 The profits involved.
3 The likely results of the acquisition.
4 Future prospects of the new concern as well as future opportunities for employees.

Press releases should be issued by the succcessful company—with the full agreement of the new partner. Separate releases to the press would be illogical and confusing. Separate circulars to respective shareholders, however, would be logical. Because although one company has won the battle, they remain separate companies for a while. A full scale public relations campaign should now be launched to sell the new and enlarged company to the financial community. The business news media should be kept informed of developments.

> 'Since Room and Wade and Holman Brothers got together just over a year ago to form International Compressed Air, a steady stream of investment experts have been taking it in turn to visit the group's headquarters at High Wycombe. No doubt helped by favourable buying decisions following these trips International Compressed Air shares enjoy a rating accorded only to the stock market favourites. What is so exciting to make people invest in something apparently so innocuous as air? To discover the answer I too took the road to High Wycombe to chat with international Compressed Air's genial but tough chief executive, Mr Alex Masters . . .'.
> (*Evening News*, 29 July 1969)

A glowing circular from a blue-chip broking giant examining the combined group and forecasting its profit potential would help enormously. Institutional managers should be lobbied by the directors of the new combined board. With 2,000 changes and around 10,000 major non-routine decisions involved in the integration of two companies—it took 400 separate steps to integrate the equipment maintenance functions alone in the Pennsylvania and New York Central railroads link—financial public relations can often be squeezed to the end of the line. Which is wrong. Financial public relations must be given high priority in any post-merger situation. Mr David Hargreaves, division director—acquisitions and mergers, PA Management Consultants, for example, has listed two financial public relations points—annual accounts and company letterheading—as among the 14 most important non-routine decisions which should be tackled when a merger has been carried through. Most important of all, shareholders should be kept up-to-date on rationalisation plans as well as future prospects.

The Monopolies Commission both stressed the importance of extending the amount of information at present available and urged companies to give shareholders more information in their General Observations on Mergers published in their report on the proposed acquisition of The De La Rue Company of The Rank Organisation (HMSO 6s 6d).

'Attention was drawn to the fact that after a company had acquired another company the increase in reported earnings arising from the acquisition itself could to some extent mask an absence of earnings arising from real growth in the profits of either company. This could lead to a false appreciation of the results of the merger (in so far as earnings per share could increase although the total profits of the two companies could remain the same or fall) and an over-valuation of the shares of the company concerned which in some cases might facilitate further acquisitions. Moreover the ability to switch resources from one section of a diversified company to another could be used to conceal weaknesses in particular sectors.'

Higher labour turnover. Absenteeism. And more demands for higher pay. These are the reactions bred by insecurity among employees in the after-math of a takeover battle. Just as progressive companies keep their employees fully informed on their annual reports, so—more than ever—should just-married companies.

Again and again, therefore, the company's policy should be spelt out. Don't forget, this is a double-edged weapon. It convinces the financial media of the value and success of the operation. It also lays the groundwork for the next battle. Cheney has spelt out the dangers of sitting back, putting one's feet up and trusting to luck:

'I have seen instances where mergers were arranged on what appeared to be too hasty a basis. Because the stockholders hadn't been adequately prepared, the mergers collapsed under the fire of stockholder dissent or stockholder suits. No stockholder is going to be happy with a management that works out mergers only to save its own skin. They want mergers that improve their investment.'

Chapter 12

Shareholder relations

The Editor, *The Times*, 8 August 1969.

Sir: I recently became a shareholder of Reckitt and Colman Limited and have today received:

1 A letter of welcome from the chairman with a general statement of the company's activities.
2 A booklet listing and illustrating the company's products.
3 An addressed dividend mandate with an envelope to return it.

In these days of impersonal takeovers and confusing diversification, it is indeed refreshing to find a company eager to inform new shareholders of what it is about—and to treat them as human beings interested in the workings of the concern, as well as the bleak annual figures of profit and loss.
Yours, etc.
T. C. BATLEY

What better proof: Stockholder relations are important. And, handled properly, tremendously effective. At the lowest level it could mean a favourable letter in *The Times*. At the highest it could mean shareholder loyalty in the face of a bitter takeover battle. The traditional two-nations philosophy dividing companies from stockholders is not only out-dated but dangerous. Not from the stockholders point of view. But from the company's. For the stockholder can always vote with his cheque book and quit the company for another, more stockholder-orientated organisation.

Some companies, for example, go as far as giving the names of their major shareholders to managers in case they should ever come across them. Smith maintains shareholder relations are 'desperately important to the fortunes of a company. A company should be open to its shareholding public. In the catering industry, for example, it is important to the manager of a restaurant to have a list of the major shareholders.'

12.1 The time to start

The time to start is the time a company goes public and discovers shareholders for the first time in its corporate life.

12.1.1 IT HELPS TO GUARANTEE A PROPERLY VALUED STOCK

This is obvious. Because it is the stockholders who fix the price of the stock. It is no good running a superb operation if nobody knows about it. By ensuring that stockholders, above all, know how well the company is being run, a company can ensure that its stock is given an accurate valuation in the market. Once that happens the market takes care of the rest. Everyone likes a good company, properly run with a properly valued stock. Stanley Sauerhaft, a senior vice-president of Hill and Knowlton has spelt out the reasons.

'A rising price curve can prove very salutary in relations with banks, suppliers, distributors and even tone up employee morale. A declining price pattern in the face of better performances by similar companies can lead to a variety of dire consequences, including the turning out of the entire management by dissident stockholders and corporate raiders.'

12.1.2 IT BOOSTS SALE

Here the company starts with a big advantage. A shareholder is automatically a company man. He has invested his money in the organisation. He wants it to prosper. What better way of helping it to prosper than becoming a customer as well. This is, however, a problem. For most shareholders forget to make the jump. They probably buy into Marks and Spencer yet carry on shopping at the corner store. It is up to the company, therefore, to point out the advantages in no uncertain way. Booklets, brochures and constant reference to new products, new displays and new stores will eventually do the trick.

The ICI research into the effectiveness of their annual reports, don't forget, revealed that five out of seven of their shareholders wanted more information about ICI products. So shareholders are already eager for such sales stimulating information.

Unilever, for example, produce a small 12-page Unilever shopping list, which covers all the principal products of Unilever companies sold in shops in the United Kingdom. The 1968 annual reports of Reckitt and Colman Holdings and United Biscuits (Holdings) both illustrate their products. Reckitt show them all in one enormous wire shopping basket while United Biscuits show then all shaped in the form of their company symbol.

12.1.3 IT MAKES EVERY STOCKHOLDER A POTENTIAL LOBBYIST

The Americans tend to look on their shareholders as lobbyists for the cause as well. During the 1962 government-steel industry battle, companies were dropping hints to their shareholders that they should also join in the affray by drumming up as much support as they could. Union Pacific Railroad made a similar point. 'It is up to all of us—railroad management, employees, stockholders and informed citizens generally—to let our representatives at Washington know of our opposition to all such discriminatory railroad legislation', said their annual report. In the United Kingdom, companies are far more restrained about enlisting the support of shareholders in a lobbying campaign—or ignorant of the powerful role shareholders could play in such a situation. But they are always there as a powerful addition if companies have to face a do-or-die lobbying battle.

12.1.4 IT IS A CUSHION AGAINST TAKEOVERS

Chapter 11 spelt this out in full. The company that lives together, stays together. Interim reports, annual reports, an effective two-way annual meeting, perhaps, even special shareholder films about the company and its development all engender confidence in the organisation and its activities. And it is confidence that counts. As Jones said:

'Probably the most effective precaution (against unwanted bids) is for management to take shareholders into their confidence to the maximum practicable extent. The company that presents its accounts in a simple, informative manner, reinforces the statutory accounts with effective explanatory statements, gives a welcome to members at general meetings and perhaps circulates interim reports at not less than half-yearly intervals, is far less likely to find itself at the wrong end of a takeover bid.'

12.1.5 IT BOOSTS THE COMPANY'S FINANCIAL PUBLIC RELATIONS EFFORT A THOUSAND-FOLD

Every shareholder is a potential PRO. If he is convinced of the standing and importance of a company, he will tell others. This will help the company tremendously. As New Zealand-born Nigel Neilson of top public relations consultants, Neilson McCarthy, says, 'Every shareholder should be a non-paid public relations man'. The effect of, say, 25,000 or, in some cases as many as 500,000 shareholders actively promoting the name of their company is bound to have a tremendous effect on a company's reputation.

With companies getting bigger and bigger and, at the same time, ordinary shareholders gaining a greater percentage holding in the company, shareholder relations are becoming more and more important. Just over 31 per cent of the ordinary share holding in Thomas Tilling at the end of 1968, for example, was in 500 shares or less. Forty-seven per cent was in 501 to 2,500 shares. ICI went a stage further and discovered by analysing their ordinary stockholder register in April 1969 that 22·75 per cent of ordinary stock holdings were of £100 or less; 25·35 per cent between £101 and £250; 23·35 per cent between £251 and £500; 16·14 per cent between £501 and £1,000 and the remaining 12·41 per cent held the rest. This makes shareholder relations critical and the following shareholder media vitally important for every company.

12.2 Welcome letters

Reckitt and Colman Limited are, of course, the past-masters. Mr Batley and other new shareholders like him always receive a letter from the Chairman, Mr B. N. Reckitt, when they first take out a holding in the company. Almost by return comes the dividend mandate he mentioned; the Reckitt and Colman guide to shopping, a 28-page booklet listing the products produced by the company's household, food, toiletries, pharmaceutical and industrial divisions; and, of course, the letter from the Chairman, Mr B. N. Reckitt.

> Dear Shareholder,
> I am very pleased to learn that you have become a shareholder in Reckitt and Colman Limited and I trust that your association with us will be long and worthwhile.
> Reckitt and Colman is a major international manufacturing and marketing organisation. In the United Kingdom the company is organised by product divisions with interests which include a wide range of household products, pharmaceuticals, toiletries, industrial cleaning products, food products and soft drinks.
> Reckitt and Colman has a long record of investment in developing markets outside Britain, and today two-thirds of our business is done overseas. Our products are manufactured in most countries of the world or exported to them. Many products sold in Britain are available overseas and in some countries we make products which are not available in Britain.
> I hope that your Reckitt and Colman shares will prove a good investment and it may be of assistance for you to know when the dividends and interest will normally be paid:
> *5 per cent Cumulative Preference Shares*: dividends paid in equal half-yearly payments on the 1st January and 1st July.
> *Ordinary Shares*: an interim dividend at the end of December and a final dividend towards the end of June, a few weeks after the Annual General Meeting.
> $6\frac{3}{4}$ *per cent Debenture Stock*: interest paid in equal half-yearly payments on 1st May and 1st November.
> A list of our main products sold in the United Kingdom is enclosed and in it you will recognise many famous names. I hope that you will try some of those you are not already using.
> Our Annual General Meeting is held in London, usually at the end of

Q

May, and I hope we shall have the pleasure of meeting you there. If you
require any other information please get in touch with me.
Yours truly
B. N. RECKITT
Chairman

Unilever, perhaps because of their size, are more formal, more concerned
with company detail and, because of the unique nature of the company, more
involved with the structure of the company and how it operates. Their letter
also comes from the company secretary, Mr H. A. Holmes, and not the
chairman.

Dear Sir,
I am writing on behalf of the Board of Directors to welcome you to this
company.

    In the normal course you will receive the Annual Report and Accounts
of the Unilever group with the notice convening the annual meeting.
This is usually held in April.

    Unilever Limited ('Limited') is one of the two parent companies of the
Unilever group. The other is the Dutch company Unilever NV ('NV').
These companies have identical Boards of Directors and are linked by a
series of Agreements of which the principal is the Equalisation Agreement. This Agreement provides for the equalisation of dividends on the
Ordinary capital and in certain circumstances for the pooling of profits
available for payment of dividends on Preference and Ordinary capital
or, in the event of liquidation, of surplus assets. The practical effect of
this community of interests and identity of direction is that the two
companies can be looked upon as one undertaking.

    Broadly speaking Limited holds the interests in the British Common-
wealth and NV those in the rest of the world.

    Unilever is engaged in the manufacture and sale of a wide variety of
goods, mainly for household consumption. Its companies manufacture
and market their products in more than sixty countries, and employ in
all some 300,000 people. The principal products are margarine, cooking
fats and edible oils; other foods, such as ice cream, quick-frozen, dehyd-
rated and canned products, meat and fish; soaps and other detergents,
and toilet preparations such as tooth-pastes and shampoos. Unilever
also has extensive interests in plantations (palm, rubber and copra); in
oilseed crushing and in the manufacture of a wide range of chemicals,
paper, plastics and packaging materials. Through The United Africa
Company's group a substantial business is carried on, mainly in Africa,
in merchandise and the production and sale of a wide range of domestic
and individual products, in the development of timber concessions and
the operation of ocean and river fleets.

It goes on to mention a booklet, which is enclosed, about the principal products manufactured and sold in the United Kingdom by Unilever companies.

'Most of the products are familiar to you from advertisements and displays in shop windows, but perhaps you were not aware of the association of some of them with this company.'

It also gives the various dates when dividends and interest payments are made. Clearly both letters have a lot in common. Successful shareholder letters should, therefore, contain the following features.

A welcome

British companies seem slightly embarrassed by the whole affair. Those that do contact their new shareholders tend to be a little restrained.

'I am very pleased to learn that you have become a shareholder in McCorquodale and Co. Ltd. . . .'

'It is with much pleasure that I welcome you as a Stockholder of Metal Industries Ltd. . . .'

The Americans, however, are much more enthusiastic.

'I cordially welcome you into the Edison Stockholder Family. It is a large and well-established group with more than 130,000 members. . . .'

'It is my hope that this letter will serve to express the very real sense of welcome that your management and Board of Directors desire to impart to you on becoming a shareholder of General Electric. . . .'

A description of the company

It is a fair bet that some people still associate Reckitt and Colman with mustard and nothing else. It comes as a shock to them to realise that the company is an international giant with its products on sale in grocers, chemists, ironmongers, shoe shops, hairdressers, garages, department stores and supermarkets throughout the world. Hence the need for spelling out the size and scope of the company's activities.

'The McCorquodale Group has experience in printing almost everything that can be printed and is always to the fore in exploring possible new applications of printing. . . .'

The value of an investment with the company

The Commonwealth Edison Company probably has the strongest claim in this department. 'As you may know', they tell all new shareholders, 'quarterly dividends have been paid on our Common Stock without interruption since 1890'. That is probably too much for most companies. But new shareholders would at least expect to be reassured that they made the right decision and plumped for a company which was a good investment. It is dangerous country, of course. So most comments are pretty low-key.

> 'I hope that your McCorquodale shares will prove a satisfactory investment.'

Few companies, however, even go as far as this for they fear allegations of share-pushing. Which is a pity. The first thing a shareholder is looking for when he buys into a new company is, of course, re-assurance. The shareholder letter is the place to give it.

What the shareholder can do for the company

Shareholders can, of course, also be customers. And the more the better. The suggestion, however, is restrained. Mr Reckitt merely says, 'I hope that you will try some of those (products) you are not already using'. McCorquodale go just a little further: 'If you yourself are a print user, I hope also that you will show your interest in the Group in a practical way by allowing us to quote for your requirements'. No such reticence for the Denver US National Bank. 'If you owned the Yankees, would you root for the White Sox?' it bellows at new shareholders.

Communications with the company

With the vast majority of companies, the only contact they have with shareholders is the dividend cheque. Then it just arrives out of the blue. The company doesn't even bother to tell its new shareholders when it is coming. The go-ahead communications-conscious company, eager for the benefits of a financial public relations programme, should not only launch a regular contact programme with the financial public, it should stress the benefits of the programme to its new shareholders as well.

General Electric spell it out:

> '. . . you will find that the company attempts to keep its share owners not merely fully informed, but informed in a way that you will find interesting and stimulating. For example, we have endeavoured to make the Annual Meeting—held the fourth Wednesday in April—an opportunity for gaining broad firsthand impressions of the Company through special programmes and plant tours as well as through the customary review of the past year's operations. We will continue striving in the years ahead to add to the Meeting's value and interest.'

The Commonwealth Edison Company used to go into even more detail.

> 'To keep you informed about your Company's affairs, various communications will be mailed to you. Among these are our Annual Report and a booklet covering the annual meeting of stockholders. You will also receive the reports we enclose with our quarterly dividend cheques.'

Requests for further information

Communication is only effective if it is a two-way communication. This means encouraging—or at least catering for—shareholder correspondence. The chairman of Metal Industries boldly claimed: 'If there is any other information I can give you at any time, please do not hesitate to get in touch with me'. General Electric are more sober: 'If you have comments or suggestions concerning the business, or if you have inquiries about it, I would be pleased if you would send them direct to us'. The chairman of Edison, however, is probably the most honest. 'If you have any questions at any time', he would write to shareholders, 'please do not hesitate to write me or our Secretary, Mr Fred N. Baxter'.

Peroration

Most people can start a letter. But ending it, they find a problem. Most shareholder letters finish with a crisp promise to handle any questions investors may have. Which is workmanlike. General Electric, however, seem to have set a standard with their rousing paragraph:

> 'I hope that . . . you will come to feel that you are indeed a member of the General Electric family, conversant with its problems, proud of its contributions to our national economy, a user and an advocate of its products. We want all who associate with General Electric to share in maintaining our emblem as a symbol of leadership in the electrical industry.'

Of course, there is little point in inviting comments from shareholders and developing a two-way communication channel with them, if the correspondence is not going to be handled as quickly and efficiently as straightforward business correspondence. But there are two problems. First, who is going to be responsible for handling shareholder mail? In most cases, it is the company secretary. In a few cases, it is the public relations adviser. The company secretary seems the ideal man, because shareholders are his number-one responsibility. The only problem is ensuring that he handles it properly. This is the public relations adviser's responsibility. Clearly, there is little point in mounting a major shareholder relations programme, preparing special welcome letters, printing company booklets and so on if the company secretary is going to reply to a shareholder's letter in a sharp, turgid rigmarole that will destroy everything. Answering letters from shareholders also calls for tact. One major company, for example, goes as far as referring some of its shareholder letters to a psychiatrist to discover the most tactful way of answering them. This is not recommended. But it is the right approach.

12.3 Welcome booklets

With the civilities over, the shareholder welcomed to the company, the investor will probably now want some solid, detailed information on the company. This involves more than a letter from the company chairman. Some companies include copies of the latest annual report. Others send copies of their house journal. Neither of which are ideal. The annual report is fine if the shareholder already knows the background, the growth of the company, its market position and so on. The house journals are ideal for employees. They are generally parochial and, again, much too general to give the investor an insight into the company itself. This calls for a special information booklet to put new shareholders in the picture. It can also, incidentally, be used as a background briefing for the press on the company.

Courtaulds, for example, publish two. The first, *Origin and Development Manufacturing Activities,* is a 20-page round-up on the history and growth of the company.

> 'Courtaulds today are world leaders in fibres and textiles, supplying a greater range of man-made fibres than any other producer and having an integrated manufacturing and marketing organisation that is unique. Courtaulds operate in eight major industries namely fibres, textiles, chemicals, woodpulp, packaging materials, plastics, paints and engineering. The parent company together with its United Kingdom and overseas subsidiaries employ some 120,000 people (95,000 in the United Kingdom) and the Group as a whole have manufacturing interests which extend to more than 350 factories in 25 countries throughout the world. Courtaulds spend some £4 million a year on research, and the Research Division functions in the United Kingdom through nine laboratories or research depts employing about 2,000 people.'

Page one covers the essentials: the share capital, the loan capital and the board of directors. Pages two and three list the main products of the organisation from man-made fibres to paints with accompanying trade names. Pages four to six cover the origin and development of the company in the United Kingdom.

> 'The Courtaulds were a Huguenot family who came to England in about 1686. Some members of the family became silversmiths in London. The first to enter the textile industry was George Courtauld (1761–1823), who was apprenticed to a silk throwster in Spitalfields and who established silk mills at Pebmarsh and Braintree, Essex . . . Courtaulds today are the largest textile group in Europe.'

Page seven talks about the overseas development of the organisation. While the remainder of the booklet (pp. 8–17) are taken up with a list of the group's manufacturing interests.

The second Courtaulds booklet in English, French and German is much more of a promotional nature covering their marketing operation in Europe.

These should not be too expensive to produce. If, however, they are, they can always be made available on request.

As part of their going-public operation, Rentokil, by comparison, produced a glossy 16-page brochure, *Rentokil . . . a profile*, which they sent to their new shareholders. For a new company with new shareholders, the booklet was a model of its kind. It was both brief, effective and, at the same time, comprehensive.

Page one carried a welcome letter from the Chairman, Mr Patrick L. Burgin: 'I take this opportunity to welcome you as a member of the Rentokil Group Limited. We have tried in this booklet to give you a glimpse of the Group; the services and products it offers and its record of development in recent years. The Group's expansion reflects the importance of its contribution to the raising of standards of hygiene and the protection of health and property. The diversity of the markets in which it is engaged, both in the United Kingdom and overseas, indicates how general is the demand for its services and how great the scope for further development.'

Page two, complete with a series of six action photographs, described the extent of the organisation behind the nationwide service to the community. 'It is the most comprehensive and widespread industrial and domestic pest control and property maintenance organisation in the world. Six hundred teams of trained servicemen are based at important centres throughout the British Isles', it said.

Page three concentrated on the scientific staff—the biologists, entomologists and chemists—involved in the company's research programme. It outlined the work of the Rentokil Film Unit, the photographic department and the series of text books on everything from wood fungi to household insect pests, which had been produced within the organisation.

Page four listed the eight divisions within the company: woodworm and dry rot; pest control; damp proofing; hermeseal insulation; production; products; wood preserving and export. A short description—never more than 100–150 words—was devoted to each one.

Page five carried a photograph of a Rentokil employee at work on the Houses of Parliament. A subtle yet superb case-history of the company at work. The accompanying caption was appropriately low-key: 'The problems of defacement of public buildings presented by birds in towns are effectively and humanely controlled by Rentokil. Bird repellent is applied to building ledges and forms a harmless, lasting deterrent to birds which normally perch or roost there. Many famous buildings—including the Houses of Parliament— are so treated.'

Page six, complete with attractive line drawing of the company's Felcourt, East Grinstead headquarters, explains the Rentokil national network of offices which 'ensures that a local Rentokil man is on the spot to deal with any problems which may arise'.

Page seven begins the more hard-sell. It covers the international side of the business, explains how it has grown and illustrates the various Rentokil companies on a map of the world.

Page eight lists the six directors of the company complete with individual photographs. It also details the secretary and registered offices; the bankers, auditors, solicitors and registrars and transfer office.

Page nine to 15 give the authorised and issued capital of the company; the principal subsidiary companies. There is a ten-year financial summary chart as well as charts showing group turnover; appropriation of profits before tax; total capital employed, and turnover and profits.

The last page—page sixteen—carries a letter from the company secretary, Mr K. A. Bridgman:

> 'This booklet has been prepared to tell you about the Group's activities, its organisation and the progress made over the ten years illustrated. It is difficult to cover every aspect of the Group in a single review. Should there be any matter on which you require additional information you are invited to enquire direct to me. Every attempt will be made to satisfy your interest. As you will see, the Group covers a very wide field of activity: if you feel that any of the services and products offered might be of assistance to you the organisation is on call.'

Both the Courtaulds and Rentokil booklets are perfect examples of welcome booklets. They immediately give the general shareholder all the information necessary. They also, of course, sell their own products and services in an effective oh-so-subtle manner as well. Which, after all, is part of the reason for welcome booklets in the first place.

The Northern Illinois Gas Company in the United States, however, has come up with a novel variation on this theme. They have produced a special booklet, *Purposes and Principles*, which covers the company's attitude to investors, customers, employees, the general public, suppliers, the Government and the gas industry. It is a Boy Scout law for managers. The section on investors, for example, pledges the company to:

> 'Strive to provide to its owners, the holders of its common stock, a growing per share value, measured in terms of both income and appreciation and to be the maximum, in the long run, consistent with the Company's responsibilities to its customers, employees and the public.

> 'Seek to continue to hold the interest of its broad, diversified, well-balanced and stable family of shareholders, and to attract others who will maintain this balance.

> 'Provide for its stock a ready, convenient and technically sound market to ensure optimum flexibility for its owners.'

And so on.

12.4 Shareholder mailings

Everything from the chairman's speech at the local Rotary Club to a company profile in *Management Today* could legitimately be sent to shareholders. The shareholder has an interest in the company. He is, therefore, interested in company activities. But there are a number of points to bear in mind.

Cost

Mailings are all very well. They are effective. But they can cost the earth. The company must decide the budget and then get as much benefit as possible from the money. There is little point sending mailing after mailing to a shareholder if there is no return. There is even less reason sending him information if he is going to get up at the annual meeting and ask how much money is spent on mailings every year. The cost of mailings to a 10-share man is different to the cost to a 10,000 share investment manager.

Value

There is no point sending out information to shareholders unless they will recognise it as valuable background detail to assist their understanding of the company. This avoids having to circularise that speech to the local Rotary Club. But it means that the *Management Today* profile would be an ideal piece of promotional material. As in most things, it is much better to adopt a wait-and-see attitude than commit oneself to a definite mailing programme without knowing whether valuable material will be on hand.

Any brokerage report, however, prepared on the company should be considered an ideal example of the right kind of material for special mailing projects. A covering letter from the chairman should draw shareholders attention to it; urge them to read and study it; and, of course, stress the benefits of such third-party endorsements.

In the United Kingdom, the dividend cheque usually falls out of the plain brown envelope in solitary isolation. The crucial moment when the stockholder is actually getting a return on his investment floats away in silence. In the United States, however, it is the occasion for a 'hitchhiker', a same-size leaflet bringing investors up-to-date on latest developments. Management changes, product development, new advertising campaigns. They can all be mentioned in the hitchhiker. And, don't forget, this is one of the cheapest ways of making contact with stockholders. The postage, after all, has already been covered.

12.5 Magazines

Horizons. Quarterly. Quarterly Memo. News and Views for Stockholders. Stockholder's Quarterly. These are all special magazines and newsletters—a cross between a welcome magazine and an annual report—being produced for investors by American companies. *Span* is a 28-page quarterly issued by the Standard Oil Company (Indiana) for stockholders and employees. The *Jersey Shareholders Quarterly* only runs to four pages but keeps investors up-to-date on the Standard Oil (NJ). Whether they are worthwhile has yet to be proved. The cost is high. It is yet more material for investors to study. But it would seem a useful communications tool for larger companies. The cost would be too prohibitive for smaller concerns.

One of the best, however, is *Spotlight*. A few years ago the American Corn Products Company switched its quarterly report into a quarterly magazine. The quarterly balance sheet remained. The accompanying report was expanded. Comments were added from the chief executive. General company news was included. And, issue by issue, a different aspect of the company was examined. First, it looked at the company's educational programme. Then a new chief officer being appointed to a subsidiary, followed by the international division, an advertising campaign and so on. As a result, stockholders have a comprehensive image of the company.

12.6 Personal visits

The Americans are far more advanced in financial PR activities than most firms in this country. They have even gone as far as arranging for management representatives to visit certain key, selected shareholders in their offices and homes. This can have a number of advantages. If the shareholder has a complaint, it means the company can answer it without the glare of publicity. It also means that the company reduces the danger of infection. If you have a rotten apple the last thing you do is put it in a barrel—or annual meeting—with all the others. Western Union, which launched its visiting programme as far back as 1939, is convinced it helps shareholders to feel like owners of the business. It also cuts down the number of irritating questions they are likely to ask. This is supported by the Bell System, who say:

> 'Shareholders respond warmly to visits from friendly and informed hometown management people and speak their minds. We have a whole new picture of what our shareholders are thinking about, their likes and dislikes, their needs and desires for information.'

12.7 Factory visits

If companies doubt the value of factory visits, they should check with Arnaud de Voguè of Saint-Gobain, who threw open the doors of his company to 120,000 visitors in the important pre-bid stage of his bitter struggle for survival against a takeover bid from rival Boussois-Souchon-Neuvesel. And it worked. BSN were beaten off. Saint-Gobain remained intact.

Many companies arrange special tours for visitors. But few companies make a special point of arranging tours for shareholders although they are one of the most important groups in the company's operation. It is a short-sighted policy. Tours for shareholders are no more difficult than tours for outsiders. In fact, they could be more effective. The best time is probably after the annual meeting providing the meeting itself either takes place in the same premises or nearby where the necessary travel arrangements can be made. Directors could then be present. Special guides could be provided. Afterwards, depending on the company, samples of the company's products could be distributed, or brochures about the company itself.

12.8 Previews

Similarly, shareholders have a vested interest in new products. If companies are inviting stockholders to the opening of new outlets, why not invite them to advance previews of new products as well? It is the same thing. Consumer-orientated companies, of course, will score more than the heavy engineering organisations. But it is still worth considering.

12.9 Special events

Investors have a vested interest in development. The more, the better. So why not invite them to be present on opening day? In America, this is becoming the practice. If a chain store is opening a new branch, they automatically invite all shareholders in the area to be present. It kills three birds with one stone. It increases the importance of the occasion itself. This, in turn, makes it more attractive to the news media. Which results in more publicity for the company. Instead of arranging special events for shareholders, preparing special material, and arranging for the chairman and directors to be present, all the work has been done. Everyone is present in any case. And shareholders are more than pleased to be invited along as well.

An American company, Chesapeake and Ohio, go a stage further. They throw shareholder parties at their own Greenbrier Hotel off-season. Dances, concerts, teas are all laid on as well as the brief essential progress report on the company. Stockholders like them so much that many have even flown in from abroad to be present. And again they kill two birds with one stone. Stockholder relations get an enormous shot in the arm. And, at the same time, the company get a much-needed off-season boost in revenues for the hotel.

12.10 Films

Major companies have on average around 250,000 to 500,000 shareholders—an ideal target audience for a film. But it depends where they are. Producing a film for shareholders when only a handful can turn up to see it is obviously absurd. BP get round this problem, to a degree, by inviting shareholders to see their films during the pre-Christmas period when they reckon most of them will be in town Christmas shopping. Films were also part of the reason for the enormous interest in Australian mines during 1969. At one time no less than four mining documentary films were being shown to shareholders, potential investors and customers in different hotel suites. One of the best was, 'Wheels of Progress', commissioned by Perth-based Bell Brothers, the contractors and manganese miners. Complete with Wild West harmonica background, it gave a mass of information about the mineral wealth of Australia. This was pressed home afterwards by Hume Holdings, the London investment trust and property company, which distributed additional information about the company including the fact that Bell Brothers, only four years after being listed in Australia, already had a sizeable United Kingdom investment holding totalling nearly 31 per cent of the company's capital.

12.11 Letters of regret

This is a way of keeping friends and influencing people. Often investors cash in their shares not because they suddenly dislike the company but because they need the money. This is part of the trend into securities and away from the more traditional forms of saving which companies will have to adjust to. A letter of regret, therefore, ensures that the company will remain favourably placed with that investor when he is in a position to return to the market. An offer should be made to continue sending annual reports to foster this interest still further.

One of the best examples of this kind of delicate operation comes from Borden Company in the US which operates one of the finest financial public relations programmes in the country:

> Dear . . .
> You are no longer listed as a shareholder of The Borden Company. This does not necessarily mean that you have sold your stock. You may have transferred your shares to the name of a broker or some other person. But if you have disposed of your stock, I would like to know your reasons —unless they are personal. I am not trying to influence any decision on investments. I would like to know, however, if company policies or activities affected your decision. Did we keep you informed about Borden's? I shall appreciate a frank reply. If you have sold stock but would like to receive our next Annual Report, please let me know. I shall be happy to send it to you.
> Cordially yours
> PRESIDENT
>
> PS. I hope that you will continue to buy Borden's products and to ask your dealers to stock them.

It has everything. An apology in case the shareholder is still a shareholder. A declaration of not wanting to pry into an investor's personal affairs. A similar move, not to influence the investor's investment decision. Yet it does invite frank criticism of the company, its activities and its communications programme. And it works. 'The response and interest shown by shareholders to our letters has proved to be worthwhile', says a director of another shareholder relations programme which features letters of regret. The response from departing shareholders is also a valuable feedback to investor opinion. It could provide the company with vital clues to public attitudes towards them. It could also provide the raw material for future promotional and shareholder campaigns.

'There is bags of opportunity for expansion in the shareholder relations field', says Leo Cavendish. It is the blank spot in the financial picture.

Part four

Corporate Advertising and Public Relations in Action

Chapter 13

Corporate Public Relations

'The Toronto-Dominion Bank is to drop the hyphen from its name to project a new corporate identity. Nothing remarkable about that, except that the cost of redesigning the signs outside its 730 branches will be £1 million.'
(*The Observer*, 17 August 1969)

Everyone has heard of Accles and Pollock—or is it Hackles and Wallop? ICI seems enormous while, to the select few, Hambros or Lazards are the leading merchant banks. That's in this country. In America, of course, British companies fare much worse. Victor J. Papanek, Professor of Industrial Environmental Design at Purdue University, Indiana, for example, has said Rolls-Royce, Triumph and Letraset have projected a very good corporate identity throughout the United States. International Computers and Minis are just good. The Thomson Organisation image, he believes, is indifferent while he has never heard of IPC. Which shows how far most companies have still to go. For in the shrinking world of international finance, corporation public relations is becoming more and more important.

'In the case of a company, it means the fostering of a good reputation with shareholders and the financial world; with employees and potential employees; with customers and potential customers; with suppliers; with neighbours and local authorities in areas where the company operates; possibly with government, trade associations and other bodies. In practical terms, such a programme provides for the maintenance of friendly relations with editors and journalists, with radio and television; the expert preparation of booklets, house magazines and other literature; the arrangement of open days, factory visits and displays; and countless other activities with—over-all—professional advice on policy and the provision of information and facilities which will bring the company or organisation the reputation which it deserves.' (Charles Barker City)

Corporate public relations is, therefore, the over-all control and direction

R

of a financial advertising and public relations programme. A company has gone public. It has published its first interim and annual report. Its first annual meeting has taken place. The shareholder relations programme is under way. But the company cannot sit back with its feet up. It must ensure that not only is it known and recognised by more and more people but that its activities and progress are closely followed as well. Similarly, with an established company. It runs an effective shareholder relations programme. It might even—like Thomas Tilling—hold regional board meetings as well. But, again, it cannot relax. It must ensure there is a continuous stream of news and information about the company and its progress.

Because it is so important to a company, corporate public relations should be the responsibility of the chief executive. Nobody else in the management hierarchy can be deputed to look after it. For, says top American public relations consultant, David Finn, his style, his manner and his interests dictates the public relations of the company. 'This can't be delegated lower and lower down.' He gives two examples.

> 'A United States automation company found that soon after its products were installed in other companies, the managements were laying off men because there was no longer any work for them to do. A natural reaction. But it was incensing the unions. The automation company chairman, therefore, decided on action. He launched a non-profit making foundation to tackle the problem of automation—and even voluntarily taxed his own products to finance it. He got the unions to chip in as well since the research was also in their interests. As a result, the company chairman became a national figure and a spokesman for the automation industry. Another company chairman was interested in art and philosophy. Because he wanted to stress the quality of life, he insisted the companies under his control ran art-oriented advertising and promotion programmes. Again, the companies became known and recognised. The chairman became a national figure. When asked whether he thought his art advertisements boosted sales, he would reply, "I doubt whether getting clients drunk either does much good. But everybody does it." '

Says Finn, 'To boost a company's corporate image, one must develop the tangential interests of the chairman. It doesn't work unless someone in top management is really interested.'

Different companies, of course, have their different approaches. Unilever, for example, see public relations as 'the protection, maintenance and development of a deservedly good reputation'. As far back as 1942, their chairman at the time, Geoffrey Heyworth, later Lord Heyworth, had come to the conclusion that it was no longer sufficient to dismiss criticisms with a shrug. They were a company with high standards of business ethics. Their behaviour was not anti-social. In future, therefore, they would take steps to keep their critics fully informed of the true facts. Wrote Lord Heyworth:

'This does not involve a change of outlook but rather that the public in general should be conscious of our attitude. This implies changing from a negative attitude in what is generally described as "public relations" to a long-term positive and progressive plan.'

In 1948 they launched a public opinion poll to discover the attitude of the public to Unilever. Around 85 per cent of the population had never heard of them. A large number had heard of Lever Brothers and knew it involved soap and Port Sunlight. But the vast majority knew nothing about the holding company, its network of subsidiaries, the washing products, toilet preparations and edible fats and foods they prepared for both animal and human consumption. And the majority didn't particularly want to know anything about Unilever either. Of those who knew about the company, a number were against it. Not because of any concrete reasons. But because of an idea that Unilever was a big financial octopus. And because it was big, it was bad.

Obviously Unilever had to fight back. They dismissed the idea of a massive, all-out public relations campaign, however, for two reasons. They thought it would do more harm than good. It would probably raise suspicions even more and, at the same time, tend to impair instead of improve relations. Instead they decided on a two-fold attack on opinion-moulders—Members of Parliament, trade union officials, journalists, authors, school teachers, university dons, Civil Servants, political organisers, etc.—and their own employees. The opinion-moulders, once they had been given all the necessary information about Unilever would obviously begin influencing other people with whom they came in contact. Similarly employees. Instead of just shrugging their shoulders and saying they know nothing about the company they worked for, they would be able to actively promote the company in their own private lives as well. Once this was under way, Unilever launched a youth programme giving young people who had reached their teens and were at an impressionable age more educative information about their activities. At the same time, of course, they were feeding out information to their 300,000 odd stockholders. But the nature, size and ramifications of Unilever presented problems.

1 Unilever was a holding company. It did not manufacture or market any products as such. The general consuming public, therefore did not come in contact with the company.

2 Unilever was one of the greatest industrial organisations in the world. It occupied a special place as a leader of British and Dutch industry. Its Report and Accounts, its chairman's statements at annual meetings were major news events in themselves. This meant the financial results were used by economists, sociologists and the press for different purposes. Governments, other industries, cultural and educational groups also turned to it for information.

3 Unilever, because of its size, had to be careful that it did nothing to encourage attacks on it as a monopoly.

The operation—and the continuing corporate public relations—of Unilever were obviously successful. For today the company is no longer regarded as some enormous financial octopus—but a motherly octopussy.

Companies should therefore be continually examining and re-examining the ingredients that make up their corporate identity—attitude surveys should be a regular feature of any corporation public relations programme—to see whether any blank spots have developed or whether there were any improvements that could still be made.

This means looking at three things: the name, the symbol (or logo) and the image.

13.1 The name

It was communications philosopher, Marshall McLuhan, who made the point: 'Love thy label as thyself'. Sony and Bell Telephone Company were superb company names, he said. They were immediately identifiable with their products. Companies therefore, should regularly check that their activities have not outgrown their label.

The Sanitus Trust, for example, found themselves in this position in August 1969. Since they first went into business 90 years ago with that traditional nursery comforter, Woodward's Gripe Water, they have answered to the name Sanitas. It was the name associated with other health-giving commodities, antiseptics and, of course, the much-revered Elsan chemical closet. But it was becoming more and more irrelevant. In the 1960's the company expanded into cosmetics and cigarette filters. Today their individual divisions include leading companies in manufacturing and marketing batteries, beauty preparations, brushes, engineering products, pharmaceutical products, plastic mouldings, print and packaging material, sanitation, cleaning and soap. It was decided to change the name to Carlton Industries.

Why Carlton Industries? Chairman, Sir Max Rayne, lives in Carlton House.

13.2 The symbol

In a world of mass communications, the symbol is valuable short-hand—if it is chosen for the right reasons. Top international designer, Henri Henrion, has given two of the more extreme reasons for commissioning symbols. 'In great organisations a symbol is in some sense a status symbol, feeding the vanity of the chief executive who commissioned it; or again a symbol is thought to be an agreeable extra to a company's name style which may have no rational justification in marketing terms', he says.

He went on to propose a methodical approach to the whole problem. First, the designer must approach every problem with a number of questions. Such as: (1) Are signs or symbols an appropriate answer to the problem we are facing? (2) To whom are the symbols addressed? (3) What will be the conditions in which the symbols are seen? Will they be monopolising the 'site'—or will they be competing with other symbols? (4) What should be the relationship between, for example, a symbol and other identifying elements such as colours, logotypes, etc.? (5) What limitations are imposed by the nature of the organisation to which the symbol is to be applied?

This is only the first step. After the symbol comes the house style. The symbol is applied to every single aspect of the company's visual corporation— from letter-headings to company transport. This ensures that once somebody comes into contact with the company, they recognise the symbol. Then ever afterwards whenever they see the symbol or come into contact with the company again, they immediately recognise the corporate identity of the organisation. In terms of products, this is the brand image. In terms of companies, it is the house style or corporate image. Milner Gray, senior partner of the Design Research Unit (*Public Relations*, May 1968) which drew up a corporate identity programme for British Rail, goes a stage further:

'It represents something more than merely a link in the public mind between one activity and another, between product and product. It implies a company's faith in the whole organisation of their business— and extension of the self-respect, once thought to be the exclusive prerogative of the craftsman, in the value of his service to the public. It encourages among the company's staff a feeling that they are working for a progressive organisation confident in their wares and their selling methods. But the prime reason for the adoption and implementation of a corporate identity programme lies in its commercial value and in its contribution to net revenue.'

13.3 Image

'We get a bit cheesed off with being the Aunt Sally of the British motor industry. In fact, we've never been in a stronger position', a Rootes spokesman told the *Evening Standard* on 25 July 1969. It was an understandable complaint. They had just reduced prices. Not out of weakness as their competitors has suggested. But because they had reduced the time it takes to make a Minx from 74 to 50 hours. In addition, they had agreed an advance pay and productivity agreement with employees and drawn up plans to fill the 1300 cc gap in their range as well. Yet the label persisted.

An image is like Coca-Cola. It cannot be created overnight. It takes years and immense patience and promotion investment to create an image. It took years and a creative design group headed by Paul Rand, Charles Eames and George Nelson to create the 'clean, impressive' image of IBM, probably the most expensive and most valuable abbreviation in history. But it worked. Whoever talks about the International Business Machine Corporation now?

A successful image should, therefore, be passive, synthetic and believable. It must also be simple.

Says Dr Max Adler, one of the most experienced market researchers in the business, 'The image is the impression, the flag, the conception, which the public has of a company'. In order to get its image across, therefore, a company must continually be in contact with the public. Not just in its ordinary day-to-day business operations. But through a host of other methods as well. Although these, to a degree, will be dictated by the nature and size of the company, they will include all or some of the following.

13.3.1 ANNIVERSARIES

The American Lead Pencil Company celebrated the golden anniversary of its Venus trade mark by staging a special cake-cutting ceremony alongside a life-size replica of the famous Venus de Milo statue. A typewriter company, by comparison, celebrated its 50th anniversary by assembling all its typewriters manufactured throughout the period and getting typists, dressed in the fashions of the time, to demonstrate they were all still in working order. Another company actually re-built the street it was founded in—complete with a replica of its original premises.

There are probably as many ways of marking an anniversary as there are anniversaries. First, they can be calculated in years of existence. Then in product years. Maybe even in man-years. The only problem must be, once the go-ahead is given, to ensure that the event is as successful as possible.

The most successful anniversary ever was probably the nine months long celebration of Ford's 50th anniversary in 1953. Plans began being drawn up in 1951—two years before the climax came with a two-hour television spectacular screened by both American television networks, NBC and CBC, and seen by an estimated 16 million homes. Within just six months *Life* magazine had carried four stories—one of them 14 pages long—on the anniversary. *Look*, *Time* and *Newsweek* carried two articles each. The old *Saturday Evening Post*, *Cosmopolitan*, *Fortune* and *Reader's Digest* carried one article each. Six institutional advertisements appeared in publications with a combined circulation of more than 82 million copies. As a result the anniversary massed 59,000 column inches of publicity within three months—a staggering achievement.

The Swiss Volksbank, one of the country's 'top five' banks marked its centenary with a difference. Founded in 1869 by a group of 53 private individuals—workers, tradesmen, civil servants and professional men—as a self-help organisation, it decided to mark the occasion with a review not of the past but of the future. Everyone from first-formers to best-selling authors were called upon to support their special campaign to 'confront the public through the mass media with opinions and questions on the future of Switzerland'. The children were asked to paint murals on the theme, 'Our Town in the Year 2000,' for exhibition in Basle, Berne, Geneva, Lausanne, Lucerne,

St Gall, Winterthur and Zurich. Teenagers were given the chance of making collages in which 'conclusions as to the future which could be drawn from the elements of today'. The younger generation as a whole were then given the opportunity to have their say about their opinions and apprehensions about the future. The Volksbank sank half-a-million francs in three films made by young Swiss film makers which together illustrated their fear whether the individual of the future will be able to retain his identity in the collectivised and depersonalised world a few years hence.

Then came the best-selling authors. They were asked to prepare short, epigramatic opinions for a series of nine posters for display throughout the country. The results were mixed. One noted that Switzerland was unable to cope with the demands of its present six million population in health and education. What would it be like in a few years when the population has reached eight or ten million? Others were more pithy: Pre-judgment is a high wall. Are we able to bring down this wall; Out of life into the ghetto of the family; and Democracy should be discussion. Another was practically unintelligible: Do you want the total future? Follow the voice of reason: stop thinking—which turned out to be an attack on admass.

Said one commentator, 'The campaign is very much more than a public relations move—although it has obviously been very good for the Volksbank's image. The bank, like many other big undertakings in Switzerland, does feel itself to be "populaire" and does feel that it has a certain duty to the public.'

Every effort in an anniversary campaign should be made to arouse maximum interest not only among employees, suppliers, customers but among the key financial public relations media as well.

13.3.2 ART

This is almost pure corporation public relations. Philip Morris Europe, for example, couldn't have expected any commercial return from sponsoring the way-out 'When attitudes become form' exhibition at the Institute of Contemporary Arts in 1969. A length of rope and a pile of rubbish were among the exhibits. But they did. And, according to Trevor Russell-Cobb, author of *Paying the Piper* (The Queen Anne Press, 1968) and an expert on patronage, other companies should follow suit. He gives two reasons.

> 'First, what the public is prepared to pay at the box-office is unlikely, even in the most affluent society, to be the sum required to furnish first-class performances by artistic ensembles kept together permanently. Secondly, due to the operation of what economists call 'the principle of indivisibility', certain types of products and services—opera houses and their casts and staff, orchestras, theatre and ballet companies—are available only as functioning units; it is not possible to buy them a part of the time.'

That's the disinterested side of the coin. There are, perhaps, other motives which would appeal to companies even more.

1 The desire to take part as a corporate citizen in the life of the community.
2 The search for prestige.
3 The need to provide amenities for staff and employees.
4 The wish to engage in a form of reminder advertising.

But even the apparently disinterested prestige argument can have some pretty compelling commercial reasons behind it. These were outlined by Sir Frederic Hooper in the May 1955 issue of the *Journal of the Royal Society of Arts.*

'Prestige advertising sets out deliberately to court the attention of that influential minority of the public which can be described as "the leadership group", or "the directive elite". They are the intelligent, the sophisticated and the cultivated, mainly found in the professional and managerial classes. Broadly speaking, they set the standards of taste and fashion which all other grades of society follow. They confer the hallmark. What this group accepts as the best will be accepted as the best by the large majority of people who do not, as a rule, form such judgments on taste for themselves, but tend to take them ready-made on the authority of those socially above them. This group of leaders is not confined to one class, but draws on the whole field of discriminating people interested in and accustomed to handling ideas.'

13.3.3 AWARDS
Mr C. N. Harris, ICI Fibres export director, received the award of Officer of the Order of the Republic of Tunisia for services to its textile industry on 14 August 1969. It made the front page of the *Financial Times.* For awards are news. Any company sponsoring an award is likely to benefit enormously. Among the many successful award schemes is the National Westminster Bank's contest for young exporters, which in its two years of operation, is already attracting more than 300 entries every year. The publicity which it attracts is tremendous. One of the winners, cattle exporter, Diana Hatfield, was pictured with one of her pedigree bulls on the front cover of the *Sun.* The *Financial Times* highlighted the award on its Export Page. The *Evening Standard* took a different angle. They reported on the 'Loneliness of a long-distance salesman's wife'. This theme was also taken up by the *Daily Mail* and the *Sunday Telegraph.* All in all the award story made more than 40 national and regional dailies as well as radio and television. Not to mention the mass of trade and technical magazines involved.

13.3.4 BROCHURES
Brochures are life-savers. In a few pages, they can cover the whole history and development of a company, its position in particular industries and its plans for the future. Not only is it long-lasting promotion, it is also an ideal

source of reference on the whole company. As a result, it is indispensable
to any corporation relations programme.

British Oxygen Company, for example, produced a glossy 16-page booklet
called 'Air to a Fortune'—ouch!—which covers everything from the launch
of the company to their range of products and world-wide network.

> 'Four-fifths of the air we breathe is of no use to us personally, so our
> bodies separate it and keep some of the oxygen and refuse the rest. It is
> a clever trick of which we are barely conscious, until the air around us
> becomes "foul" and breathing difficult. Then and at other times we can
> be grateful to those scientists who have made it their work to understand
> all the elements of air, and use them for our wellbeing. Back in 1886 a
> company called Brins Oxygen (later British Oxygen) had found two
> uses for "pure" oxygen—one vital, the resuscitation of hospital patients;
> the other dramatic, the burning of limelights, an old stage lighting
> technique which has left a metaphor behind. The story began with
> oxygen, the life giver. It continues.'

From there, the booklet went on to speak about air separation, tonnage
oxygen for steel, medical equipment, the gas that does nothing—'When you
make oxygen by the ton you have to separate four times as much nitrogen.
It used to be wasted, but gradually BOC built a business on this by-product,
providing services to industry which has become indispensable.' Then came
cryogenics, rare gases and notes on chemicals, metallurgy and high vacuum.
Finally, a description of BOC management and central services.

> 'There is little doubt that the world of the 70's and 80's will depend on
> far fewer companies than today. But they will be much larger and more
> important companies, many of them global in their scope and diversified
> in technologies hardly glimpsed today, so greatly has the rate of change
> increased. BOC intends to be one of them.'

Price, Forbes (Holdings) Limited, international insurance brokers, produced a lavish 28-page brochure that neatly managed to look backwards and
forwards at the same time. Perhaps, because it was based on T. S. Eliot's text,
'Time present and time past are both perhaps present in time future'. It began
with a comment from Chairman, Mr I. H. F. Findlay, and went on to tell the
story of insurance.

> 'Insurance began with exports, shipping risks and coffee. The first
> recorded British policy was drawn up in 1555 following Vasco da Gama's
> voyage in the *Santa Cruz*—the first vessel to round the Cape of Good
> Hope and sail to India, thus bringing in its wake the first prospects for
> insurance of both vessels and cargo covering long voyages.'

Then came the story of the founding of the company, how it developed and
expanded into an international insurance service. It explained the role of the
broker, how the client benefits by his specialist knowledge and experience.

It described the company itself, its offices in London, in North America, Africa, Australia, New Zealand and Europe. There is a section on Lloyd's and a section on the staff, 'Our staff are our assets'. And finally, the guts of the brochure, the principal companies and offices in the Price, Forbes Group together with its management structure.

Investors Overseas Services, however, went a stage further, in their glossy 'This is IOS' brochure. Instead of just listing their top executives, they gave full biographical details as well. And a tremendous impact it made. More companies should follow suit. IOS also publish a series of magazines for their investors. These are glossy, high-class magazines produced in English, French, German and Spanish. On the surface they are like any other topical publication, full of interesting features and good photography. But, of course, the underlying message is I—O—S.

Unilever, by comparison, are less flamboyant and more comprehensive. In addition to the chairman's speeches (see Chapter 9) they publish a whole series of leaflets on different aspects of the company ranging from Margarine, Edible Fats and Oils in Unilever to The United Africa Company Group. There are booklets on Unilever products, research and careers; catalogues on films and educational material; and magazines and news sheets for both internal and external readership. In fact, there are so many that they have even had to publish a special leaflet on all the brochures available.

13.3.5 EDUCATIONAL PROGRAMMES

An American company sponsors an Annual Science Talent Search by inviting high-school seniors to compete for important science and scholarship awards. Finalists are given a Grand Science Scholarship for four years tuition with all expenses paid. The runners-up get smaller Science Scholarships. Unilever contributes over £300,000 to various establishments including Churchill College, Cambridge; the College of Science and Technology at Manchester University; University College, London; St Catherine's College, Oxford; Trinity College, Dublin; and the Universities of Liverpool, Leeds, Edinburgh, Leicester and Oxford. A further £10,000 went to the Delhi Engineering Trust and another £7,000 to the University College of the West Indies. In addition they contribute to university prizes and the buying of scientific equipment. They also sponsor Unilever research fellowships worth £500 a year.

All educational programmes, however, do not have to be as ambitious as this. Some companies produce different series of booklets on important subjects likely to appeal to students. Some even go as far as organising special teenage club nights. For, the more companies are well regarded by universities and technical colleges, the higher their reputation will be and the more likely they will attract first-class recruits.

13.3.6 HISTORY

'A major work ... compulsively readable.' That was *The Economist* on Dr

D. C. Coleman's 846-page two-volume economic and social history of Courtaulds. Few companies have been as lucky as Courtaulds to find such an able business biographer. Few company histories have been so extravagantly praised. The official history of the old AEI, for example, fails to mention profits at all during its coverage of the first 50 years of the company's existence. Yet for the right company, with a long tradition and history of development behind it, a history can be an important and invaluable boost to its reputation. Obviously there are two ways of doing it. Either, casually with the help of one or two home-grown company historians. Or professionally, with a writer of the standing of Dr Coleman. This is naturally far better. A special historical committee, however, could be set up to ensure the project proceeds at full speed with every facility being given to the writer. Records, files, documents, etc., must be made available together with outside surveys. If a history is being published, it must be objective.

13.3.7 LECTURES
Again, a pure corporation public relations activity. The sponsoring company has nothing directly to gain. It sponsors the event as a genuine service because it has the facilities and the opportunities. Ford, for example, sponsor an annual lecture for sixth-formers 'to widen their horizons and to promote interests outside their curricula'. The 1969 speaker was Director of the Bank of England, Sir Eric Roll, who spoke about the City of London and its effects on the economy, British and the world. Selection Trust Limited, by comparison, sponsor the annual Chester Beatty Lecture at the Royal Society of Arts on every aspect of metals and their service to mankind. The objective: to bring home to the general public the everyday importance of minerals and metals.

Lectures, therefore, have a dual purpose: they pack a punch at the immediate audience concerned and, at the same time, they are yet another opportunity for catching the attention of the business public generally through the business news media.

13.3.8 LOBBYING
Lobbying is nothing more than information promotion. An open society lives by the information it generates. Therefore, it must have a vested interest in not only more information but better and better channels of communication. And lobbying is a vital channel.

'Pressure groups are necessary to the government of our complex society. They have become the means by which many individuals contribute to politics. It is important that the system of government be such that their role can be carried out with responsibility', says J. D. Stewart in *British Pressure Groups—their role in relations to the House of Commons*, 1958.

If a company finds that its interests should be represented in Parliament, it should set up a special parliamentary liaison operation. Regular information should be fed to MP's covering the constituencies in which it is based. More general information could be sent to MP's as a whole. Then there are the government departments. They should be kept informed as well.

13.3.9 SPORT

The Sunday Times sponsor round-the-world yacht races. Coca-Cola sponsor English Table Tennis. More and more companies are going in for sport sponsorship. Yet they do so for different reasons. A one-year research programme into the whole area of sport sponsorship at Manchester Business School revealed two outstanding opinions among sponsoring organisations (*Financial Times*, 3 September 1969). First, organisations sponsor sport to generate public awareness for their company, product or brand. Great emphasis was put on getting extra media time or editorial comment at low cost. Second, organisations were becoming more concerned with the cost benefit equation of sponsorship. As a result they tended to prefer events which involved direct media coverage; 'national' interest; and a high volume of editorial comment. Taking this into account, sponsorships are probably one of the most delicate areas of any corporation public relations programme because it calls for an ideal relationship between the sport and the sponsor. Sports and companies do not usually mix. It is a lucky organisation which finds an ideal sport. If it does the results can be enormous.

13.3.10 UNIVERSITY CHAIRS

A more and more popular form of corporate promotion among major companies. It is serious. It is worthwhile. And it is immensely valuable in developing a reputation for a genuine concern for education. The National Westminster Bank, for example, financed Manchester Business School's first chair of business finance, now held by the Canadian and American educated former lecturer at Massachusetts Institute of Technology, Professor Geoffrey Clarkson.

These are the more conventional corporate public relations media. But there are others. Matsushita Electric, the Japanese electronics colossus, for example, has produced its own company song:

'For the building of a new Japan,
Let's put our strength
and mind together,
Doing our best to promote production,
Sending our goods to the people
of the world
Endlessly and continuously,
Like water gushing from a fountain.
Grow, industry, grow, grow, grow!
Harmony and sincerity!
Matsushita Electric.'

Effective, it undoubtedly is. But the chances of company songs in the West are, perhaps, a little restricted.

Chapter 14

Corporate News

Twining, the tea and coffee company, held its first press conference in a 263-year history yesterday. It lasted under three minutes, taken up by Mr John Parkin, Chairman and Managing Director, giving a fast-talking sales routine as he made a cup of coffee with one of his new coffee bags—proper ground coffee, not the instant powder. Finished, he invited us to taste some and bounced about saying, Well, how was I? Did you like my spiel? Not the greatest coffee, but it ain't bad as they say. Do you think I would get a job demonstrating in Selfridges?
(*Financial Times*, 8 October 1969)

Not all companies are as slow as Twinings. Although most chairmen and managing directors are just as excited as John Parkin when it comes to meeting the press. For companies are still not used to living with the news media.

Charles Clore, the first real takeover king to make his debut in the United Kingdom still refuses to see any journalists. Harry Hyams, the brains behind Oldham Estates and owner of the still tenantless Centre Point skyscraper at the junction of London's Tottenham Court Road and Oxford Street, seems to grow more and more silent the higher the rents of property in central London seem to rise. Only one photograph has ever been taken of him. He is even said to get up and leave meetings and dinners once he knows a journalist is present. Chairman of Robert Fleming, the merchant bank, Mr Richard Fleming, is almost as bad. While Hyams never gives interviews, Fleming despite being the brother of the late Ian Fleming, creator of the legendary James Bond, only rarely meets the press. Not that this has stopped any of them from getting publicity. Probably the reverse. The more they have tried to avoid publicity, the more they have hit the headlines. Yet, in spite of this anti-communication backlash, it is still wrong to deliberately avoid the press.

Companies are part of the financial community. They have a duty to keep that community informed. And this means keeping the financial news media informed of their activities. Not for the press's sake. But for their own sake. It would obviously be a waste of resources for a company to court the financial community before going public, to produce valuable interim reports and comprehensive annual statements, and then to retreat into its shell without a word. Once a company is a public company, it has responsibilities to that public. The press are also interested in the company itself. It wants as much information as possible about its activities. The nature of the media, however, demands not just straightforward information. But news.

'News', said Arthur MacEwan, the Randolph Hearst-appointed first editor of the *San Francisco Examiner*, 'is anything that makes a reader say, Gee whiz'. There are plenty of things companies are doing every day of their life that will make people sit up. Instead of making them say 'Gee whiz', company news can turn readers into investors and small investors into large investors. It will also bring all the other benefits of a financial public relations programme.

There is one slight problem, however. If companies are going to launch a company news operation, they must launch an efficient operation. There is little point in arranging press conferences, fixing interviews and mailing press releases if the company is not prepared to throw its whole weight behind the operation. If a journalist wants to interview the managing director, the managing director should do everything in his power to be present. If a press release is being issued on a new management structure, it must be explicit. It is no good hiding the facts under a mess of verbiage. Says City Editor of the *Evening News*, David Malbert:

> 'So and So Group is recasting its structure because of growth. New companies will each be responsible for one of the Group's major activities, and each managerially autonomous under its Managing Director and Executive Directors, subject to the Group Board.
>
> 'This recasting of Group structure will allow concentration of management and provide a firm base for continued growth, as well as providing further opportunities. The vertical control up to Group Board level will be more clearly defined and horizontal integration between companies facilitated.
>
> 'Now what exactly was this company trying to convey. If I hack my way through the heavy boskage of verbiage I suppose I discover that it had decided to make public, no doubt after a day-long agonising board meeting, that it was going to decentralise control. Having made the decision to promulgate this information I would have thought a form of words might have been devised that was less flatulent and pompous.'

Then there is the other extreme: too much information for a non-specialist audience.

> 'The Instrument Division of So and So has announced the availability of a two-page, two-colour leaflet on their new CDV. 200 digital voltmeter. This unit has five ranges, from 0·2 V to 1000 V full-scale reading, with an accuracy of 0·05 per cent and a resolution of 100 microvolts . . .'

or worse still the correction, as put out by Monsanto in November 1969:

'Santoflex N–isopropyl–N–pheny–p–phenylenediamines should be substituted for the term Santoflex diphenyl–p–phenylenediamines . . .'

What does the City Editor want? Malbert puts it in one word: truth. He wants to know what is happening and why. This is a valuable invitation for the communications-conscious company. In order to exploit the offer to the full, however, the company should observe some preliminaries. First, it must be able to define itself. Malbert showed the drawbacks of too generalised information. It means nothing. If, however, a company can describe itself, its operation and its position in the industry in one neat thumbnail sketch, it should do so. Director Mr T. M. Gullick, for example, describes his company, Clarkson Tours as:

'The biggest organisation in air charter operating in the world, about 50 per cent bigger than the biggest of the German operators, and ten times the size of the nearest US company.'

It is difficult for people to remember that passengers have shot up from 80,000 in 1967, that profit is just $3\frac{1}{2}$ per cent of turnover and so on. It is not difficult to remember that the company is the biggest in the world and, at the same time, streets away from international competitors. Hence the value of a thumbnail sketch. It helps establish the name and importance of the company in the eyes of the press and the public generally. Similarly, Sotheby's is always known as 'the biggest fine art auctioneering firm in the world'. GKN, however, have gone a step further. Instead of just a thumbnail sketch they have produced a brief 32-page booklet packed with facts and figures about the company:

'Guest Keen and Nettlefolds is one of the world's largest international engineering groups with sales of £1·8 million ($4·32 million) per day, and out of its total annual sales of £434 million ($1040 million) it exports £113 million ($271·2 million) direct and indirect from Great Britain to 130 countries throughout the world. By sales it ranks 42nd in the top industrial companies of the world outside the USA, while in England it is 14th largest in terms of capital employed. The Group supplies 35 per cent of its sales in high precision component parts to the world's automotive industry and, although well-known by consumers for its predominance in the bolts, nuts, screws and fasteners market, this now accounts for only 8 per cent of its turnover. It is by far the largest steel user in Great Britain, buying 2·4 million ingot tons every year; its annual world consumption is 4 million ingot tons.'

It covers the principal products and activities of the group; their trade marks and business names and masses of facts and figures about every aspect of the group—packed into 32 brief pages. This is invaluable for the company. It means journalists can have the relevant details in a matter of seconds. It is also extremely useful for the news media.

Second, financial public relations advisers must study the media. Newspapers and television do not publish stories about companies because they have either a space to fill or a few minutes going spare. They use the material because they feel it is both important and of interest to either their readers or their viewers. This means PR people should study the media, see which stories they use; which ones get more treatment than others and when. Timing is almost as important as the subject itself.

Third, he must investigate the sources of news, the mechanics for getting news to the newsmen. This means checking on local correspondents of national newspapers, finding the people who represent the different radio and television news services; contacting freelance journalists and specialists. This will help him to deliver the stories as quickly and as effectively as possible.

Fourth, and probably the most difficult of all, he must make the company communications-conscious. This means training everyone in appreciating news. Clearly, it is no good a sales director banging the desk and demanding publicity for an export order six months after the final delivery took place. Similarly, there is little point in trying to promote a new finance director three weeks after he started. Once news-conscious, however, the company has to become media-conscious. This means being prepared to dig out relevant facts and figures for the press. A journalist cannot pull a story out of thin air. It also means, especially in the case of top executives, being prepared to drive half way across London to be interviewed on radio or television. And, if the interview was a failure, being prepared to attend special training courses in mastering the media.

This done, the scope for corporate news is enormous, as ICI demonstrated in October 1967 when they mounted one of the largest-ever corporate news operations to promote their just-completed mammoth two-year £377 million programme on building new plant. Both 1965 and 1966 had been difficult years. Profits were falling. Margins were tightening. As a result of Mr Callaghan's 'July package' in 1966 over 1,000 men had been declared redundant in their fibre-spinning plants. ICI then came to the market to raise money for their capital projects. And immediately more criticism broke out. Their approach was badly timed said the city editors. They would have to pay too much interest. And so on.

ICI decided to fight back—if their half-yearly figures for September 1967 were encouraging. The message was simple. Their £377 million investment programme would save production costs and pay dividends.

ICI's Public Relations Department, began work towards the end of 1966. First, they had to decide what production centres and/or laboratories they would throw open to the press. Second, which journalists would be invited. And third, how could it be arranged in the maximum two-to-three days journalists would be prepared to be away from their offices. The result was a three-day tour of ICI's European centres at Teesside, Rozenburg, Cestringen and Cheshire by 160 journalists from 15 different countries. More than 70 stories appeared in the British press as a result, with a further 130 in Continental newspapers. Altogether a total 5,000 column inches in newspapers with a combined circulation of 45 million—with only two examples of stories unsympathetic to ICI. 'The cost of the trip, in relation to what I believe to be its total value, will be what I would regard as microscopic', said the Chairman at the time, Sir Paul Chambers, afterwards. In fact, it was less than £20,000.

Not all corporate news operations need be as enormous as that. There are scores of opportunities for hitting the headlines.

14.1 Advertising campaigns

Many companies seem to think that the only people interested in their advertising are their advertising agents. That is not true. Advertising is a £500 million-plus industry with its own trade press and its own specialist writers on the national press. A good advertising story, therefore, can attract wide publicity—and additional attention for the company over and above the space they are actually buying for the campaign.

The British Steel Corporation, for example, scored twice-over with their 'Steel can do anything' campaign, which featured an attractive girl wearing a £250 durable steel wig. Not only did the wig appear in a series of full-page advertisements in newspapers and magazines, it also turned up in the editorial columns. For the Corporation took the wig on tour.

> 'The workmen on the Embankment wolf-whistled at my new wig. I turned to glare—and was nearly decapitated. My fringe scratched my eyelids and my curls dug into my shoulders. I tried to wriggle my head into a more comfortable position—and was viciously swiped on the nose. I thought of trying to comb my new locks into shape, but only a screwdriver could get through the glorious steel-grey strands. Clearly, my new wig was becoming a dead-weight—all $15\frac{1}{2}$ ozs of it.'
> (Sally Wilkins, *Daily Mail*, 9 September 1969)

Obviously not every advertising campaign will yield such publicity. But the opportunities should be considered.

14.2 Appointments

Almost a certainty. Run-of-the-mill appointments are likely to attract the relevant trade, business and local press publicity. Without fail. Most publications will include a single-column photograph as well. If, however, the man—or woman—taking over the new position can also be built into an interesting news-worthy figure, the scope for publicity increases as well. Capers, for example, is a small company selling around £250,000 worth of mini-dresses and trouser suits a year at Harrods, most of the big London stores and well-known boutiques as well. It plans to double its sales as soon as possible. Nothing very exciting about that. But the story becomes interesting because one of the directors is Leila Croft.

> 'Remember the curly haired blondes in the "which twin has the Toni" advertisements? Well Leila Croft, the one who DID have a permanent wave, has come up smiling again as a design director of a successful new dress firm. Now smooth-haired, mini-skirted and married to City banker Panton Corbett, who financed the venture, Leila is a maker of changing fashions. She is the female partner in a bright young trio who started a brand new clothing firm four months ago.'
>
> (*Daily Express*, 8 September 1969)

Valuable publicity for a small firm in the right media as well. Not only small companies can benefit by this kind of publicity. It is open to all comers. Moss Empires, the theatre chain company, was the centre of attention when a new managing director took over. Again there was a story behind the story.

> 'The man who started work as a 12s 6d a week office boy with Moss Empires is to take over as managing director of the theatre chain company. Mr Louis Benjamin takes over as head of the group, whose London theatres include the Palladium and Victoria Palace. He said today "When I first started as an office boy in 1937 variety was in its hey-day. I became determined to get to the top of the profession." '
>
> (*Evening Standard*, 16 October 1969)

Rags-to-riches stories always go down well with the press. In fact, one can almost guarantee that a rags-to-riches story will always get twice the publicity an ordinary appointment would attract.

> 'It's a pretty long way from starting out as a £350-a-year insurance clerk at 18 to earning "well over £20,000", but this is what 30-year-old Mr Alan Phillips has achieved, and he has done it in a little matter of 12 years. A South Londoner educated at Bec School, Tooting, Mr Phillips is manager of the West End office of Abbey Life, and he tells me that he has achieved such a high income by "producing an enormous amount of business". Now he is starting on what might be described as phase two of his clearly lucrative career. On Monday he joins Property Growth Assurance, the company master-minded by estate agent Mr Peter Hutley to bring property bonds to the public.'
>
> (*Evening Standard*, 25 July 1969)

Women are, of course, the other passport to appointments publicity. If a woman is taking over a man's job, becoming the first woman ever appointed

to such-and-such a position or even just being made a d.
sure-fire opportunity for press coverage.

> 'Muriel Ward-Jackson, the John Lewis Partnership's ne
> director, is not one of those ladies in business whose portra.
> likely to find on the feature pages of women's magazines. For a .
> female executives in the partnership are no novelty. There are six oth.
> of senior rank, including the company secretary. Possibly for this reason
> she is not overconscious of being a woman in a predominantly man's
> world.'

(*The Times* Business News, 28 July 1969)

The publicity, of course, depends on the information. If there is a lot of
interesting background material, the publicity is practically automatic. If not,
one can reckon on a line in the appointments column—at the most.

14.3 Cut-backs

Stories about cut-backs are more often the stories that companies can do
without. Occasionally, however, comes a cut-back which can be turned to
advantage and used as a peg for an all-out promotion in the process. Advertising agents Papert, Koenig and Lois relinquished £1 million worth of business
overnight in August 1969. Instead of regretting the move, they took the bull
by the horns and hammered the reasons home. Chairman, Mr Nigel Seely,
maintained that 'by 1975, it is likely that there will be only two kinds of
advertising agency—the giant American-owned operation turning out
indifferent work for international clients, and the small agency, which will
survive because it produces interesting and effective advertising for a small
number of accounts'. PKL clearly wanted to be one of the small, specialist
outfits. Judging by the way the business news media reported their decision,
it seemed everyone was in sympathy with their aims.

14.4 Dedication

A special event to mark the opening of a new centre. One dedication arranged
by Chrysler in the United States called for 150 organisers and a whole day
programme of sporting events and new car tests.

14.5 Exhibitions

Exhibitions and fairs are great publicity occasions. An original and well-
designed stand can attract enormous attention from visitors. Its effect on a
company's corporate image can be startling. But it can also provide the basis
of a series of stories about the company, its staff and its products. Apart from
the home business media, a special service should concentrate on handling

stories aimed at the general and specialised press in other countries. A feature service could aim at passing information to radio and television.

14.6 Extra-curricula activities

A businessman is not only news in his business. He is news outside it as well. If he addresses a conference or opens an exhibition, he is not only attracting attention to himself but also to his company. The choice of activities he follows, therefore, is of vital importance to the company.

On this basis, 1969 was a very good year for Sir Val Duncan, Chairman of Rio Tinto-Zinc. At the beginning of July, he gave the first annual lecture to the Institute of Directors. He urged Britain to enter the Common Market. The forecast of a gloomy £600 million a year set back to the balance of payments, he dismissed. He went on to urge the establishment of a European currency and full European political unity. The speech, before 850 members of the Institute, attracted wide national press, radio and television attention. It was even discussed in a Business News leader in *The Times* the following day.

At the end of the month came the Duncan report—chaired by the Rio Tinto-Zinc chairman—which discussed the functions and scale of British representational efforts overseas. Once again, Sir Val Duncan and Rio Tinto-Zinc were in the headlines.

At the other end of the scale comes Mr Monty Moss of Moss Bros. He described the history of the company to members of the Round Table at Streatham Constitutional Club.

'Mr Moss traced the history of the firm, from the time when a Mr Charles Pond, a friend of his great uncle, Alfred, first borrowed clothes from the firm, to the new One-Up shop, just opened by the fifth generation of Moss Bros. in the person of Mr Stephen Moss. To Moss Bros. the watchword has always been quality, says Mr Monty Moss. He described some of the more unusual aspects of the firm. He said, "We were able to help out a great number of people who attended the Coronation with various items of uniform and the American commentator who said, "If it had not been for Moss Bros. the Coronation would not have taken place", was not a mile out.'
(*Streatham News*, 15 July 1969)

14.7 Exports

ICI exports are running at around £166 million a year. Ford are close behind with £164 million. Next comes British Leyland with about £157 million closely followed by Rolls-Royce, General Electric, Massey-Ferguson, British Petroleum, Vauxhall Motors and Hawker Siddley. But a company doesn't have to be one of the top exporters to get export publicity. Brian Hart and John Whiteley of Koraz are invading America, with a process as old as 11th Century Persia and as young as a secondary school art class.

'With partners Mike Nolan and Ann Akroyd, they are firing off 100 catalogues of their dramatic marble wallpapers for the US Clarence House collection. It all started when they rushed up five-walls-worth overnight for Mike Fish of the Mr Fish boutique two years ago, and has since developed to a fine art involving eye-droppers, squeegees and a 1½-ton tank of cellulose. Operating from the site of Jack the Ripper's last murder in London, Koraz now hopes to make a killing by under-cutting its only known rival by around 60 per cent.'
(*The Sunday Times* Business News, 27 July 1969)

Few companies could beat that. It has everything. But it proves that every company, no matter what size, which products they are manufacturing or where they are based can have a crack at getting export publicity.

14.8 Factory visits

War correspondents like getting to the front. Business journalists like getting to the work bench. Hence the appeal—and success—of factory visits. An at home visit for specialist journalists can create enormous impact and lasting goodwill. The Board of Trade in 1967 outlined the ingredients of successful factory visits: 'A welcome by a senior executive. A short introductory talk about the firm, its history, organisation, products and overseas markets. Models, charts and photographs put life into statistics. A brief tour of the plant pin-pointing the highlights of the production methods. It may be worthwhile isolating and explaining the essence of a manufacturing process which is particularly newsworthy. An opportunity at the end of the tour to question executives and production experts. In addition, correspondents should have the chance to talk informally to executives and develop individual themes of special interest to them. Press material and photographs including basic facts on the size, structure, and development of the company should be provided.'

14.9 New premises

New premises mean expansion. And expansion is news. Every company should seize the publicity opportunity of moving into a new centre. The news media are automatically interested in development. They will automatically be interested in any move. They will also want to examine the implications. For an article in the January 1963 issue of *The Statist* called 'Buildings don't lie' suggested a variation to Parkinson's law: Good buildings go with good companies; bad buildings with bad companies. The author, 'Actaeon', first checked the criticisms of new buildings found in the *Architects Journal*. Then he discovered that whenever they praised any new buildings of companies such as Thorn or Castrol, the shares subsequently shot up. And whenever they damned any new buildings such as English Electric or Shell, the shares went down.

Similarly, all the other groups the company comes into contact with should be told about the move. Existing clients and suppliers will have to be told. Potential clients will have to be persuaded that the move means better opportunities for providing them with the services they are looking for. Wells Fargo Bank crystallised all the reasons for opening their first over-seas branch at 2 rue Heine, Luxembourg-Ville, Luxembourg in a special advertisement at the time:

'The purpose
To receive and place Eurocurrency deposits.
To provide short and medium term financing in Eurocurrencies.
To participate in term loans with other banks.
In short, to serve you.
The plan:
To complement the operations of our affiliates, Western American Bank (Europe), Limited, a merchant bank, and Eurofinance, a consultant in finance and research.
To broaden the capabilities of our worldwide network of correspondent banks, affiliates and our other representative offices in Mexico City, Tokyo and Central America.
In short, to serve you.'
(*The Economist*, 5 July 1969)

Sandeman's had a different story to tell altogether when they moved from their old headquarters in the City of London's St Swithin's Lane after 164 years. And they made the most of it. They moved on St Swithin's Day.

'The ancient vaults with their arched roof of square chalk blocks dating from Roman times had a strange and empty air when I visited them this week. The Sandeman brothers, Tim and David, have had to put sentiment aside and throw out many old ledgers, documents and papers, including the cheque which one long dead Sandeman started to sign but "was too drunk to complete" as the bank was told in no uncertain terms. He, added Tim Sandeman, was not one of the best of the Sandemans, and hastily passed on to the ancestor who was once a much respected director of the Bank of England.'
(*Investors Chronicle*, 11 July 1969)

Because of the St Swithin's Day connection, the company benefitted even more by the repetition of the Sandeman alternative to the doggerel by St Swithin.

'Three-thousand score days with three hundred more
All pray to the Saint on St Swithin's Day.
If the dividend falls below last year's score,
There's hell to pay on St Swithin's Day.'

14.10 Off-beat stories

They are impossible to define. They just happen. When they do, a company
can expect to get some startling results. Take the story of Benedictine. Most
people would think it's drunk by the After-Eights set throughout the smooth,
affluent stockbroker belt of the South East. In fact, no less than 40 per cent
of its United Kingdom sale is taken up by a string of Mill towns throughout
East Lancashire.

> 'Burnley, Nelson, Colne, Accrington and Blackburn, seem unlikely
> locales for legions of Benedictine tipplers. Yet in King Cotton's cradle,
> drinkers swig 50,000 bottles a year (retail price 79s)—as many as in
> London. What are they doing with it—oiling the looms? Williams and
> Humbert (the Dry Sack sherry people who distribute the liqueur
> here) mounted a fact-finding mission.'
> (*Sunday Times*, 27 July 1969)

The results were bizarre. A 100-year old asked to account for his age some
years back apparently replied, 'It's the Benny'. Since then its been drunk as a
chaser to—believe it or not—Guinness topped up with concentrated orange;
as a stomach-settler to nine pints of ale, and as a celebration whenever a
local's whippet wins a race.

There was a similar off-beat story linking Lloyds, the insurance centre, with
the Apollo moonshot:

> 'No, the spacecraft is not being insured in Britain. What is believed to
> be the first risk contingent upon the success or otherwise of the moon
> landing has been arranged at Lloyd's for a London firm proposing to
> strike medallions to commemorate the moon landings. Striking of the
> coins will begin as the lunar module touches down at its destination.'
> (*The Times*, 15 July 1969)

Leonard Matchan, the millionaire President and Chairman of Cope Allman,
was involved in a different type of off-beat story, which landed him in the
news. As owner of the island of Brecqhou, he runs his own postal service as
there was no collection or delivery to his island. Under a plan drawn up by the
Guernsey Post Office, however, he would face £25 fines for carrying a
single postal packet. A private issue of stamps 'he was having specially
printed would lay him open to further charges. The story made the national
papers.

14.11 Photographs

Chairman of Klinger's, William Castell, was pictured lying in the sun. Mr S. T. Ryder, Chairman of the Reed Group, was seen leaping out of a helicopter during a flying visit to a £1 million stationery factory site at Washington, Co. Durham. Both Chairman and Managing Director of Glass and Metal Holdings, Alf Bowman and Bertie Webber, were photographed, jackets off, sleeves rolled up, helping to move into new premises after closing down their East End factory.

Photographs are news. The standards are getting higher and higher all the time. The news media are no longer prepared to accept the standard picture of the chief executive sitting at his desk with his ear to the telephone and a blank sheet of blotting paper in front of him. It's old hat. Instead, the financial press are looking for lively, interesting photographs. This has its built-in advantages for the companies concerned. If a company can offer the press newsworthy pictures, they now stand far more chance of getting them used.

14.12 Plans

Everybody likes plans except, of course, the company making them—in case they go wrong. But if things look reasonably safe, there is no harm in releasing the information to the financial public relations media. Plans for a new factory, for example, could affect the financial community's long-term view of the company. Plans for a new product could affect the short-term view. Rio Tinto-Zinc, for example, gained a great deal of publicity with the announcement of plans to build a huge low-grade copper-gold project on Bougainville Island in the Territory of Papua and New Guinea especially as it seemed to herald the era of capital intensive mines. Huge Eurodollar loans had to be arranged, backed up by two powerful syndicates of 35 international financial institutions.

> 'Bougainville could be the toughest technical challenge yet to be undertaken by the RTZ group. Situated in a hilly jungle terrain, the open-pit proposition is estimated to contain 760 million tons of ore grading a low 0·47 per cent copper together with a sweetener of 0·4 cwts gold per ton of ore, around which there are additional quantities of lower grade material.'
> (*Financial Times*, 29 July 1969)

14.13 Polls

The important thing about polls is to come out on top. If you do you can wring every last drop of publicity from being in the number-one spot. For polls are the quickest way to a journalist's heart. If not, its best to forget about the whole thing.

'The fast-growing North Country textile machinery concern, Ernest Scragg, has been declared officially Britain's champion company for 1969 by *Management Today*, the monthly magazine. The phenomenal profits growth of Scragg mainly through the fast expansion of world-wide sales of one machine have given the company in its latest trading year a massive 35·2 per cent return on capital growth. It has pushed the company up to the number one position from number five in last year's growth league table of Britain's top 200 companies.'
(*Evening Standard*, 19 August 1969)

An accolade like that is worth stressing again and again. There are many opportunities for drawing it to people's attention—just as companies always stress their Queen's Award for Achievement.

14.14 Product publicity

Virtually any form of publicity for a company's products rather than for a company's personnel, premises and so on.

'Lesney, the Matchbox firm, is all set to counter the American toy companies who have been winning orders around the world for the latest schoolboy craze—model cars with friction-free wheels. Within the next week or two, the first export shipment of the British firm's answer Superfast cars—will be leaving Lesney's factories in East London, bound for the United States, where the craze was started 16 months ago by Mattel.'
(*The Times*, 14 July 1969)

Product publicity is a specialist field in itself. It calls for knowledge of all sales promotion and merchandising skills. Yet every time a new product is featured, it automatically reflects on the company. Product publicity is, therefore, vitally important to an effective financial public relations programme.

14.15 Re-organisation

It depends, of course, on the results of the re-organisation. If a company is re-organised and still loses money, it is dangerous to make too much fuss about it. If, however, a company is taken by the scruff of its neck and shaken back into life again, it is worth shouting from the roof tops. Take Associated Fire Alarms. Five years ago, they didn't even have a Stock Exchange quotation. The shares had slumped from a peak 22s 6d to 2s 6d. The company was losing £885,000 and it owed the bank £2 million. Then in came Ian Morrow, an accountant, as chief executive. He set to work. Within a year the quote was back. The price on the first day was 8s 6d. After 12 months the company came up with a trading profit—and a dividend. By 1968 profits had risen 20 per cent to £545,000. AFA was back in the glamour stakes. This made a superb re-organisation story for the financial press. Morrow was described as the 'Man who beat the alarm bell'.

Kenneth Fraser came in for similar praise with his re-organisation of Hall-Thermotank. Within two years he had liquidated seven companies and closed down a number of factories. The whole group had been reconstructed. A new board appointed. And a new logo assigned to the group. Again, an important story for the business press.

Birmid Qualcast went a stage further when they completely restructured the group into three new divisional companies in July 1969. They took a two-page advertisement in the *Investors Chronicle*.

> 'The Board of Birmid Qualcast Limited announce a major development in their plan for the future organisation and management structure of the Group. The changes affect the membership of three new Divisional Companies, which between them will embrace all the subsidiary operations of the Group. The Divisions will be complemented and directed by a corporate structure at the centre. These arrangements establish a framework for the future planning and profit growth of the Group and reflect the final stage in the integration of Birmid Industries Limited and Qualcast Limited.'

Alongside, they listed the full 33 companies in the Group and which Divisions they had been classified under. The names of the executive directors of the new main board were also given together with their responsibilities.

14.16 Sales

Companies live by sales. So sales should be the basis of a wide range of financial public relations activities. They are also especially interesting to the news media because not only the companies own future depends on the success or otherwise of its sales campaign but the future of its competitors as well. A successful drive which boosts a company's share of the market can mean a headache—and, perhaps, set-backs for the opposition.

From a financial public relations point of view there are three different opportunities for sales publicity.

14.16.1 TEST MARKETING

The more companies try to keep test market campaigns a secret, the more people hear about them. It is absurd to think one can clamp a net of secrecy around any commercial operation nowadays. Most companies know more about their rivals than the rivals ever imagine. It is not difficult to find out the straightforward commercial information about any company. The best way of tackling a test market operation therefore is to bang the drum and put the fear of God into the competition. This will be done with the aid of all the usual sales promotion, advertising and display material attached to every test drive. It can also be done through the financial public relations media.

'With its Scottish test marketing on the new, longer life, higher priced, chromium blade a success, Wilkinson Sword is now ready to open a second front in the razor blade war. I also hear that chief executive Roy Randolph has got an even bigger surprise in store for the competition and that he will be making his move soon. Both developments could not come at a better time . . . Wilkinson has had takeover approaches galore, but the controlling Randolphs have always put up a strong independent front. They have been in business since 1772 and they have a lot of pride. But views have been known to change before, and in Wilkinson's case there are at least half a dozen big companies patiently waiting with their cheque books ready.'

(*The Observer*, 6 July 1969)

14.16.2 EXPECTING THE ORDERS

This could be risky. Although generally the news only gets out if an order is practically 99 per cent certain. If it is possible, it is a superb technique. The company demonstrates its confidence by letting it be known that it is on a short-list. It also ensures that it gets twice the publicity. First, when it is expecting the order. Second, when it arrives. If a newspaper or magazine carries the first story, it is practically duty bound to confirm or deny whether the company subsequently landed the order or not.

'Upper Clyde Shipbuilders hopes to announce soon a new order for a ship slightly under £3 million in value. It is for overseas owners and negotiations are in their final stages. Mr Anthony Hepper, Chairman of the Group, also confirmed today that "active negotiations" were in progress with five other potential customers, one of whom would be interested in a "serial" order.'

(*Financial Times*, 1 August 1969)

Jensen, the small luxury car company owned by merchant bankers, William Brandt, went a stage further. Not only did they publicise the fact that sales were roaring ahead, they were able to spotlight the business-getting organisation behind the sales figures as well.

'It is much in line with the big plans they have on at Jensen Cars that the current Miss World—Australian beauty Penny Plummer—should have been their lunch-time guest at the West Bromwich plant this week. For Jensen is getting very world-minded. Managing Director, Mr Carl Duerr and other top executives are busily flying around Europe, Australia and the United States preparing the ground for a sales development aimed at lifting production from its modest 15 cars weekly now up to 60. Only one a week on average goes for export so far.'

(*Evening Standard*, 9 July 1969)

The story went on to explain how one distributor had been appointed in Switzerland so far. Another was lined up for Austria. While motor men all over Europe were anxious to get their hands on a Jensen franchise.

14.16.3 GETTING THE ORDERS

The logical extension to expecting the orders—with two variations. If a company lands a major contract, that in itself could be an opportunity for publicity. Relatively small contracts tend to attract little attention in the main financial press while the trade press—again depending on which industry they are covering—generally go overboard. Either way the company benefits. The other alternative is waiting until the end of an intensive selling period or, say, until the end of the year and then releasing information about sales. If sales are up dramatically, publicity is practically guaranteed.

> 'On Friday, Sotheby's, the biggest fine art auctioneering firm in the world, holds its last sale of the season. It has been an enormously successful one for the firm—so successful that I believe Sotheby's will prove to have broken all records. Turnover in what a spokesman describes as a "triumphant" year, will top the £40 million mark—£10 million more than last year. And around £28 million of the current year's turnover will have been earned in foreign currency. The sort of overseas earnings that Sotheby's manages to tot up are impressive and in America alone sales brought in more than £15 million. Over the past year, Sotheby's has extended its overseas network, opening six new offices. This brings the total up to 11, with one deep in the heart of Texas, in affluent Houston.'
> (*Evening Standard*, 28 July 1969)

Getting the press coverage is only half the battle. Merchandising the clippings is the other half. For, clearly, it is a waste of time and effort to fight like mad for press coverage only to see the story published and disappear from sight. First, because a company cannot be sure that the very people they wanted to see the story actually saw it and studied it. Second, because press coverage confers authority. And authority means reassurance. Companies should, therefore, gather the clippings together and reprint them to form the basis of background mailing shots to specific publications. Or they can distribute them to potential clients and customers as a sales aid. Either way is effective.

Chapter 15

Corporate advertising

The third side of the corporate triangle: corporate advertising. Corporate public relations is the over-all promotion of the company as a company. Corporate news is news of the company as a company directed at the relevant news media. And now, corporate advertising is the paid-for promotion of the company as a company. Says Beveridge:

> 'Almost as varied as the companies that use it, corporate advertising is defined as being any advertisement whose primary purpose is to sell an idea or a theme rather than a product or a service.'

Take one or two examples:

> 'Dear Chancellor of the Exchequer,
> If you ever get to feeling down in the mouth, our end of term report and a few facts and figures should buck you up. As you know, we haven't been doing too badly in the home market. But much nearer your heart is the way our exports have been going. In 1968 we earned a record £208,000,000 for Britain. In fact, more Ford cars were exported than any other single British marque. And in the first six months of this year, we added another £130,000 of exports. Opening up new markets (in places like Korea, Indonesia and Peru) in the process. All this didn't just happen. It is one of the results of the biggest capital expenditure programme in the history of the British motor industry. £185 million over the last five years . . .'

That's a corporate advertisement. Ford are not selling cars—just the company.

> 'Introducing the fantastic big Fords for 1970. The new Zodiac and Executive for 1970. More style outside. More style inside. And more comfort too. Zodiac £1,477. Executive £1,795.'

This time Fords are selling cars—and selling them hard. It is not a corporate advertisement. But an ordinary sales advertisement. Take another example.

'Who's in on practically every deal and never mentioned
Morgan

Name a dozen companies at the top today. Without realising it you've
got yourself a baker's dozen. The extra one is Morgan . . . Morgan are
diversified. And diversifying. And growing, world-wide. £25 million
sales last year. 46 per cent overseas. Three major divisions: Carbon,
Thermic, Electronics; 25 subsidiaries in the United Kingdom, 15 overseas;
200 agents in 80 countries. Morgan. A name to remember.'

Obviously they are not selling carbon brushes to the transport industry,
radiants to gas-fire manufacturers or even ceramic fibre to nuclear power
stations. They are selling the name Morgan—just that. Notice the difference
with another advertisement, such as the very clever oh-so-soft sell of the
Algemene Bank Nederland, which tells the story of how the Jhaveri brothers
went to their Bombay office in 1964, how they worked with their limited capital
and how the Bombay office helped them with financing and gave them advice
about arranging foreign contacts.

'It wasn't long before their diamond export doubled again. We advised
them on foreign exchange transactions and the risks involved. Their
diamond export kept on doubling. The Jhaveri brothers had come to us
in 1964 owning a factory employing 15 craftsmen and producing a
diamond export of a few hundred rupees. By 1968 their staff had risen
to 500 and their exports had exceeded 10 million rupees. Their diamond
exports had doubled more than 5 times in less than 5 years. If you have
an import or export problem, contact one of our 70 branches . . .'

Deceptive at first. But in the end just as much sell-sell-sell as the hard-hitting
no-nonsense advertisement for Ford's Zodiac and Executive.

Corporate advertising is, therefore, different from the other forms of
advertising.

15.1 It is public relations advertising as opposed to advertising advertising

Straightforward advertising is interested in speaking to only one group:
potential customers. And it is interested in persuading them to do only one
thing: buy. Corporate advertising prefers to sell the company as a whole—
not a particular product or service—and to 'sell' it to not only potential
customers but employees, both present and future; suppliers; shareholders;
banks; the City and the public generally. It is, therefore, a vital aid to any
financial public relations operation.

British Leyland, for example, used a whole page advertisement to hammer
home not only the scope of their research but the practical application as
well. First came the drum beating:

'An idea is only as good as you make it.

Some of the best ideas often end up as some of the
worst ideas, because nobody knows how to make them work.
At British Leyland, we pride ourselves in doing justice to good ideas.'

Then the story about the gas-turbine engine:

'After spending years developing these engines for aeroplanes, we've now
perfected them for trucks. They'll be the quickest, cleanest, quietest
trucks on the road.'

And the story about both the small and bigger-engined cars as well:

'British Leyland revolutionised it through front-wheel drive and the
traverse engine. The engine which enabled us to make the world's
first small car that was really big inside. Coupled with hydrolastic suspension (the most sophisticated form of suspension ever invented) our
small cars have helped us to become Britain's biggest exporter. And on
bigger-engined cars, we experimented with fuel injection. Fuel injection,
as every good mechanic knows, is very efficient.'

Admittedly, all this will be of interest to all the lucky owners and buyers of
British Leyland cars, but it was not the primary objective. Clearly the advertisement was talking to the community generally. As a result anyone who
reads the advertisement is immediately convinced of the reasearch and
thoroughness of the company.

Another public relations advertisement, probably a pure public relations
advertisement, appeared in the *Financial Times* on 9 July 1969, backed by the
Cleveland, Ohio-based giant, Eaten Yale and Towne Incorporated. It did not
even mention a product. Instead it concentrated on President, Mr E. M. de
Windt's recent tour of Europe and listed some of the comments he had made
at various meetings with government groups and leading editors. Said the
headline:

'Our multinational company looks at the world as one big global
market and it looks great!'

And one of the quotes:

'Each of our Divisions and Subsidiaries is a profit center and its management has board authority to make decisions. Our multinational employees
receive intensive training in our management philosophies, policies and
techniques. Programs defining objectives and goals are reconciled at
corporate levels.'
(Industrie-Club and American Chamber of Commerce of Germany,
Dusseldorf, Germany.)

The Reed Group ran a highly effective series of corporate advertisements
in the principal European financial media in 1969 prior to raising money by

means of European Units of Account. They were, in fact, the first industrial concern and the first United Kingdom borrower to raise money that way. Each advertisement took the form of a quiz—about the Reed Group. And, according to publicity controller, Barrie Powell Jones, was 'extremely successful'.

15.2 It is advertising for the record

Prospectuses are not the only form of advertising that companies book for the record. Although it is probably the most frequent. There are plenty of other opportunities during the life of a company when it should go in for corporate advertising. Mergers are one example. When two companies link up, they should launch an all-out campaign to set the record straight—otherwise they will find that few people realise they are no longer separate entities. Labour disputes are another. Often the issues involved in a labour dispute can become so obscured that the management is forced to take advertising space to re-state their case, develop their argument or to put a proposition to employees. It is not selling advertising. It is corporate advertising.

15.3 It is image-changing advertising

Gone are the days when companies passed from father to son and to grandson without a change in their make-up. Most, the most dynamic, are constantly evolving. Others find they have to drop one line, modify another and develop a third. As a result, a company can start out with a progressive image in one field and end up, years later, as a laggard in a completely different industry. Similarly, a company can plough its furrow for so long that it is taken for granted and virtually ignored. When that happens, it needs a corporate advertising campaign to re-vamp its image and begin to fight back.

Probably the most successful comeback, in these terms, in recent years has been the British Steel Corporation's re-launch of steel. The problem was painfully simple. Stainless steel apart, steel was regarded as old-fashioned, heavy, ugly and likely to rust. If you wanted good design, the last thing you thought of was steel. Aluminium, plastic and even glass were far more with it than steel. The result: a campaign for steel appeal, backed by a series of first-class, modern, compelling advertisements.

> This cobweb isn't made of the solid strands that the spider spins. It is steel tube. It is hollow, and the hole in it is only ·007″ in diameter. Compared with some steel tubes, it is still pretty coarse stuff. A stainless steel tube has been made so fine that the hole in it is invisible except through a powerful microscope. But ·007″ steel tube is commonplace. . . . Steel is the only material strong enough to be worked with such infinite precision. That's steel appeal.

Steel has great strength and endless variety. Bridges and fridges. Cars and bikes. Pots and pans if you choose wisely. And humble cans. All sorts of things will always be made of steel because nothing else has quite the same qualities. Only steel combines such strength, lightness and value for money. Think of that when you're shopping. And give your home steel appeal.

Steel can. Others can't. Tin cans are steel. They give stronger, longer protection than anything else. . . . Cans are steel because nothing else combines such strength, lightness and value-for-money. The qualities that add up to steel appeal. You'll find it in a wonderful variety of practical, beautiful things in your home. From cruets to cookers. Next time you're shopping remember to bring home more steel appeal.

Now think of steel as being old-fashioned, fuddy-duddy and out-of-date. Hence the value of a corporate campaign such as this. But that's only one side of the image problem.

Singer had a similar problem. They had diversified world-wide. But still they were 'the sewing machine company'. They decided to fight back with an advertisement which featured their '999 other products serving 179 other countries'.

The moon. Singer was landing on the moon years ahead of Apollo 11. Because Singer built the computer-fed Apollo 11 and lunar module simulators used to train the astronauts. Plus, 50 other products that helped to put man on the moon.

The sea. Singer did six weeks of business at the bottom of the sea last year—testing systems that will eventually free Man to work effectively in the oceans' depths. Singer is also pioneering undersea communications and perfecting infra-red photography for use in combating water pollution.

The air. Singer makes virtually every type of conventional heating and air conditioning equipment. And some highly unconventional ones. Like Incremental comfort conditioners that individualise temperature room by room. Or the system that extracts heat from one side of a large building and uses it to heat the shady side.

And so on. But it works. Anyone who reads that advertisement soon loses the image of the company as a one-product outfit. In its place they get a dynamic picture of a company constantly developing and expanding in a whole range of specialist areas. Similar companies labelled with an out-of-date image can fight back just as well.

Some of the Gas Council's advertisements are also a good example of this genre. A company is rightly or wrongly blamed for creating a particular problem. Instead of just sitting back and trying to shrug it off, a company must give its side of the story.

T

Similarly, a company which changes its name. Perhaps it has been taken over or submerged by its giant parent. Either way, it means it must start life afresh. It is no good relying on people remembering the old name, remembering the change and remembering the new name. The company must start life all over again—and re-sell its new name. This calls for a different style of corporate campaign.

15.4 Leading corporate advertiser

Probably the leading exponent of corporate advertising in this country is ICI which has been running corporate campaigns for more than 25 years from the early years of the last war—they booked advertisements selling nothing except the idea that, as an industrial giant, it was honest, responsible, important to the country's economy and conscious of both its reputation and profits—up until their 1969–70 Pathfinder series of television commercials, the first purely corporate advertising to appear on television in the United Kingdom.

ICI's earliest essays in corporate advertising were aimed at opinion-formers and managers and then different sections of society. After each operation, they would research to discover whether the message was getting across. It was during one of these surveys that they discovered that while the higher income groups, like the A's and B's, knew a great deal about the company— and liked what they knew—the C's and D's and E's were much less well-informed and by no means ready to think favourably about them. This was particularly noticeable among the 18–35 age group, which had grown up while ICI's previous corporate campaign had been directed at higher audiences. On top of that, the C's and D's especially, found it difficult to warm to the 'image' of the organisation.

Ogilvy and Mather, ICI's advertising agency, blamed this on the company's remoteness from the affairs of ordinary people: ICI's vast programmes of research and investment brought enormous benefits to the man-in-the-street but their products were swallowed up by other industries in the process. Hence, they lacked personality.

Television, it was decided, was the solution. It was the only medium to capture the necessary target audience. It would also inject warmth and personality into the ICI image. For this reason it was decided not to mention any product names. That would only turn a soft-sell commercial into a hard-selling one. Thus look like all the others on the screen. As a result, the stories ranged from farming where a new chemical spray enables poor pastures to be renovated without ploughing to medicine where new anaesthetics have been developed for the benefit of both surgeons and patients. There was also a link between Concorde and ICI's household paint. But all the time the message was clear: ICI was not cold and remote. It was composed of people with a concern for other people's problems.

ICI then went a stage further and researched the effect of the campaign. People from the target C2D range were wheeled into special screenings of a number of films. Those who had seen them before were then subjected to a series of questions putting ICI on a five-point image rating scale. Was the image a warm image? They gave ICI a 3·4 rating. Others who had seen the films for the first time in a similar experiment gave 3·7. A question about being modern yielded a 4·4 rating; whether the company was go-ahead, 4·6.

'The public feels it has a right today to know something of what goes on in boardrooms and on shop floors', says Gordon Long, ICI's Head of Public Relations. 'As a result a company's success depends now, and to an extent it never did before, on the sort of reputation it acquires in the world at large. If that reputation is good, people will be inclined to buy its products, to want to invest in it, to try to gain employment within it for themselves or their children. If its reputation is malodorous, the climate in which it conducts its business will be very unfavourable on every score.'

That applies to every company.

Part five

Benefits of Financial Advertising and Public Relations

Chapter 16

Getting Value for Money

To the Editor, *The Times*, 8 September 1969
Sir—There must be many small investors like myself who wonder if it is really necessary to be burdened with such detailed documents from companies. . . . The cost of printing must be considerable, and is, I presume, borne indirectly by, the investors . . .

Of course there are objections to a deliberate, planned and sustained financial advertising and public relations campaign. There will always be shareholders who will put the reverse end of the telescope to their blind eye and swear black and blue it is not worth the money. But they are wrong. And, more and more, in the minority. For companies are beginning to recognise the need for financial advertising and public relations. Says the public relations adviser to a world-wide mining and investment company: 'If all our financial advertising and public relations means that we are offered just one mine in 20 years which we wouldn't otherwise get then the whole programme has been worth it'.

Mines apart, there are more manageable ways of measuring the success of a financial advertising and public relations programme.

16.1 By attendance at annual meetings

Obviously, the more stockholders attend an annual meeting, the more they are interested in the company. The less likely, therefore, they will drop out at a difficult moment. This, of course, could be crucial in any takeover battle. But it could also mean a boost for sales, especially for a consumer company with a wide range of stockholders.

16.2 By turnover of shareholders

Every public company faces a turnover of shareholders. There would be something wrong if it did not. But the important point is: Why? If shareholders sell because they need the liquid funds or because they have spotted a better bargain, although it involves risk, that is fair. If, however, they sell because they no longer trust the company or because they fear they are being misled or because they simply got bored with the company's lack-lustre performance that is something a company should fear—and do something about. Shareholders are more prepared to stock with a company if they share its confidence, if they understand the short-term problems and if they are convinced that all will be well in the long run. Similarly with new shareholders. It is much better from a company point of view to have shareholders joining the ranks because they accept the company for its performance, its plans and its personnel rather than because they have a hunch they stand to make an extra 6d over the following three months.

16.3 By outside comment

If the press switches its attention from one company to another and follows its activities closely, quoting its chairman from time to time, it obviously reflects on that company. Similarly with stockholders. The more interest financial analysts and stockbrokers take in a company, the more special reports they will prepare. These, in turn, will attract still greater attention.

16.4 By being free from rumour

Lack of information breeds doubt. And doubt breeds rumour. If a company runs a financial public relations operation which is constantly feeding out the relevant facts and figures to the relevant financial public relations media, there will be little room for doubt. Other companies running a closed-door policy will be the subject of rumour. A company with an open-door policy will not.

16.5 By research

If a big company conducts a massive financial advertising and public relations programme, it can mount a research operation to discover the success of the drive on different sectors of the financial community. It can also afford it. A smaller company, however, need only bother about certain specific sections of the financial community.

16.6 By having a share price that reflects the financial and trading position of the company as well as its future prospects

This does not mean rigging the market. It means reducing the chances of unjustified fluctuations in the share price. If the share price remains steady without being subjected to wild 'highs' and 'lows' like other companies, it means that the financial public relations programme is getting across. Investors know the full facts of the company's position. They are confident in its operations.

16.7 By better executive material

A company which is in the news and which is recognised for its abilities is a company that people want to work for. Blue-chip companies have little difficulty attracting the right kind of executive material. They can have the pick of the bunch. It is the less attractive, more unknown companies which have trouble. And then if they get the right men, they have difficulty keeping them. There is always the lure of that blue-chip on the horizon. The solution, of course, is to become a company, whatever the size, with a blue-chip reputation.

16.8 By the P/E ratio

The P/E ratio is essentially a confidence index. The more confidence investors have in the company's ability to meet its targets the higher the ratio. And investors can only be confident if they are fed the right information at the right time.

16.9 By money raising

A company which is well known to the investing public certainly finds it easier to mount new issues. It also faces lower underwriting costs. This is important in the United Kingdom. But it is becoming more and more important in Europe. One company has already run a major financial public relations operation in Europe prior to raising money. It worked and paid dividends in return. Other companies will be following suit. Banks are also more inclined to help companies with established reputations, perhaps, more than companies still struggling for recognition.

A financial advertising and public relations programme is, therefore, indispensable for any company. It can be a time-consuming operation. But it is worth every second. It can be expensive. But it is worth every penny. It is certainly not uneconomic. For the budget can easily be counted against the benefits.

Financial Glossary

Ideally, of course, financial public relations practitioners should be as conversant with financial jargon as the hardened Stock Exchange professional. Unfortunately, space is limited. The following terms are among the most useful, as far as public relations is concerned.

ACCOUNT The 14-day periods of the Stock Exchange year. Account dealings are dealings made during the Account. And Account Day is the day on which accounts for dealings made during the previous Account are presented.

ACCUMULATION The transfer of stock from minority into majority holdings. An all-out buying spree.

ACTIVE STOCKS Securities in the Stock Exchange Official List for which there has been the highest number of bargains.

AFTER MARKET Trading after the market has closed. Initial dealings after a launch.

ARBITRAGE An American term for buying and selling stock, which is convertible, when the market prices are different from the official rate.

ARITHMETIC MERGER A merger by a low multiple company with a high multiple company. Thus the earnings per share of the original company are boosted—without any boost to the company's income.

AUTHORISED CAPITAL The nominal capital of a company outlined by the Memorandum of Association.

AVERAGING Buying more of a particular stock, even though at a high price, so that taken with the existing holding the average cost is much lower.

BARGAINS AT SPECIAL PRICES This is the meaning of ‡ in the Stock Exchange Daily Official List. A deal, which is either larger or smaller than usual for which a special price different from the ordinary market price has been struck.

BARGAINS DONE PREVIOUS DAY Or ø. Deals made after 2.15 pm which are too late to appear in that day's Stock Exchange Daily Official List and so have to appear—with the hieroglyph ø—the following day.

CASH FLOW The increase in a company's liquid resources. It is obtained by adding retained earnings to depreciation.

CASH TENDER A third-party offer to buy stock for a particular price within a particular time limit.

CLEAN Ex-dividend.

CREEPING ACQUISITION Takeover by stealth. An oh-so-quiet and oh-so-slow takeover by a raider through the open market—with the aid of other interests.

CUM-DIVIDEND If a stock buyer has the right to the next interest payment, the stock is cum-dividend.

DILUTION The watering down of a share's earnings.

DIRTY A similar term for cum-dividend—especially when the stock is about to become ex-dividend so that it is full of dividend.

DIVIDEND The amount of profit a company distributes to shareholders, generally referred to as a percentage of the nominal value of the original capital.

DIVIDEND COVER The number of times available profit covers the sum needed for dividend.

EARNINGS YIELD Multiply the nominal value of the shares in shillings by percentage earnings and divide by the price of the shares, also in shillings. This is the return from investing in a company if all the latest annual profits were distributed to investors.

EQUITY After providing for debenture, creditors and preference shareholders claims comes the equity, the assets for which the equity shareholders have a claim.

EX Without. Ex All: without the advantages. Ex Cap: without any rights to scrip or capitalisation issues. Ex Div: without the current dividend. Ex Rights: without the right to any shares issued for cash to existing shareholders.

GO-GO Dynamic, Successful. Capital gains at all costs.

HEDGE FUNDS Go-Go funds in an highly volatile market.

NET ASSET WORTH Divide the net equity assets by the number of Ordinary shares. This gives an indication of the value of the shares.

NOMINAL SHARE VALUE The original face value of a share—not its market value.

ON THE BLOCK Ripe for picking. Ready for takeover.

PAINTING THE TAPE Share-pushing to get investor interest.

PLUGGING THE MULTIPLE Boosting the share price. Either to make an attempted takeover too expensive for the raider. Or to boost the earnings per share figure in an arithmetic merger.

POOLING OF INTEREST One company takes over another and promptly merges its own year's earnings with those of the acquired company—even though the acquired company had only been merged for a part of the year.

PREFERENCE CAPITAL Capital which carries prior rights to fixed interest payments out of profits.

PREFERENCE DIVIDEND COVER The degree to which the preference dividends are covered or exceeded by earnings or profits.

RAIDER A takeover merchant.

SELF TAKEOVER Using the cash and assets of the victim company to take it over.

SIDESTEP A defensive merger. Instead of being swallowed by a devil it doesn't know, a company prefers to merge with a devil it does know.

SYNERGISM $2+2=5$. A total that is greater than the sum of its parts.

Bibliography

Company-Investor Relations, James Derriman,
University of London Press (1969).

Financial Public Relations, Oscar M. Beveridge,
McGraw-Hill (1963).

Guide to Company Balance Sheets and Profit and Loss Accounts, Frank H.
Jones, Heffer and Sons (1964).

The City Code on Takeovers and Mergers,
The Issuing Houses Association (1968).

The International Public Relations Encyclopedia,
Peter Biddlecombe, Grant Helm (1968).

Advertising for the Advertiser, Eric Webster,
John Murray (1969).

Disclosure in Company Accounts, Harold Rose,
Institute of Economic Affairs (1963).

Current Thoughts on Public Relations, by members of Hill and Knowlton Inc.,
M W Lads Publishing, New York (1968).

The City, Paul Ferris,
Victor Gollancz (1960).

Business Adventures, John Brooks,
Victor Gollancz (1969).

Index

v

Wilson, Sir Reginald, 135
Winner, Paul, 94–5
Wolfson, Sir Isaac, 7
  and takeovers, 197
Wolseley-Hughes Ltd., 10
Woodhead (Jonas), and Sons, 217
Wyly, Sam, 188

Yawata Steel, advertising in *The Economist*,
  39

Yorkshire Evening Post, 38
Yorkshire Evening Press, 57
Yorkshire Post, 36, 37
Youdale, Peter, 75
Young and Co's Brewery, 135
Young and Rubicam, 103
Young, John, 135
Young, R. D., 148, 152

Zilkha, Selim, 102, 103

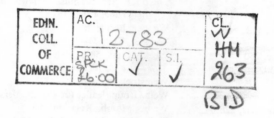